Occasional
Prose

Occasional Prose

by Mary McCarthy

HARCOURT BRACE JOVANOVICH, PUBLISHERS

San Diego   New York   London

Requests for permission to make copies of any part of the work should be mailed to: Permissions, Harcourt Brace Jovanovich, Publishers, Orlando, Florida 32887.

Some of these essays previously appeared in *The New York Review of Books, The New York Times, Saturday Review of Literature: Arts* (September 16, 1972), *The Observer, The Sunday Times;* "The Very Unforgettable Miss Brayton" in *House & Garden,* "On F. W. Dupee" in his *King of the Cats* (University of Chicago Press, 1983), "The American Revolution of Jean-François Revel" in *Without Marx or Jesus* (Doubleday, 1971), "*La Traviata* Retold" in *La Traviata* (Little, Brown, 1983).

Library of Congress Cataloging in Publication Data
McCarthy, Mary, 1912–
    Occasional prose.
    I. Title.
PS3525.A1435O3   1985   818'.5208   85-765
ISBN 0-15-167810-3

Designed by Dalia Hartman

Printed in the United States of America

First Edition

A B C D E

For Patricia Fowler and Margo Viscusi

Contents

OBITUARY

Philip Rahv
(1908–1973)

So HE'S GONE, that dear phenomenon. If no two people are alike, he was less like anybody else than anybody. A powerful intellect, a massive, overpowering personality and yet shy, curious, susceptible, confiding. All his life he was sternly faithful to Marxism, for him both a tool of analysis and a wondrous cosmogony, but he loved Henry James and every kind of rich, shimmery, soft texture in literature and in the stuff of experience. He was a resolute modernist, which made him in these recent days old-fashioned. It was as though he came into being with the steam-engine: for him, literature began with Dostoyevsky and stopped with Joyce, Proust, and Eliot; politics began with Marx and Engels and stopped with Lenin. He was not interested in Shakespeare, the classics, Greek city-states, and he despised most contemporary writing and contemporary political groups, being grumblingly out of sorts with fashion, except where he felt it belonged, on the backs of good-looking women and girls.

This did not overtake him with age or represent a hardening of his mental arteries. He was always that way. It helped him be a Trotskyite (he was a great admirer of the Old Man, though never an inscribed adherent) when Stalinism was chic. Whatever was "in" he threw out with a snort. Late in his life, serendipity introduced him to the word "swingers," which summed up everything he was against. With sardonic relish

3

he adopted it as his personal shorthand. If he came down from Boston to New York and went to a literary party and you asked him "Well, how was it?" he would answer "Nothing but swingers!" and give his short soft bark of a laugh.

Yet he had a gift for discovering young writers. I think of Saul Bellow, Elizabeth Hardwick, Jarrell, Berryman, Malamud. There were many others. He was quickly aware of Bob Silvers, editor of the *New York Review of Books*, and became his close friend—counselor, too, sometimes. To the end of his life, he remained a friend of young people. It was middle-aged and old swingers he held in aversion; young ones, on the whole, he did not mind.

He had a marvelous sensitivity to verbal phrasing and structure. What art dealers call "quality" in painting he would recognize instantly in literature, even of a kind that, in principle, ought to have been foreign to him. I remember when I first knew him, back in the mid-thirties, at a time when he was an intransigent (I thought), pontificating young Marxist, and I read a short review he had done of *Tender Is the Night*— the tenderness of the review, despite its critical stance, startled me. I would not have suspected in Rahv that power of sympathetic insight into a writer glamorized by rich Americans on the Riviera. Fitzgerald, I must add, was "out" then and not only for the disagreeable crowd at the *New Masses*.

That review was delicately, almost poetically written, and this too was a surprise. I would have expected him to write as he talked, pungently, harshly, drivingly, in a heavy Russian accent. It was as though another person had written the review. But as those who knew him discovered, there were two persons in Rahv, but solidly married to each other in a long-standing union—no quarrels. It would be simplifying to say that one was political, masculine, and aggressive, one feminine, artistic, and dreamy, but those contrasts were part of it.

Perhaps there were more than two, the third being an unreconstructed child with a child's capacity for wonder and amazement. Philip marveled constantly at the strangeness of life and the world. Recounting some story, seizing on some item in a newspaper, he would be transported, positively enraptured, with glee and offended disbelief. His black eyes with their large almost bulging whites would roll, and he would shake his head over and over, have a fit of chuckling, nudge you, if you were a man, squeeze your arm, if you were a woman—as though together you and he were watching a circus parade of human behavior, marvelous monstrosities and curious animals, pass through your village.

His own childhood in the Russian Ukraine had stayed fast in his mind. He used to tell me how his grandmother (his parents were Jewish shopkeepers living in the midst of a peasant population) ran into the shop one day saying "The Tsar has fallen," and to him it was as if she had said "The sky has fallen"; he hid behind the counter. Then, when the Civil War began, he remembered staying in the shop for weeks, it seemed, with the blinds pulled down, as Red and White troops took and retook the village. His parents were early Zionists, and, after the Civil War, they emigrated to Palestine, where in the little furniture factory his father opened he got to know those strange people—Arabs. Just before or after this, he went to America, alone, to live with his older brother. There, in Providence, Rhode Island, already quite a big boy, he went to grade school still dressed as an old-fashioned European schoolboy, in long black trousers and black stockings, looking like a somber little man among the American kids. Starting to work early, as a junior advertising copywriter for a small firm out in Oregon, he had no time for college and got his education, alone, in public libraries. In the Depression, he migrated to New York. Standing in breadlines and sleeping on park benches, he became a Marxist.

This education—Russia, the Revolution, Palestine, books read in libraries, hunger—shaped him. He read several languages: Russian, German (his family on its way to Palestine had spent a year or two in Austria), probably some Hebrew, and French, which he picked up by himself. He had a masterly sense of English and was a masterful copy-editor—the best, I am told by friends, they ever knew. American literature became a specialty with him; he had come to it curious and exploratory like a pioneer. Hawthorne, Melville, James, these were the main sources that fed his imagination. His insights, never random but tending to crystallize in theory, led him to make a series of highly original formulations, including the now famous distinction between redskins and palefaces among our literary men. He himself, being essentially a European, was neither.

Though he knew America intimately, he remained an outsider. He never assimilated, not to the downtown milieu of New York Jewish intellectuals he moved in during his early days, not to the university, although in time he occupied a professor's chair. When he lived in the country, which he did for long stretches, he was an obstinate city man and would hold forth darkly on the theme of "rural idiocy." He never learned to swim. This metaphorically summed up his situation: he would immerse his body in the alien element (I have nice pictures of him in bathing-trunks by the waterside) but declined or perhaps feared to move with it. His resistance to swimming with the tide, his mistrust of currents, were his strength.

Remaining outside the American framework, his mind had a wider perspective, and at three critical junctures in our national intellectual life, its reflections were decisive. First, at the time of the Moscow trials, when he and William Phillips broke with the Communists and "stole" *Partisan Review*, which they had edited as an organ of the John Reed Club. Second, during the War, when he broke with his former collaborators Dwight Macdonald and Clement Greenberg on the issue of whether the war against Hitler should be supported by American radicals or not. We had all been affirming the negative,

6

but Rahv in a long meditative article moved toward the opposite position: I remember the last sentence, with which I did not agree at the time but which struck on my mind nevertheless and reverberated: "And yet in a certain sense it is our war." Third, in the McCarthy time, when so many of his old friends of the anti-Stalinist left were either defending McCarthy or "postponing judgment," Rahv, alone in his immediate, *PR* circle, came out, in print, with an unequivocal condemnation and contemptuous dismissal. On Vietnam, so far as I remember, he did not pronounce at any length but maybe he did and his characteristic voice is lost to my recollection, having mingled with so many others.

The words "radical" and "modern" had a wonderful charm for Philip; when he spoke them, his sometimes grating tone softened, became reverent, loving, as though touching prayer beads. He was also much attached to the word "ideas." "He has no *ideas*," he would declare, dismissing some literary claimant; to be void of ideas was, for him, the worst disaster that could befall an intellectual. He found this deficiency frequent, almost endemic, among us. That may be why he did not wish to assimilate. I said, just now, that he was unlike anybody but now I remember that I have seen someone like him—on the screen. Like the younger Rahv anyway: Serge Bondarchuk, the director of *War and Peace*, playing the part of Pierre. An uncanny resemblance in every sense and unsettling to preconceived notions. I had always pictured Pierre as blond, pink, very tall, and fat; nor could I picture Philip as harboring Pierre's ingenuous, embarrassed, puzzled, placid soul—they were almost opposites, I should have thought. And yet that swarthy Russian actor was showing us a different interior Philip and a different exterior Pierre. Saying good-bye to my old friend, I am moved by that and remember his tenderness for Tolstoy (see the very Rahvian and beautiful essay "The Green Twig and the Black Trunk") and Tolstoy's sense of Pierre as the onlooker, the eternal civilian, as out of place at the Battle of Borodino in his white hat and green swallow-tail coat as the dark "little man" in his long dark East European clothes eyeing the teacher from his grammar-school desk in Providence.

February 17, 1974

The "Place" of
Nicola Chiaromonte
(1905–1972) *

When Chiaromonte died in January 1972—of a heart attack, just after taking part in a discussion program on Italian radio—there was a remarkable outburst of emotion. As news of the event spread, to his widow, in their Roman apartment, came a continous flow of telegrams and letters expressing the grief of people of the most varying kinds, from the head of state to the old woman who used to sell him newspapers in the village in Liguria where he once spent his summers. One of the most moving was from a young member of Potere Operaio *(an extreme leftist group), which read something like this: "He has been a model for everyone of intellectual and moral lucidity." When he died, Chiaromonte was in his late sixties and far in his thinking from the extreme left. The memorial tributes that followed during the next weeks in the press were, again, from the most varying sources: ranging from the centrist* Corriere della Sera *and* La Stampa *to the communist-inclined* Paese Sera. *Most interesting was the fact that in all those words written and wired there was scarcely a one that had an official*

---

* In the medieval theatre the "place" was the central stationary acting area, or *platea*, usually free of scenery, around which were grouped the various "pageants" and "mansions" representing Herod's palace, Pilate's hall, and so on.

or conventional ring, even those sent by official "personalities."

Chiaromonte would hardly have guessed that he had "stood for something" to so many and might even have tried to refute the evidence as it poured in. He had left Italy as a young man to become an anti-Fascist exile in Paris, where he was close to non-violent Anarchist groups. He took part in the Spanish Civil War, enlisting in André Malraux's air squadron; he is the character who is always reading Plato in Man's Hope. At the time of the Nazi invasion, in 1940, he fled with his Austrian wife to the south, his wife died in Toulouse, and he eventually continued on, reaching the United States, via North Africa. It was there that he met Camus, who became his close friend. In America, he wrote for the New Republic, Partisan Review, *and Dwight Macdonald's* politics. *His friends here were Macdonald, Meyer Schapiro, James T. Farrell, Lionel Abel, Niccolò Tucci, Saul Steinberg, and—less close then—me.*

In the late forties, he went back to Europe, working first for UNESCO in Paris (for which he was very unsuited). He returned finally to Rome, where he started doing a theatre column for the old Il Mondo, *a liberal (in the American sense) weekly. In the fifties, with Ignazio Silone, he founded the monthly* Tempo Presente. *When he died, he was doing theatre reviews for* L'Espresso *and writing political and philosophical reflections about once a month for* La Stampa. *His ideas did not fit into any established category; he was neither on the left nor on the right. Nor did it follow that he was in the middle—he was alone. Though his thought remained faithful, in its way, to philosophical anarchism, he had long lost the belief in political "effectiveness."*

In America, after the forties, he was not well known. He sent occasional "Letters" from Europe to Partisan Review *and wrote occasionally for* Dissent. *In 1966 he gave the Christian Gauss lectures at Princeton. They dealt with the novel and the idea of history in it, and were published, as a volume, in*

London under the title The Paradox of History. *In Italy, his volume of theatre essays,* La Situazione drammatica, *had won a prize in Venice, and his Gauss lectures were published in book form as* Credere e non credere.

The present essay is a preface to a selection of his theatre reviews and essays, not including those in La Situazione drammatica, *to be published in Italian following a selection of his political writings. It is characteristic, probably, of our period that his death should have prompted what might almost be called his "discovery." Consciousness of a loss has awakened curiosity as to what exactly was in the vacated space.*

Nicola Chiaromonte deeply loved the theatre. The fact was surprising, "out of character," to those who knew him as a man attached above all to ideas and principles, a theorist and reasoner, and—perhaps more important in this connection—a detester of artifice. He *was* every one of those things, though it did not follow that he was also, as some imagined, a puritan and therefore a natural enemy of the stage. Yet grease paint and footlights, the makeshifts of illusion and impersonation, were scarcely, you might have thought, his element. The glamour of the theatre, long recognized as one of its essential attractions (a collection of theatre pieces by the excellent American critic Stark Young was called simply *Glamour*), ought to have been a source of repulsion for Chiaromonte, even as a youth. And, unlike many or most play-reviewers, he had never, so far as I know, cherished any ambition to tread the boards himself.

It is hard to imagine him dressing up as a child to take part in home theatricals or school pageants, indeed to picture him in any sort of costume or disguise. Nor can I hear him declaiming poetry at a Prize Day to the admiration of teachers and parents. There was nothing histrionic in him; when he spoke in public, he was certainly no orator, though sometimes forceful when angered by incomprehension of what to

11

him intellectually or morally was clear as day. If he was "stage-struck" at any period in his life, collected theatre programs, pored over photos of stars, this cannot have come about through a process of identification with objects of fame and applause. No one could have been less desirous of shining than Chiaromonte, and the hero-worship of actors common in his and my day among young people should have been totally foreign to him who had so little interest in the immediate satisfactions of the performing, capering ego.

Nevertheless not only was he a continuous playgoer, by profession and inclination, but he loved actors and actresses. To go backstage with Chiaromonte after a performance, say at the Eliseo, was a delightful and entertaining experience; though a modest and shy man, he basked in the atmosphere of good will and affection that he seemed both to bring with him into the actors' dressing-rooms and to find there waiting to meet him. As his theatre criticism shows, he was a friendly critic of actors and a respecter of their art—encouraging to young people and beginners but fond too of the old idols even when compelled to remonstrate with them for some misguided interpretation of a scene or role. He had a great simplicity of heart, and if perhaps he looked on actors as children, something childlike in him responded, so that often he seemed more at home, more easily himself, in the green-room than at any soiree of his fellow writers and intellectuals.

Few theatre critics can have taken the pains Chiaromonte did to go to see what small groups of actors, amateurs or novices, were essaying, usually in some remote, inconvenient part of the city and in a semi-empty hall or room. Whether in Rome, Paris, or New York, he could be counted on to have a sympathetic look. He was not so indulgent with "name" directors. He deplored the ascendancy of the director and blamed most of the evils of the contemporary theatre on a system in which the director was the star, usurping the place of the actors as well as that of the text.

The promotion of the director to top billing coincided with the rise of the movies (of which Chiaromonte was no fan), and the overwhelming emphasis in the contemporary theatre on staging, on décor and "effects," reflected the influence of the movies, in which the virtuoso director is all-powerful, everything being grist to his mill, capable, that is, of being processed as in a giant factory. There is a film industry, but there can never be a theatre "industry"—a point not understood by hubristic stage directors—because every performance is inevitably one of a kind and cannot be reproduced the following night. Chiaromonte's love of the theatre must have sprung partly from the love of handcrafts and dislike of mass production, and the poor ephemerid players with whom he sympathized were its artisans.

Yet this does not altogether explain his fascination with the stage—a love affair constantly frustrated and almost doomed to disappointment, for the theatre, among all the contemporary arts, is the least flourishing. Why go to the theatre at all nowadays, since most plays and most productions are so bad? If you do not care for the movies, why not stay home and read a book? Or watch television or listen to records. And in fact people, by and large, do *not* go to the theatre any more. A study made last spring in the United States showed that only a minute fraction of Americans under thirty had ever seen a live play. The results would probably be similar in Western Europe; it is only behind the Iron Curtain that the theatre is still valued as an instrument of socialization. In capitalist countries, those of us who continue to go to *le spectacle*, as the French call it, are conscious of belonging to an ever-dwindling minority—not an elite, really, but a peculiar species of animal nearly extinct.

No doubt there is a vicious circle. The decline in public interest means that playwrights and actors, who must eat, turn to films and television, which means fewer and poorer stage productions, which in turn causes public interest to decline

13

still more. The theatre is dependent on numbers, both to produce it and to consume it. Far more than the novel or, say, the sonnet, it is keyed to demand. A sonnet, requiring only one hand to produce, may be composed for a single reader—its addressee—and a novel, also a one-man job, may be written to be read by posterity or circulated in manuscript to friends, but even street theatre demands a troupe, a vehicle, a permit usually, and some curious spectators.

Chiaromonte seems sometimes to have hoped that the theatre might be kept alive by groups of amateurs putting on shows, like children's plays, for audiences of family and friends. Yet going to a professional performance is a voluntary, spontaneous undertaking ("Let's get tickets for Sunday's matinee") while amateur theatricals, like children's plays, are to some degree compulsory on members of a small immediate circle, who feel duty-bound to attend, and duty, in the long run, is a feeble incentive to spur one to take part, regularly, in what is supposed to be a pleasure.

The sociability of the theatre distinguishes it from films, where one sits in the dark, and from concerts, where many listen with eyes closed, shutting out the environment the better to take in the sound. One is never lonely in the theatre, whether one holds a single ticket or not. The play is a social event, and watching the audience arrive, observing it during intermissions in the bar or foyer, is one of the playgoer's privileged diversions, like gazing around at a party and ticking off the guests as they come in. To take one's seat early and crane one's neck waiting for the hall to fill up, sometimes with painful slowness, initiates one into suspense, a mixture of dread and longing very like what one will experience when the house lights finally dim and the curtain rises: one inspects the balcony and the gallery—still too few there—follows the usher's quickening footsteps up and down the orchestra aisles—two more, three more, *four!*

At the movies, it does not matter if you are the only

spectator present; except for the inconvenience of having other people stumble past you, your enjoyment is not affected one way or the other. But at a play it is sad to be surrounded by empty seats. I think I could not bear to be the solitary member of an audience and not just because I would feel sorry for the actors. At a play everybody wants the pride of a packed house. Sitting together with others, intent on a performance that will never be precisely the same, even if you occupy the same seat the next night and for a dozen nights thereafter, makes going to the theatre an immersion into community, like the yearly mass baptism that used to be performed on every baby born in a parish. A theatre audience is a self-constituted assembly and, unlike an anomic film audience, generally has a civic character. Something of the sort happens also at sporting events—people go to the stadium, rather than watch on television, not just to eat hot dogs but to bear joint witness to some feat or dramatic contest—with the difference that in the theatre you are simply absorbed in the spectacle and do not take sides.

Yet in the theatre nowadays that exalting sentiment of community, of civic participation, and the sense of privilege it carries, has ceased to elate the remnant of playgoers, just because we are a remnant, because we are such freaks, such a minority, so unrepresentative. At any given moment, we were always a happy few, since a theatre has a limited seating capacity and does not "project," but now we are not even envied. The community we take our place in, as the usher leads us down the aisle, has no civic or statistical significance; we might as well be installed around a Ouija board. Uniting to watch a play, whether it is *Hamlet* or *Hair,* we recognize ourselves as veteran members of an obsolescent cult or fraternity, some of us, in the stalls, wearing the old class uniform—or vestment—of dinner jacket and evening gown, others in ancient shawls or queer rusty hats; even the children, if it is a matinee, seem to have been freshly exhumed from mothballs to enact, with their parents and schoolmates, the archaic boring rite of being-at-the-play.

Chiaromonte was well aware that some mystery attached to his faithful attendance at this charade. In the essay written after a heart attack had caused him to drop his theatre column for nearly a year, he asked himself why in the world he was starting it up again. What was the use? Writing about the theatre in Italy (where things were even worse than elsewhere), you found yourself saying something negative seventy percent of the time. Since the theatre was clearly dying, what was the point of going on?

His answers to these insistent questions do not wholly dispel the mystery: he likes writing his column and likes the paper (the old *Il Mondo*) it appears in and the liberty the paper gives him to write about whatever he wants, using the theatre as a springboard. He likes having a part to play, a role assigned to him, that of the critic, whose mask he wears, in the common drama of society, where we all play our parts, and the theatre is not just a microcosm of the real world, it is a cosmos in which all that is lived in the real world may be clarified and purified to a point where it can acquire significance. Finally, there is not only the real theatre, as it exists today, but also the idea of the theatre, and abominable as the real theatre is, it still fascinates him *because* of its hideous deformity, as we continue to love an altered, disfigured being and refuse to acknowledge that the creature is beyond redemption. What he is saying, in short, is that he cannot tear himself away from his seat in the stalls since he is in love with the *idea* of the theatre, even in its fallen state, as one might be with a fallen woman. In sheer horror, if nothing else, he remains in his place, unable to turn his eyes away.

Something like this is what most of us who love the theatre feel, though no one, I think, has expressed it so forcibly. Despite all we know, despite our better judgment, we keep coming back to it. In my own case, I ought to add, it is more in perpetual hope than in despairing fascination. I can never quell a stir of anticipation when the curtain parts. But, unlike Chiaromonte, I have never had the dream of reforming the theatre—only the dream that it would somehow reform itself—which probably means that my passion for it has been less than his.

In any case, though, why the theatre? What caused him to fall in love with that sad strumpet in the first place when he might have chosen a good woman—painting, sculpture, poetry, instrumental music—or even that demi-rep, opera? And if he wanted to suffer, what about films, which offer plenty of opportunities for exasperation to anyone who has a pure "idea" of the cinema? The truth is he was allergic to the silver screen. Like most people who care about the stage, he would rather see a play, *any* play, providing it was serious, than a film "masterpiece" that everybody was talking about. On the screen, not being a puritan, he appreciated ribald farce and fast-moving comic extravaganzas (on the order of *Dr. Strangelove, Divorzio all'Italiano*); it was the "art" film he could not tolerate and the widely diffused belief that the cinema, with its greater powers of representation, had superseded the theatre *qua* dramatic art, as though the limitations of the stage had been a mere matter of technical incapacity, which the camera had rendered otiose—the oft-voiced idea, that is, that if Shakespeare had only been born in the age of the moving picture he would have been the first to write movie scripts, grateful for the exciting possibilities of a medium that would free him from the cramped makeshifts of the Globe.

Still, if Chiaromonte obstinately resisted the seduction of films, he was genuinely fond of music and poetry and more than fond of painting—he even practiced it a little—and his first long work, lost in France in 1940 during the mass exodus of political exiles fleeing from the Nazis, was a manuscript on Michelangelo. He also had a gift for journalism and might have become, like Victor Hugo *(Choses Vues)* and

Dostoyevsky *(Diary of a Writer)*, a regular critic of the national life, including crimes of the passionate sort: as readers of his "Notes" in *Tempo Presente* and his "Letters" in *Partisan Review* know, he had a great relish for the "small" human event buried in a news item or spread out in the headlines of a tabloid. Yet with all these capacities and endowments (which were the reflection of an unusual inner activity; his soul had no dead areas, calluses, or proud flesh), not to mention his philosophic interests, centering on history and politics, he elected the theatre as, you might say, his scene of combat, his preferred arena.

It was combat from the very beginning. A note passed on by a friend and Roman contemporary of his informs me that Chiaromonte, as a young man of twenty or perhaps still a boy of nineteen, belonged to a group that called themselves *I Sciacalli* (the Jackals) and went to the theatre to hiss fashionable bourgeois plays and applaud Pirandello and other writers of the avant-garde. The playwrights they were hooting hired "provocative elements" to put on counter-demonstrations, but without much effect. The Jackals prevailed; then gradually young Fascists added their voices to the ensemble, and bit by bit Nicola's group broke up. It is strange now to think of Chiaromonte playing jackal, i.e., running in a sportive pack to hunt prey, but to come upon the name Pirandello suddenly throws light. Here we may have the clue, finally, to what caused his young emotions to fasten so inflexibly on the stage.

Chiaromonte's championship of Pirandello never lost its vigor. If he comes back again and again to worry the case of Bertolt Brecht, for him symptomatic of what was basically wrong with the theatre of today, he returns again and again to Pirandello to illustrate what was—or might have been— right. Commenting on current productions, Chiaromonte was not satisfied to praise or condemn. He always saw lessons to be learned, for the director and playwright, and Brecht was the great negative lesson whose anatomy he patiently dissected, while Pirandello he perceived as a model, not of course to be copied but to be studied in depth and understood.

Even Pirandello's weaknesses are instructive for Chiaromonte in that they show him in the act of *mis*understanding his own strength. Or, as he himself puts it in the long review of *Vestire gli' ignudi (Clothe the Naked)*, there are times when Pirandello does not accept in full the logic of his own inspiration: seeking a pathetic effect, he falls into the very staginess from which he ought to have set the theatre free with *Six Characters*. For Chiaromonte, it could not be enough to state this. He must make us see it, and, using the same components of character and event (a seduced and abandoned girl tries to kill herself), before our eyes, as if at a drawing board, he brilliantly sketches out the play as it would have been, had the Pirandello of *Six Characters* rigorously thought it through. This careful demonstration, which almost makes us laugh aloud at the ease and simplicity of its means, is an object lesson itself in the *how* of theatre-reviewing.

He did not hesitate to call *Six Characters* a "milestone" of the modern theatre—an assertion that may startle a foreigner. For us, Pirandello has been more of a curious bloom on the tree of modernism that anything as solid and perduring as a milestone on a road leading into the future. Even twenty or thirty years ago, to us he appeared as old-fashioned as the dark suits and widow's crape worn by the automata that were his characters. His "psychology" or "philosophy" (an extreme relativism or, vulgarly, "It's all in your mind") had pasted him for us in a period album of the twenties. Indeed, he seemed a prime example of a writer who had been locked into a set of once-current notions and sealed off from posterity as though in a time-capsule, and the very theatricality of his plays, while it encouraged their revival with period costumes and accessories, identified him as a dramaturge, i.e., an old-time

19

wizard and prestidigitator skilled in theatre magic and particularly in the art of "freezing" actors in a tableau.

Reading and rereading Chiaromonte on him, I have become convinced that we missed the point. But whether the
Pirandello he teaches us to see is the real Pirandello or Chiaromonte's own ideal construct, it is clear that the Pirandello
he expounds to us is indeed a crucial and disquieting contemporary figure. A line can be drawn from Pirandello that
will pass through Artaud, Ionesco, Beckett, Genet, and skirt
altogether Brecht, Sartre, T. S. Eliot, Peter Weiss's *Marat-
Sade*, and the American realists. Strindberg and Shaw have
a place in the line, which can be extended backward to Chekhov and Ibsen. Those two (and behind them the Greeks) are
the playwrights Chiaromonte dwells on with love, from whom
he has learned, to whom he goes back, as if for a refresher
course and to reassure himself of his bearings.

On nearly every page of his commentary, however big
or small the occasion that prompted it (Genet's *The Blacks* or
a hippie version of Euripides), we find a reaffirmation and
testing of principles. And yet what principles, the reader might
ask, looking down an inventory of the blessed that embraces
Pirandello, Beckett, Sophocles, and Jean Genet? What can
they have in common? In fact how can Chiaromonte's principle of the theatre as reasoning action (*azione ragionante*)
accommodate Artaud's notion of the stage as a concrete physical space to be filled with spectacular violence, sound, and
gesture? Is it not capricious, then, a sheer matter of taste, to
draw the line at Brecht?

Our wonder has something familiar about it. We are
feeling the same mystification as we did at the outset when
we confronted the fact of his theatrical "calling" or vocation.
Perhaps the two enigmas are bound up together: if we can
find a common factor or factors among the objects of his
preference, we may be close to the idea Chiaromonte formed

for himself of the theatre—the idea he espoused for better or for worse on first meeting it in the work of Pirandello.

Well, one common factor gradually becomes discernible; from the Greeks through Genet, all those figures are non- or anti-realist, or so Chiaromonte argued. He had a bias against realism (which, since I do not share it, I consider a prejudice) and seldom lets pass a chance to vent his feelings on the subject. A good deal of his sympathy with Genet comes from the playwright's insistence on "an absolute break with representation" and his expressed desire for "a declamatory tone"—in production often denied him by directors. Artaud's Theatre of Cruelty attracts Chiaromonte for a number of reasons, among which he lists first, as a cardinal point, its remoteness from any kind of realism or naturalism. It is no problem for him to find the same virtue in Shaw, whom he cites once as the true inventor of distancing.

Yet at other times Chiaromonte's reprehension of realism is selective: determined to make his case, he relies on a certain wilfulness, not to say contrariness, of definition. In exculpating Ibsen and Chekhov from the sin, he concedes that in these authors there is something that may look like realism or faithful representation (the telegraph poles in *The Cherry Orchard*, Trigorin's checked trousers and Uncle Vanya's splendid neckties, the declared prosaic intention of Ibsen's great middle works), but, with them, he maintains, it is tempered by something else—lyricism in Ibsen and, in Chekhov, a kind of immateriality. One can agree that there is a lyric strain in the middle Ibsen and that in Chekhov there is a loving perception, filtered through pity, of a world beyond Trigorin's ephemeral checked trousers but yet comprising them. Still, you and I might call this realism—what else?—in its purest distillate. Or, as Chiaromonte puts it himself, writing of *Hedda Gabler:* "In these dramas of ordinary bourgeois life, destiny strikes through the ordinary, the mean, the petty."

To come closer to today, Chiaromonte is able to admire Beckett and Ionesco (able to censure them too, on occasion), both for themselves and for the imprint of Chekhov he perceives on them. What other theatre critic would have had the acuteness to notice that "Beckett's maggot-men seem to come straight out of a sentence in *The Sea Gull*" (in the play-within-a-play, at the opening, when a time 200,000 years from now is foreseen, on an empty cold planet where "all living things have completed their sad cycle")? In Ionesco he also notes traces of Pirandello. Yet what he may have failed to see is that both Beckett and Ionesco, after their fashion, are latter-day realists. In comparison with Genet's *The Screens*, Beckett's *Happy Days* looks like a "slice of life": if you take the postulate of a fifty-year-old woman buried up to her waist in the sands of time, this is how she would be, down to the last, harshly observed detail of handbag, toothbrush, lipstick—a bundle, to use Chiaromonte's words, of "small satisfactions, habitual gestures, false triumphs, held together with animal selfishness."

Something similar could be said of Ionesco's *Amédée ou Comment s'en débarrasser*: if you postulate a foot belonging to a corpse in an adjoining, unseen room that keeps growing and inching its way into the family dining room, that is exactly how the family would behave toward it. In both cases, the inability of the characters to "rise" to an enormous exterior fact such as the silting in of the world or the slow intrusion of a dead body enhances the horror and monstrosity of their daily, "realistic" circumstance. Or put it the other way around: representation in an eschatological context (the ever-present doomsday of those playwrights' vivid metaphors of burial and encroachment) survives, like Winnie's toothbrush, at the cost of becoming caricature.

In fact, thinking it over, I am not sure that Chiaromonte failed to see the realistic component in Beckett and Ionesco. Perhaps the reservations he felt about them can be attributed to a suspicion on his part that the break with representation there, despite appearances, was something less than absolute—reservations he never felt about Genet. Yet we will not understand his reprehension of realism unless we understand that the term for him meant something less and more than the rules and conventions of lifelike stagecraft. By that standard, Ibsen would be more of a realist, i.e., a culprit, than his epigone Arthur Miller, who violates time sequences, lets his archetypal characters declaim and soliloquize, and embodies dreams and memory fragments on a bare or near-bare stage.

When Chiaromonte anathematizes realism, he has in mind the error of mistaking the surface of life—or lives—for reality. Surface conceals while, in his view, the theatre's function is to strip and lay bare. In the light of this, we can see his objection to elaborate stage settings, multifarious props, studied costumes—the whole ponderous deployment of illusionist stage machinery, including the machinery of plot. What he held against the illusionist theatre was the naïve or else false importance given to externals, not only of dress and furnishings but of events and happenings. An importance lent these latter by suspense, as though in *The Three Sisters* the question agitating the audience were the same as the one working in the sisters at the curtain's rise: will they get to Moscow or not? That they will not is for Chekhov a foregone conclusion, and to invite the spectators to "identify" with the sisters in their disappointment would have trivialized the drama, which shows us the irreducible reality they face, of which not-getting-to-Moscow is only the tiniest and most superficial part.

The plots of such plays as *Death of a Salesman* (which treat destiny in terms of averages and statistical expectations) turn on questions of success or failure—realistic questions in that they appear vital to the principals, as they would to us in their place in real life. But not on the stage, Chiaromonte insists, where success or failure in an enterprise—will Romeo

23

get to marry Juliet?—is neither here nor there. Except, I would add, in determining whether the nature of the genre is comic or tragic: comedy has a resolution, a happy wrapping up, usually signified by a marriage or multiple marriages, where tragedy has none—the death of Macbeth, while doubtless a happy solution for Scotland, settles nothing for Shakespeare. This glad wrapping up of an awful tangle of cross-purposes is improbable and often incredible (as people are wont to complain of some of Shakespeare's darker comedies), but this only means that the characters' getting together cannot be taken as a permanent resolution of anything; it is a moment of joy and celebration such as reality also contains and on which the play chooses to stop. The pairing off that signals the finale of *Love's Labour's Lost* (or *The Marriage of Figaro*) makes us laugh and clap because, among other things, it is so funny, too Noah's Ark good to be true.

It was not, then, that Chiaromonte wished to see the stage draconically purged of such common objects as easy chairs, kitchen sinks, baby carriages, ironing boards (though, given his bias, an ironing board, stage center, in a contemporary play was likely to provoke a defensive reaction, whereas the baby carriage wheeled across stage rear in Act 4 of *The Three Sisters* entertained him). Nor was it an insistence on ideal types, even if it may be true that, as an Italian, that is a man of the south, he found warty realism of portraiture deeply uncongenial: compare the ugly, grinning peasant bystanders surrounding an Adoration or a Nativity in northern painting with the ideal figures assisting at Italian holy scenes. For him, reality was, above all, sad, even in its humors and extravagances.

He quotes Pirandello's definition of humor as the "sentiment of the contrary"—a feeling in which critical recognition of what ought to be mingles with compassion for what is. Pirandello had used as an example Manzoni's parish priest, Don Abbondio, in *I Promessi Sposi*, asking: "Who is Don

Abbondio? He is what you find in the place of what you would
have wanted." The contrary of your expectations of the ideal
figure of the perfect priest. "The down-to-earth, dispirited
shadow of cautious Don Abbondio falls across the sacerdotal
ideal." But that definition of humor—or the comic—comes
very. close to Chiaromonte's own definition of the real. Don
Abbondio is a little piece of reality, and pity, as with Chekhov, is the agency that allows us to perceive it. "Pitiless realism" was detestable, clearly, to Chiaromonte and as remote
in his eyes from the real, which would shrink from its touch,
as any other form of "graphic" representation that took itself
for the truth.

Chiaromonte, it must be remembered, was a modern, a
deep-dyed modern, going tirelessly into battle against the fal-
lacy of representation. That is, he was very much an "engaged" intellectual of his time, having entered the fray in the
twenties to do his bit in the vanguard onslaught on the con-
tinuum of appearances which the majority still took to be solid
and durable, despite the shock of the First War that had
demonstrated—as plainly, one would have thought, as an
earthquake—the crack or "fault" in the substratum. The
demolition work had already been begun by the cubist sap-
pers before the war, but in the theatre Pirandello was the first
to expose the fissure, which was why he was the hero of the
Jackals. Chiaromonte notes the fragmentation of the Six
Characters (1922), as after an explosion.

For those who came later it is hard to appreciate the passion
and valor of the modernist undertaking; we forget its unpopularity. And when we remind ourselves that it had no evident
political overtones and yet evidently voiced a protest of some
radical, disturbing sort, we are puzzled to determine where
that protest, almost a war cry, was coming from. The rejection of old forms—i.e., of old ways of seeing—was proclaimed in martial language reminiscent of field dispatches;

there was continual news of "break-throughs" on one front or another, and the term "vanguard" or "avant-garde," having been borrowed from the military, was appropriated with bold finality by artists. In fact, as Duchamp made clear, the movement was aimed at subverting Art, perceived as a bundle of tricks, and it often took its cues from science and advanced technology. The discrepancy between appearance and what lay underneath was repeatedly "proved" by modernists in a variety of fields. There was no "break" with reality—only a tremendous shattering of surfaces. Honesty, an ever-greater honesty, was the rallying cry responded to by architects and furniture designers as well as by wordsmiths like Joyce and Pirandello. What had happened to the Six Characters, Chiaromonte notes, was that a *fact* had exploded among them.

Anyone who knew and loved Chiaromonte will recognize that an intransigent and fearless honesty was a basic trait of his character. Still the value he set on modernism in the theatre (when he could dispense with it more readily in the other arts) may seem bewildering if we do not grasp what he conceived the theatre's function to be. His ideas on this score were highly independent, at any rate not current in his profession, where few ideas of what the theatre is or could be are ever framed in the shape of a thought. Meditation had convinced him that the theatre, among the arts, had a special, privileged position in that its forms—comedy, farce, tragedy—constitute means by which reality is met and accepted for what it is, i.e., that which is ineluctable and cannot be altered. No other mode of seeing and rendering experience possesses this capability.

Among literary forms, the novel deals with the subjective ego and its dreams and reveries, which in principle are only limited by the exhaustion of the novelist's imagination, but the theatre deals with men and women acting and interacting in a physical space and hence rigorously limited in their outward motions. Each, as he moves, encounters the boundaries that define the others' outline. These boundaries, at the start of the play, may go unperceived by the characters, who picture themselves as free; it is the discovery of them, swift or gradual, the knocking up against them, rebounding, attempting to circumvent them, that make up the agon, never a straightforward contest between two individuals (Antigone vs. Creon), but between the one and a dense plurality. This plurality may be conceived as Necessity, the Law, the Divine, or simply the Others (Sartre's *Huis Clos*)—whatever name is given under the prevailing dispensation to a limit felt to be *there*, outside, constraining human action, and which, when accepted and measured, in some way liberates the higher faculties for an act of contemplation.

Agon (though I do not recall that Chiaromonte says this) originally meant an assembly, a gathering, rather than what took place in it, and the social character of the theatre, the being together for a limited space of time in a limited but populous space, surely comprehends both the audience and the drama or interplay they watch. The silent participation of the spectator in the give-and-take of dialogue, which is nothing less than a continuous *exchange*, emphasizes the togetherness (if the word can be excused) of the dramatic situation, just as the solitude of the reader engrossed in a book mirrors the subjectivity, represented often by the narrative "I," of the novel's consciousness.

Dramatic action, being circumscribed, has a logic far more compelling than that of the strung-out incidents in a novel or tale; within a closed circle, everything follows *necessarily*, unfolds from what is implicit. This is just as true of comedy as of tragedy, in fact, I would add, more evidently so, since the comic turnabout demonstrates as exquisitely as any syllogism the sequence of somebody's chickens (Tartuffe's, Count Almaviva's) coming home to roost. Chiaromonte's principle of the drama as reasoning action can be extended, moreover, to fit the characters, who are often logicians,

27

reasoners, even hair-splitters (*vide* Shakespeare, Shaw), liti-
gants, like Bérénice, like Antigone, forcefully stating their case,
pleaders like Uncle Vanya.

Yet if the theatre, as Chiaromonte says, has a unique
relation with what is and cannot be otherwise, this relation—
strangely enough, as it would seem at first glance—has always been posed in terms of masks and illusion. Not only are
the playactors pretending to be what they are not—Oedipus
or Caesar—but the theatre loves disguises ("Enter Duke disguised as Friar"), in other words travesty, double impersonation, for the "Duke" disguised as a friar is an actor twice dis-
sembled. Worse still, Viola, in *Twelfth Night*, traveling about
disguised as a youth, Cesario, is not just a girl dressed up in
boy's clothes but a boy (the actor) dressed up as a girl dressed
up as a boy. The sphere of ultimate, irreducible reality which
is the stage is also the licensed sphere of illusion. Actors, flesh-
and-blood creatures, induce our belief in immaterial brain-
products, inventions of an unseen author. Meanwhile the
reasoning, debating action pursues its irreversible course
through a mirage of false semblances, error, mistaken identities, till it arrives at anagnorisis: the knowledge that nothing
can be done to controvert that which is laid down (doom)—
Oedipus is the slayer of Laius; Birnam Wood has come to
Dunsinane.

Chiaromonte liked to contrast masks with illusion, preferring
the mask (characteristically) because it is frank: the man in
the mask is clearly an *actor*, not someone who is half-per-
suading you with grease paint and false whiskers that he is
King Lear. For my part, I do not see that the difference is
important except in terms of styles. The masked actor will be
skilled in histrionics—the mode of declamation, close to song
or chant; the actor in grease paint will be skilled in the mode
of mimesis. But nobody is really deceived in the second case:
we know that Laurence Olivier in blackface is not a real

Venetian general. And in antique comedy and tragedy there must have been some force of illusion working *through* the mask; otherwise why would the Greek word for actor be "hypocrite," one who plays a part, who pretends?

It appears to me that the whole business of dressing-up and make-believe, the "magic" of the theatre, must be a prime ingredient. We consent to the pretense, just as children consent to the notion that the man in the red suit and white whiskers is Santa Claus down from the North Pole even when they are sure there is no Santa Claus and pretty sure that they recognize their uncle. The longing to be deceived, to "dress up" or otherwise alter reality, is both satisfied by the stage and dispelled, as we are obliged to watch it objectively, at work in the dramatis personae. If my contention is right, it does not undermine Chiaromonte's fundamental thesis; it confirms it.

The stage, he says, is the place where men who, unknown or known to themselves, have no choice but to play parts (of king or model housewife or gallant, it does not matter) are slowly divested of their outer garment—the protective casing of hopes, dreams, fictions—and confronted with naked reality. The actor, willing or unwilling, in each of us perceives his prototype on the stage, a walking shadow, the shade of a shade. The theatre is seen finally to be its own subject: a cleansed, stripped model of the world of the watchers beyond the proscenium arch, who, led to examination by the dramatic logic, recognize their lives as they truly are. When this recognition is forcible, the theatre becomes a tribunal, as in Ibsen and Genet: the watchers, the bourgeois of the audience, are on trial.

Now insofar as we are all actors or doers (it comes to the same, for doing, as exposed on the stage, is mere feinting, shadow play), the mask we put on is only a metaphor for the illusion we project whenever we appear among others—Yeats's "sixty-year-old smiling public man." The incomprehensible mixture of reality and unreality that we are aware of in the acts we perform is dramatically present in the situation of the actor, who consents for our pleasure to be someone both real and unreal. In short, he is a voluntary scapegoat, and if it is his own face—flashing eyes, noble brow, jutting chin—he uses to fabricate the mask, the nightly sacrifice can be more moving. This indeed is the theme of Pirandello's *Trovarsi (Find Yourself)*, whose pitiful heroine is a famous actress. Still, I do not deny that mimesis is more suited to comedy than to tragedy, where to observe the play of facial gesture, judge the "rightness" of this or that bit of stage business, agree that this is just the hat Tesman's well-meaning aunt would wear, may become as distracting as taking a quick inventory of the contents of Claudius's wassailing hall.

Chiaromonte probably owed to Pirandello his original insight into the theatre as a sequence of actions performed by actors—a fact so obvious that nobody had taken note of it. Shakespeare's "All the world's a stage" and "Life's a poor player" might have pointed in the right direction if those soliloquies had not passed into schoolroom commonplaces, so that what was being said in them, like the purloined letter, was overlooked. The persistent application Chiaromonte made of this seemingly simple and self-evident idea led him to discoveries that illuminate the whole nature of dramatic art, ancient and modern, and that throw light too on the nature of narrative.

On a bare rehearsal stage, *Six Characters* confronted a troupe of actors with, so to speak, a troupe of actees. What Chiaromonte applauded, with emphasis, in this play was that Pirandello had dismantled the theatre of its bourgeois trappings and restored it to something like its primary form, as though a Romanesque church had been cleared of the accumulated rubbish of baroque chapels and Victorian marble angels and returned to its original intention of worship.

Heuristic too for Chiaromonte, who could be said to have gone to school to Pirandello, was the play's approach to time.

The *fact* that had exploded among those six people, reducing them to modernist-looking bits and pieces, fragments of their former "academic," illusionist personalities, had already exploded before the start of the play. At the curtain's rise, the action had finished; what remained was to rehearse it, go over and over it in the hope of searching out its meaning amid the debris. With this stroke, we are back in Attic drama, where the action, so to speak, has already happened when the first strophes are pronounced. It is not just a matter of the dramatist plunging swiftly *in medias res*. For the Attic spectator, the story he was going to witness was over and not to be tampered with; it lay in the sacred past of myth and, in Oedipus's case, even antedated the unwitting protagonist, having been told before his birth by prophecy. What remained was to re-enact it and, with the aid of the Chorus, search out its meaning.

To a lesser extent, this was still true of the Elizabethan theatre and the theatre of Corneille and Racine. The plots of *Hamlet* and *Phèdre* presented no surprises to the audience, whose detailed foreknowledge of what was going to happen next made suspense of the modern kind impossible. The spectator of Shakespeare's time who went to see a tragedy or a chronicle play (it was different with comedy, which offered new or little-known plots that had the effect, almost, of improvisation) entered the theatre in a frame of mind that freed him from care about externals. He had left behind the anxiety so common in his daily life as to how things were going to turn out; he could not hope that Lear would get his crown back or Regan and Goneril reform, as he might with his own disagreeable daughters.

I stress this point because it is crucial to Chiaromonte's thought and yet all but inexplicable, I fear, to today's playgoer, even one repeatedly exposed to the "alienation effect." How can a big question like Lear's getting his crown back (with the aid of the French alliance and a landing at Dover) be regarded by anybody in his right mind as non-momentous? Is this critic utterly indifferent to the things that concern us, that we struggle for—power and daily bread and the rights of old age? Certainly such matters, embracing the whole political realm, are a subject of legitimate concern. But not, I repeat, for the stage. True, for those people on the stage we feel something akin to suspense—a kind of fear and agonized longing that the thing we know is coming will not arrive. Also a natural wish to see the wicked punished—that much at least—which comedy usually satisfies; tragedy more rarely. In tragedy the wicked man will often turn simply into a sufferer (Macbeth, Claudius at his prayers), so that you hardly know how to tell him from a good man. In bringing its actors face to face with an ultimate reality, tragedy purges them of faith in norms and outcomes. "Ripeness is all," King Lear was led through madness and the experience of extreme violence to conclude. The spectator, reconciled by foreknowledge to the irreparable, arrives, ideally, at the same vision. The unpopularity of the theatre with contemporary people is a warning sign that King Lear's point of view is now pretty well beyond comprehension.

Brecht's theatre, in appearance, aims at establishing a clear demarcation line, something like the old classic distance, between audience and spectacle. The audience, alerted by the "alienation effect" to the fact that this is theatre, is meant to assume an objective stance. Chiaromonte's quarrel with Brecht was based on the conviction that this whole procedure was self-deceiving. Brecht's scenic images, seemingly objectified and held at a distance, were in fact "plastic symbols of predetermined ideas." The epic theatre, as is plain from its self-chosen name, is not even dramatic; it is staged narrative of a spectacular kind, dependent on scenic effects and living pictures. Closer, in a curious way, to realistic representation, which also cannot do without décor, than to drama, which depends only on speech.

Chiaromonte's ideas about Brecht and his forerunner Piscator are more various and subtle than I can indicate here; in effect, he respected Brecht's talent but denied his claim to be anything more than a prodigious impresario of the stage. But it should be plain from what has preceded that an avowed materialist with commitments to social agitation and historical progress could never see human action dramatically—*sub specie aeternitatis*. For a Brechtian, the very conception of reality as the ineluctable, that which is and cannot be altered, would be bound to be either repellent or of marginal concern. The individual fate, in the epic theatre, has scarcely any meaning in comparison to the happiness of the species. The spectator's emotions and power of empathy are transferred from the unheroic heroes of the spectacle to a large opaque social unit, represented in the most famous instance by Mother Courage's speechless wooden cart.

In this essay the initial paradox of Chiaromonte—a man who hated artifice and loved the art of the buskined performer—has not been altogether resolved into a non-contradiction. Yet at least we can now see, I hope, that the paradox is not just a quirk or quiddity of his character but corresponds with the fundamental reality-unreality synergism at work in the drama itself. Chiaromonte was not the first stubborn truthlover to be drawn as if by tropism to a world of mountebanks (see, again, Shakespeare, and Shaw and Ibsen) and he accepted it as his personal fate, to be borne with philosophy.

To write about him and his ideas, now that he is dead, has been a hard undertaking. I should have liked him to be able to listen, approve, dissent, modify. Above all, *help*. Yet in reality, as I suddenly recognize, he *has*—on the principle of God-helps-those-who-help-themselves—by being absent, beyond recall or consultation. Having been myself a theatre reviewer, off and on, for nearly forty years, shared a lot of Chiaromonte's judgments, followed his column during periods when I lived in Italy, I have now been made to ponder for the first time on the deeper motives of the dramatic art. Rereading the essays about to be republished and the earlier collection, *The Dramatic Situation*, rushing back to have a look at Chekhov, Pirandello, Ibsen, dipping into Shakespeare and the dictionary has been an experience like those rare ones of student days when all at once everything thought and studied hangs together. In other words, one has learned something. It is too much to hope for anything like Elijah's mantle—even a little piece of it—to fall on me as a reward for industry. But, as you remember from your student days, those moments when everything fitted (even though there was much more to learn and never enough time) left you feeling very happy.

February 20, 1975

Saying Good-bye
to Hannah (1907–1975)

HER LAST BOOK was to be called *The Life of the Mind* and was intended to be a pendant to *The Human Condition* (first called *The Vita Activa*), where she had scrutinized the triad of labor, work, and action: man as *animal laborans*, *homo faber*, and doer of public deeds. She saw the mind's life, or *vita contemplativa*, as divided into three parts also: thinking, willing, and judging. The first section, on thinking, was finished some time ago. The second, on willing, she finished just before she died, with what must have been relief, for she had found the will the most elusive of the three faculties to grapple with. The third, on judging, she had already sketched out in her mind and somewhat explored in lectures; though the literature on the subject was sparse (mainly Kant), she did not expect it to give her much difficulty.

I say "her last book," and that is how she thought of it, as a final task or crowning achievement, if she could only bring it off—not only filling in the other side of the tablet of human capacities but a labor of love in itself for the highest and least visible of them: the activity of the mind. If she had lived to see the book (two volumes, actually) through the press, no doubt she would have gone on writing, since her nature was expressive as well as thoughtful, but she would have felt that her true work was done.

Being Hannah Arendt, she would have executed a service or mission she had been put into the world to perform. In this sense, I believe she was religious. Hannah had heard a voice such as spoke to the prophets, the call that came to the child Samuel, girded with a linen ephod in the house of Eli, the high priest. One can look on this more secularly and think that she felt herself indentured, bound as though under contract by her particular endowments, given her by Nature, developed in her by her teachers—Jaspers and Heidegger— and tragically enriched by History. It was not a matter of self-fulfillment (the idea would have been laughable or else detestable to Hannah) but of an injunction laid on all of us, not just the talented, to follow the trajectory chance and fate have launched us on, like a poet keeping faith with his muse. Hannah was not a believer in slavish notions of one's "duty" (which may be why she had so much trouble with the section on the will) but she was responsive to a sense of calling, vocation, including that of the citizen to serve the common life. She was also a very private person, and I think (though we never spoke of it) that *The Life of the Mind* was a task she dedicated to the memory of Heinrich, a kind of completion and rounding out of *their* common life.

Heinrich Bluecher, her husband and friend, was the last of her teachers. Though he was only ten years older than she, in their intellectual relationship there was something fatherly, indulgent, on his side, and pupil-like, eager, approval-seeking, on hers; as she spoke, he would look on her fondly, nodding to himself, as though luck had sent him an unimaginably bright girl student and tremendous "achiever," which he himself, a philosopher in every sense, was content, with his pipes and cigars, not to be. He was proud of her and knew she would go far, to peaks and ranges he could discern in the distance, while he calmly sat back, waiting for her to find them.

For her, Heinrich was like a pair of corrective lenses; she did not wholly trust her vision until it had been confirmed by his. While they thought alike on most questions, he was more a "pure" philosophic spirit, and she was more concerned with the *vita activa* of politics and fabrication—the fashioning of durable objects in the form of books and articles. Neither was much interested in the biological sphere of the *animal laborans*—household drudgery, consumption of goods; though both were fond of young people, they never had any children. When he died, late in 1970, quite suddenly, though not as suddenly as she, she was alone. Surrounded by friends, she rode like a solitary passenger on her train of thought. So *The Life of the Mind*, begun in those bleak years, was conceived and pondered for (and she must have hoped *with*) Heinrich Bluecher, not exactly a monument but something like a triptych or folding panel with the mysterious will at the center. Anyway, that is what I guess, and she is not here to ask.

I spoke of a crowning achievement, but Hannah was not in the least ambitious (absurd to connect her with a "career"); if there was some striving for a crown, it was in the sense of a summit toward which she had labored in order to be able to look around, like an explorer, finishing the last stages of an ascent alone. What would be spread out before her were the dark times she had borne witness to, as a Jewess and a displaced person, the long-drawn-out miscarriage of a socialist revolution, the present perils of the American Republic, where she had found a new home in which to hang, with increasing despondency, the ideas of freedom she had carried with her. From her summit she would also look out at the vast surveyor's map of concepts and insights, some inherited from a long philosophical tradition and some her own discoveries, which, regarded from a high point, could at least show us where we were.

In the realm of ideas, Hannah was a conservationist; she did not believe in throwing anything away that had once been thought. A use might be found for it; in her own way, she was an enthusiastic recycler. To put it differently, thought,

37

for her, was a kind of husbandry, a humanizing of the wilderness of experience—building houses, running paths and roads through, damming streams, planting windbreaks. The task that had fallen to her, as an exceptionally gifted intellect and a representative of the generations she had lived among, was to apply thought systematically to each and every characteristic experience of her time—*anomie*, terror, advanced warfare, concentration camps, Auschwitz, inflation, revolution, school integration, the Pentagon Papers, space, Watergate, Pope John, violence, civil disobedience—and, having finally achieved this, to direct thought inward, upon itself, and its own characteristic processes.

The word "systematically" may be misleading. Despite her German habits, Hannah was not a system-builder. Rather, she sought to descry systems that were already *there*, inherent in the body of man's interaction with the world and with himself as subject. The distinctions made by language, from very ancient times, indeed from the birth of speech, between *this* and *that* (e.g., work and labor, public and private, force, power, and violence), reveal man as categorizer, a "born" philosopher, if you will, with the faculty of separating, of finely discriminating, more natural to his species than that of constructing wholes. If I understood her, Hannah was always more for the Many than for the One (which may help explain her horrified recognition of totalitarianism as a new phenomenon in the world). She did not want to find a master key or universal solvent, and if she had a religion, it was certainly not monotheistical. The proliferation of distinctions in her work, branching out in every direction like tender shoots, no doubt owes something to her affection for the scholastics but it also testifies to a sort of typical awe-struck modesty before the world's abundance and intense particularity.

But I do not want to discuss Hannah's ideas here but to try to bring her back as a person, a physical being, showing her-

self radiantly in what she called the world of appearance, a
stage from which she has now withdrawn. She was a beautiful woman, alluring, seductive, feminine, which is why I said
"Jewess"—the old-fashioned term, evoking the daughters of
Sion, suits her, like a fringed Spanish shawl. Above all, her
eyes, so brilliant and sparkling, starry when she was happy or
excited, but also deep, dark, remote, pools of inwardness.
There was something unfathomable in Hannah that seemed
to lie in the reflective depths of those eyes.

She had small, fine hands, charming ankles, elegant feet.
She liked shoes; in all the years I knew her, I think she only
once had a corn. Her legs, feet, and ankles expressed quick-
ness, decision. You had only to see her on a lecture stage to
be struck by those feet, calves, and ankles that seemed to keep
pace with her thought. As she talked, she moved about,
sometimes with her hands plunged in her pockets like somebody all alone on a walk, meditating. When the fire laws permitted, she would smoke, pacing the stage with a cigarette in
a short holder, inhaling from time to time, reflectively, her
head back, as if arrested by a new, unexpected idea. Watching her talk to an audience was like seeing the motions of the
mind made visible in action and gesture. Peripatetic, she would
come abruptly to a halt at the lectern, frown, consult the
ceiling, bite her lip. If she was reading a speech, there were
always interjections, asides, like the footnotes that peppered
her texts with qualifications.

There was more than a touch of the great actress in
Hannah. The first time I heard her speak in public—nearly
thirty years ago, during a debate—I was reminded of what
Bernhardt must have been or Proust's Berma, a magnificent
stage diva, which implies a goddess. Perhaps a chthonic goddess, or a fiery one, rather than the airy kind. Unlike other
good speakers, she was not at all an orator. She appeared,
rather, as a mime, a thespian, enacting a drama of mind, that
dialogue of me-and-myself she so often summons up in her

writings. Watching her framed in the proscenium arch, we were not far from the sacred origins of the theatre. What she projected was the human figure as actor and sufferer in the agon of consciousness and reflection, where there are always two, the one who says and the one who replies or questions.

Yet nobody could have been farther from an exhibitionist. Calculation of the impression she was making never entered her head. Whenever she spoke in public, she had terrible stage fright, and afterward she would ask only "Was it all right?" (This cannot have been true of the classroom, where she felt herself at ease and among friends.) And naturally she did not play roles in private or public, even less than the normal amount required in social relations. She was incapable of feigning. Though she prided herself as a European on being able to tell a lie, where we awkward Americans blurted out the truth, in fact there was a little hubris there. Hannah's small points of vanity never had any relation to her real accomplishments. For example, she thought she knew a good deal about cooking and didn't. It was the same with her supposed ability to lie. Throughout our friendship, I don't think I ever heard her tell even one of those white lies, such as pleading illness or a previous engagement, to get herself out of a social quandary. If you wrote something she found bad, her policy was not to allude to it—an unvarying strategy that told you louder than words what she thought.

What was theatrical in Hannah was a kind of spontaneous power of being seized by an idea, an emotion, a presentiment, whose vehicle her body then became, like the actor's. And this power of being seized and worked upon, often with a start, widened eyes, "Ach!" (before a picture, a work of architecture, some deed of infamy), set her apart from the rest of us like a high electrical charge. And there was the vibrant, springy, dark, short hair, never fully gray, that sometimes from sheer force of energy appeared to stand bolt upright on her head.

40

I suppose all this must have been part of an unusual physical endowment, whose manifestation in her features and facial gestures was the beauty I spoke of. Hannah is the only person I have ever watched *think*. She lay motionless on a sofa or a day bed, arms folded behind her head, eyes shut but occasionally opening to stare upward. This lasted—I don't know—from ten minutes to half an hour. Everyone tiptoed past if we had to come into the room in which she lay oblivious.

She was an impatient, generous woman, and those qualities went hand in hand. Just as, in a speech or an essay, she would put everything in but the kitchen stove, as if she could not keep in reserve a single item of what she knew or had happened that instant to occur to her, so she would press on a visitor assorted nuts, chocolates, candied ginger, tea, coffee, Campari, whiskey, cigarettes, cake, crackers, fruit, cheese, almost all at once, regardless of conventional sequence or, often, of the time of day. It was as if the profusion of edibles, set out, many of them, in little ceremonial-like dishes and containers, were impatient propitiatory offerings to all the queer gods of taste. Someone said that this was the eternal Jewish mother, but it was not that: there was no notion that any of this fodder was good for you; in fact most of it was distinctly bad for you, which she must have known somehow, for she did not insist.

She had a respect for privacy, separateness, one's own and hers. I often stayed with her—and Heinrich and her—on Riverside Drive and before that on Morningside Drive, so that I came to know Hannah's habits well, what she liked for breakfast, for instance. A boiled egg, some mornings, a little ham or cold cuts, toast spread with anchovy paste, coffee, of course, half a grapefruit or fresh orange juice, but perhaps that last was only when I, the American, was there. The summer after Heinrich's death she came to stay with us in

Maine, where we gave her a separate apartment, over the garage, and I put some thought into buying supplies for her kitchen—she liked to breakfast alone. The things, I thought, that she would have at home, down to instant coffee (which I don't normally stock) for when she could not be bothered with the filters. I was rather pleased to have been able to find anchovy paste in the village store. On the afternoon of her arrival, as I showed her where everything was in the larder, she frowned over the little tube of anchovy paste, as though it were an inexplicable foreign object. "What is that?" I told her. "Oh." She put it down and looked thoughtful and as though displeased, somehow. No more was said. But I knew I had done something wrong in my efforts to please. She did not wish to be *known*, in that curiously finite and, as it were, reductive way. And I had done it to show her I knew her—a sign of love, though not always—thereby proving that in the last analysis I did not know her at all.

Her eyes were closed in her coffin, and her hair was waved back from her forehead, whereas *she* pulled it forward, sometimes tugging at a lock as she spoke, partly to hide a scar she had got in an automobile accident—but even before that she had never really bared her brow. In her coffin, with the lids veiling the fathomless eyes, that noble forehead topped by a sort of pompadour, she was not Hannah any more but a composed death mask of an eighteenth-century philosopher. I was not moved to touch that grand stranger in the funeral parlor, and only in the soft yet roughened furrows of her neck, in which the public head rested, could I find a place to tell her good-bye.

January 22, 1976

F. W. Dupee
(1904–1979)

JAUNTY, wry, rueful. Flash of kingfisher blue eyes. Edmund
Wilson liked to say there was something French about him.
A person of courage and irony. Much self-irony. Voice ironical with a sort of slide in it. Wrote particularly well about
elegant, dandyish writers—James, Nabokov, Malraux—if
anyone as elephantine as James can be thought of as a dandy
or fop. He himself had a quality of elegance, but mixed, very
appealingly, with innocence, the Joliet, Illinois, of his youth.
Though he had the normal quota of parents, there was a sense
of the orphan about him—he and his sister as two orphans in
the big wide world. Was always like the boyish hero of a *Bildungsroman*.

Unsuitable, often comic things were always happening
to him, as when he worked as an organizer for the Communist Party on the waterfront while being literary editor of the
New Masses. Or his being on the protective picket line for
the students at Columbia in 1968, the day he got a new and
expensive set of the finest porcelain teeth—example of rueful
courage, since he expected to be hit by a night stick. On that
occasion he stood up against his respectable friends of the
faculty. Wrote about it—including the teeth, I think—for the
New York Review of Books.

There was something permanently subversive about him,
and he was attracted to the modern literature he taught so

well—Proust, Joyce, Mann, Kafka, etc.—by the sense that it was subversive of established values and forms. Yet he was never a bohemian; he was too much attracted to style for that. Hence he was continually finding himself in incongruous positions. He was a lightning rod for the absurd and the incongruous. Or you could say that the dryness of his mind—he was very intelligent—accorded strangely with a wild streak in him, with curiosity and with an impressionable soul.

It was through him I came to Bard College to teach, and I think he was more at home at a place like Bard than he was later at Columbia—for one thing, Bard was more amusing, more incorrigible, like himself. Yet he was not, and never could have been, a cult figure. In his own way, he was an upholder of order and legitimacy, or, let's say, a wry sympathizer with their efforts to stay in place. Not vain, unprejudiced, fair-minded.

March 8, 1979

REPORT

On the Demo,
London, 1968*

IT WAS VERY English to call it "the Demo," and no wonder the pet name stuck, conjuring up the specter of "demos," the people (sometimes pejorative), but on the other hand "democracy" (good), which withstood the test of the demonstration. Small family-style states are fond of making up diminutives, whose effect is to diminish, make cosy; compare "the telly" to big gross American "TV." Yet the striking fact about the October 27 dual march was that it was organized and directed by aliens in competition with each other: Tariq Ali, a young moustached Pakistani, leading the way to Downing Street, and Abhimanya Manchanda, a middle-aged clean-shaven Indian, to Grosvenor Square.

For the English, these rival pied pipers were difficult to swallow, let alone assimilate. A well-fleshed, somewhat lachrymose police sergeant sought to explain his obscure sense of injury relating to the Demo, which in principle he did not exactly oppose but saw as a conflict of rights: the right to push your pram, undisturbed, down the Strand on Sunday and the right, slightly less hallowed, to march. We were standing in a pub near a Central London police station on the eve of the

*The *Sunday Times* of London had invited me to come over from Paris, where I lived, to report on a big demonstration against the war in Vietnam.

47

demonstration. What stuck in his craw, he confided, leaning forward and lowering his voice, was "those foreigners." "It's the bill you're paying for Empire," I replied. He appreciated the point (English fair-mindedness) and laughed. The discussion continued. I made some feeble joke about seeing him tomorrow, in jail. "You don't mean to say you're going to *march?*" "Certainly!" "Stay home and watch it on the television. Take my advice." He made a face, leaning forward in another burst of confidence and wrinkling up his broad manly nose. It wasn't the "pushing and shoving" he minded in those demonstrations. "It's the BO. Phew!"

Just then, a police car siren blew. "That's my tune," he said, grinning. Then another. Outside, cops were racing out of the police station, pulling on their coats, clapping on their helmets, and boarding police wagons. The sergeant hastily left his glass of lager on the bar. We left our drinks too and ran. A large force of alarmed bobbies was converging on Westminster Abbey, where some pink-cheeked, tow-headed schoolboys from Manchester, wearing red-and-white scarves, in town for the football match, had been apprehended on the sidewalk; their average age was maybe fourteen. A flash had come through that some unknown persons were breaking into the Abbey; possibly one or two of the little Manchester rooters had tried to climb the fence. In a minute, the police, embarrassed, were returning to base. In preparation for the Demo, they had been sleeping in at the police station, with a barrel of beer, occupying it, in short, like the students on guard at the London School of Economics. Both sides were nervous, gloomy, and gay. It worried me that with all that beer the police might have hangovers the next day, which would make them irritable. The sergeant complained that the pigeons under the eaves of his "dormitory" had been keeping him awake.

In the occupied LSE, which we had just visited, the only drinks being served were coffee and tea. As at the Sorbonne last May and June, you could buy apples and sandwiches.

Some students were already asleep in the corridors, but most were just milling about or reading the posters and slogans on the walls, many of which seemed to be copied from the French slogans. A local touch was a small notice: "Babies and Children Cared for during Demonstration. Please apply," etc. In the big auditorium, movies were being shown of previous demonstrations: the May-June French marches and street fighting and the March 17 rally against our Embassy in Grosvenor Square. This made me think of the Marines at Da Nang watching old Hollywood Second World War movies—the hair of the dog. There were fewer jokes here than in the police station—less irony. An infirmary to receive the wounded was being prepared, and the next morning there would be an ambulance standing outside the entrance hall—a camouflaged truck from Cardiff. It was plain that they expected casualties.

"What do you hope to accomplish by this demonstration?" I had been asking Tariq Ali in the offices of the *Black Dwarf* on Carlisle Street, which was placarded with art work of Fidel and Che, back issues of the magazine, provocative slogans. There were photos of the enemy: Axel Springer, Paul Getty, Howard Hughes. There was a striking photo of U.S. Marines in bristling combat formation resembling a human porcupine ready to throw its quills. There was an art photo involving a discarded condom, and a typed list of first-aid stations by districts. In this show window of pop politics, like a vision from another world, hung a very big photograph of Trotsky, with his clear, intelligent, spectacled, professorial eyes ("What are *you* doing here, old friend?" I wanted to ask "the Old Man.") A new issue of the magazine had just been printed, and young distributors were hurrying out with it. Someone ran in to say that one of the sellers had been arrested in Piccadilly Circus for "causing an obstruction." (The British guardians of order, off camera, were still up to their old tricks; see "Freedom of the Park" in *The Collected Essays, Journalism, and Letters of George Orwell* commenting on the arrests for "obstruction" of five people selling *Freedom* [Anarchist], *Peace News,* and other left-wing papers in Hyde Park. That was in December 1945, under an earlier Labor Government, and Orwell wondered how it was that you did not hear of newsboys being run in for selling the *Daily Telegraph,* the *Tablet,* or the *Spectator.*)

The *Dwarf* office, temporary staff headquarters for the Vietnam Solidarity Campaign (Trotskyist, as opposed to the British Vietnam Solidarity Front, Maoist), suggested a *stage set* of revolution, with supernumeraries like spear-bearers entering stage right and left, bit players speaking lines of studied rudeness as in some up-dated Wildean comedy, breathless messengers, and a general atmospheric litter, the floor serving as a communal ash-tray. I could not resist the feeling that I had been cast in the role of audience and ought to have paid an admission. At the pub around the corner, just off stage, Special Branch men were posing as customers.

The words "What do you hope to accomplish?", etc. had, I quickly discovered, the effect of a negative password. It virtually invited the bum's rush. How narrowly I had escaped that, I realized the next morning during a pre-march briefing at the London School of Economics when a middle-aged man in a hat addressed that question to the chairman. "Get the hell out." "Infiltrator." "Spy." "Get stuffed." "There's ladies present." "Give him a chance, for Christ's sake." "This bugger didn't come here to ask a *bona fide* question. He came here to cause chaos." In fact, from the sneer in his voice, I too concluded that the man in the hat was there for no good purpose. His hat itself was a provocation. Yet whatever his intention (or mine), the question was a natural one, which the very scale of the preparations on both sides (forty doctors and nurses and four ambulances at the LSE alone) necessarily brought to the mind of the ordinary perplexed Londoner: "What do they expect to *gain* by it, I ask you?" the sergeant had mused, in the pub.

I had been thinking about the problem myself, in a U.S. context—would it do any good to march again on the Pentagon?—and it seems to me that there is a law of diminishing returns that applies to demonstrations, though nobody can be sure at what point it will begin to operate. But if a demonstration reveals your weakness, rather than your strength, it may not be a good plan to hold it. And built into demonstrations, as into any kind of warfare, there is the tendency to escalate, to make up in increasing violence what you lack in force, till the number of injured on both sides becomes the measure of the success of a march, and this is particularly true when modern means of publicity are focused on the combat. Here—the opposite of regular warfare—each side tends to overestimate its own casualties and to underestimate those of the enemy. Or, as a police inspector said: "We will be trying to *minimize* arrests. The students hope to *maximize* them."

Tariq Ali, though he did not express it so succinctly, was aware of being caught in a dilemma implicit in the war games of street protest. Having attacked Grosvenor Square in March, he did not wish to "repeat himself" in October, for the only way of topping the previous performance there would be by a heightening of violence. Hence he spoke of Grosvenor Square as a "death trap," to which he was unwilling to commit his followers. De-escalation, according to this reasoning, then became inevitable—a change of pace and direction, to Downing Street and Hyde Park, rather than to the U.S. Embassy, and in disciplined, orderly formation, instead of in fighting salients.

He was thinking, clearly, in terms of showmanship, and in these terms he may have been right, except that the London police stole the show on him. Moreover, in his concentration on the *manner* of the demonstration, he lost sight of the matter: the U.S. war in Vietnam. Indeed, the Demo, which might have been a tragedy, turned into a comedy of manners. He did not foresee that, of course, on the eve of the march, nor perceive it later by hindsight. What the demonstration had already accomplished, he told me, was that all over England, in pubs tonight, people were talking about Vietnam, which had been practically forgotten since March. Did he really believe this? According to my guess, people in pubs were talking about the Demo all right and about *him*, but not about Vietnam and this could not be blamed exclusively on the press. The oncoming confrontation between the police and the marchers was viewed as a domestic sporting event in which you chose sides and took bets, but also, if you were fearful, as a sort of invasion from Mars or D Day, D standing for doom. With a tense contest like that right on their doorstep or scheduled live, on video, how could people be expected to turn their attention to a war in a remote country and to which the sole active British contribution was training police dogs to track down Viet Cong? Like many fiery and histrionic persons, Tariq Ali seemed to have no sense of the impact of the drama he was mounting on the ordinary clowns in the gallery. In short, no common sense. "What do you hope to accomplish, etc.?" is a commonsensical question, which was why it was an unwelcome interruption in a theatre of revolution.

In his bed-sitter in Hampstead, Mr. Abhimanya Manchanda, the leader of the Maoist group, accepted the question as perfectly legitimate. "I do not know," he said, and then added, with a mischievous giggle, "but I know we are giving the Government the jitters." This was incontestably true. The effect of the march, he went on, more formally, would be to call the Vietnamese question to public attention, which was the same as what Tariq Ali had said and yet quite different. Indeed, to my pleased surprise (for on the basis of rumor and press reports I had been expecting a frightening super-left irrealist in comparison to whom the burning-eyed Tariq Ali would look like a board meeting of the Fabian Society), Mr.

Manchanda, small and rather merry, had his feet very much on the ground. When we telephoned on that Saturday night to check up on the address, we were told that he was out, which was a blow, because we had an appointment with him for an interview. "Oh, he'll be right back," an American girl's voice said. "He's just gone to the Laundromat." In the entry hall of the two-story house, not far from where Karl Marx had lived, there was an empty baby carriage and outside on the steps were some milk bottles. The baby evidently belonged to the family upstairs, perhaps his disciples; we met two American girls and a young Canadian man in the small bed-sitting room whose chief article of furniture was a large duplicator. These young people, unlike the supernumeraries at the *Black Dwarf*, were not wearing the costumes, hair styles, and fashion accessories of the pace-setting New Left. They were dressed in plain ordinary clothes; one of the girls was in pants. The furniture was old and losing some of its stuffing, but the room was neat and there were ash-trays. Mr. Manchanda went out to make us some coffee in the kitchen. Behind me, above the Regency-style sofa on which I was sitting, was a sight familiar to me from North Vietnam: Marx, Engels, Lenin, and Stalin. Above them was a big colored photograph of Mao and on the opposite wall a nice one of Ho. No slogans, no poster art. The girls were bending over a tract they had just taken out of the duplicator.

Mr. Manchanda, a former teacher, was an old-fashioned classical Marxist. Like many of those men, he had a witty mind, referring to Tariq Ali as a "revisionist playboy," and remarking, after the march was over, that he had not cared to join Tariq Ali's "guided tour of the West End." He explained with patience the doctrinal differences between them. It was a question of correct slogans about the Vietnamese war.

For a long time, the Trotskyists of the Vietnamese Solidarity Campaign had refused the slogan "Victory for the NLF," on the ground that the NLF, a coalition of a number of class elements, had a bourgeois nationalist complexion; *their* slogan was "Support for the Vietnamese Revolution," i.e., for a non-existent phenomenon. Similarly with the Maoist slogan "Long Live Ho Chi Minh," rejected by the Trotskyists on the ground that Ho had betrayed the revolution at Geneva in 1954, also that he exemplifed the cult of personality and was a "bureaucrat." "If Ho is a bureaucrat," observed Mr. Manchanda, with glee, "I wish we had more bureaucrats in this country."

I must say that on these issues, which had no direct bearing on the march, I considered the Maoists to be completely right. As for the march itself, here too I found myself agreeing with Mr. Manchanda: the main enemy is in Grosvenor Square; march on him there; never mind if you are repeating yourself. On the issue of violence vs. non-violence, there did not seem to be a real theoretical difference. The Manchanda group had been described in the newspapers as favoring violence, and the Tariq Ali group not, but actually Tariq Ali was organizing dramatically for violence (that list of first-aid stations, manned with doctors and nurses) on the supposition, amounting to prophecy, that the police would start or "provoke" it, whereas Mr. Manchanda, when I asked him whether it was true that he planned to storm the U.S. Embassy, shrugged and said simply, "We are too few." In Grosvenor Square, the next day, a lilting voice I thought I recognized as his could be heard urging restraint on the crowd, though possibly this was merely *pro forma*. In fairness to the sincerity of Tariq Ali's position, it should be added that the sheer fact of marching on Grosvenor Square contained a potential of violence, which handing in a petition at Downing Street did not. Grosvenor Square, if not a death-trap, is a box in which pressures build up almost by themselves. Once you have marched into it, you find yourself waiting for something to happen, and the next stage is to *wish* for something to happen; you cannot just stand there all afternoon, looking at the police while they look back at you. That wish, incidentally, was shared by TV viewers and by the press at large; the contemptuous descriptions of the march as a "fizzle," the "non-event of the year," and so on, by people who *opposed* it, reveal an acute disappointment with the relative peacefulness of the encounter. Instead, one might take heart from just that. The fact that so little did happen in the interior of that box is probably a lesson in the effectiveness of Gandhian techniques. For the first time perhaps in history a massed police force practiced "passive" resistance, and it worked. Thus if the police are brutal, as in Mayor Daley's Chicago, it is not from necessity, as they insist, but from choice.

What came out of our meeting with Mr. Manchanda, following on our meeting with Tariq Ali, was a series of paradoxes. The Trotskyists, in slogans and stance to the left of the Maoists, in practice were to the right of them. The Maoists, generally thought of as inflexible revolutionary extremists, showed empirical wisdom and adaptability. The *style* of Tariq Ali was radical; the style of Mr. Manchanda was modest petty bourgeois, recalling the home lives of Marx, Lenin, and Trotsky himself. Maoist China, they say, is hermetic, suspicious, hostile to foreigners, yet the Maoist cell in Hampstead was as open as the Laundromat where Mr. Manchanda had been doing his smalls. Though we came from the bourgeois press, we were not treated as trespassers but simply as guests— the reverse of what had happened in Carlisle Street. It was even possible to take exception, as I did, to the icon of Stalin; "We can continue that discussion another time," said Mr. Manchanda after a few words defending Stalin's place in the history of revolution.

This too was perhaps a lesson in the persuasiveness of non-violent techniques on the plane of ordinary human relations, for the next afternoon, marching up from the Embankment, when we came to the crossroads of choice at Trafalgar Square, whether to turn left with the Trotskyists down

to Whitehall and Downing Street or right with the Maoists to
Grosvenor Square, I had no real hesitation in making up my
mind, and what slight hesitation I had was purely journalistic, for the police had told us the previous night that Grosvenor Square might be a "decoy," to draw Her Majesty's forces
off from the real site of battle. Innocent of the sectarian character of left-wing politics, they seemed to think that Mr.
Manchanda could be in cahoots with Tariq Ali to execute a
master coup.

Scotland Yard was alert, almost comically so, to all contingencies. They gave themselves full credit for the elaborate
precautions they took, to screen buses of demonstrators arriving from the country and make sure there were no hidden
marbles or other weapons aboard, to screen airports and other
points of entry for agitators arriving from the Continent, to
screen the universities and uncover the identities of potential
"troublemakers." An inspector told us there were Special
Branch men assigned to every university as a matter of course—
a piece of news, casually delivered, which as an American I
found disturbing and unpleasant, for if we have FBI men on
all our campuses, it is kept dark, and, if known, would cause
a national uproar. I am against police spies on campuses.
Despite appearances, the English are tougher than the Americans, more pragmatic and cool-headed—the result probably
of having a seasoned ruling class trained in the public-school
system. There was nothing crude or inefficient in the handling of that march; and the punishment that followed, like
the advance precautions, was swift and almost silent. On
Monday, five youths, three of them unemployed, were given
sentences up to three months' imprisonment for "possessing
offensive weapons": one had allegedly thrown a bottle, one
was carrying a flag-stick, one a walking-stick, one admitted
possessing three bags of marbles, and one, who got two months,

was accused of having "a piece of wood" and assaulting a constable, which he denied. This summary justice (the other side of the coin or, let us say, of the shiny merit badge) rated a tiny inconspicuous item in the *Times*, about an inch high; no details were supplied, not even names or ages. The above information comes from the *Guardian*, which, like the *Telegraph*, printed a fuller story but gave it no undue prominence. Several other persons received suspended sentences, and two "men," aged eighteen, were remanded in custody till the following week for using "an electronic device" to interfere with police radios.

It is true that at certain moments flag-sticks were flying about "like spears," the press said; if they had said "like toy spears," it would have been more to the point, for the flag-sticks I saw launched into the air were so thin and light they almost floated. Some firecrackers were thrown, causing the police horses to rear. Pennies were hurled at the police and at windows of flats, but no window I saw was broken except a big plate-glass one on South Audley Street, which looked as if it had been smashed in a charge. Once there was an incident that for a moment looked like trouble: when a fat, short, middle-aged woman wearing a bright-green embroidered mandarin coat began prowling along her balcony, somebody threw an object at her which proved to be a cardboard disc; a middle-aged man, probably her husband, came out from the flat and twice inspected it with a concerned, moral air. It was impossible to feel sympathy for people like that, who were making a parade of looking down in a figurative and literal sense on the crowd of protesters below, nor for the spectators in the windows of the American Embassy, out of range of any missiles. One man in a left Embassy window was busy photographing throughout; even when night came, his lens, evidently infra-red, was pointed at us—impossible to guess whether he was an Embassy security officer duly identifying the "troublemakers," or just a camera nut, like the G.I.s in Vietnam who are said to go into combat snapping pictures to send home as souvenirs.

But it was not hard to sympathize with the police and their frightened, rearing horses. It was Sunday, a day off for most of them, and it is not pleasant to have things thrown at you, harmless or not, and to have your helmet knocked off and tossed about as a trophy, when you are only doing your duty. Guarding an embassy is not a wicked action *per se*, but just routine in all countries when circumstances call for it, and if the demonstrators had broken through the police cordons, they might have met something decidedly worse inside: a chief inspector from Scotland Yard assured us that the Marine guards were armed with Mace and machine guns—a recurring rumor strongly denied by the Embassy, which can point to the fact that even in Moscow, when the U.S. Embassy has been besieged by crowds, the Marine guard has not had machine guns. Only the regulation pistols.

There is no doubt that the British police behaved with amazing self-control and good humor, under a certain amount of provocation. It is stupid to deny this and to assign the credit to the order and "discipline" of the demonstrators, who, at least in Grosvenor Square, were not especially orderly, even in terms of their own aims. They could probably have broken through the police lines if they had had better organization and leadership. The majority plainly did not wish to or only half-heartedly, but they would have followed if a breach had been made. As it was, only the Anarchists were serious about mounting charges, from the direction of South Audley Street, one of which was nearly successful. The Anarchists that afternoon were the best fighters, and among them must have been some of the young unemployed workmen who got sentenced in the magistrates' court; they were fairly easy to pick out in the crowd, which was mainly middle class or upper middle and student, by the Rocker-style leather jackets they wore and by their expressions of intent, concentrated fury. "If you're just here to look, push off," one of them said to me.

They were angry not just with "the fuzz" (their term) but with the whole demonstration for its idle and frivolous affability. We older people laughed and joked a good deal, greeted friends; some pretty women exchanged fashion notes: "No, it's not new. I wore it in the last demonstration." Gravity succeeded as a fair-haired boy, retreating from the police lines, bent double and retched; he had evidently been punched in the stomach. A respectful space was cleared for him, but he staggered off toward the rear of the square. Improvised ambulances drove through, with students riding on the top, from the LSE, to pick up the wounded. An occasional regular ambulance, with a blue light flashing, came to pick up injured bobbies. We were not near enough to the actual fighting to see punches exchanged—only the results.

It occurred to me that the more militant students might think of using an ambulance as a Trojan horse (or *kamikaze*) to penetrate the police barrier, but this did not happen. Respect for the rules of war. On the other hand, quite early, some youths who did not look like demonstrators (more like fascists, someone said) scaled one of the surrounding buildings that was in scaffolding. The police declined the gambit, whereupon the idea caught on; soon agile boys from the march were swarming over the scaffolding, up to the roof, on to the neighboring balcony, pursued eventually by somewhat heavy-footed police. A handsome young black man in a brilliant red sweat shirt who was in the grip of a constable twirled free and leaped from the balcony to the next building; everybody cheered, and the cops gave up the chase. These human-fly acrobatics suggested that the demonstrators might have done well to employ a cat-burglar to enter the Embassy through the roof or a back window while police attention was focused on the front; despite its grim moat, the Embassy cannot be as impregnable as it looks, and with a little ingenuity plus possibly some inside help, a North Vietnamese or Viet Cong flag or a red-and-black Anarchist banner might have been planted on the roof or in a top-story window.

What was wanted, clearly, was a symbolic victory of that sort, a miming of the Tet offensive when the Viet Cong briefly occupied a piece of American soil—the ground floor of the Saigon Embassy. Of course this Grosvenor Square assembly was powerless, just as preceding ones had been, to alter the foreign policy represented by the impersonal grey building flying the Stars and Stripes. Powerlessness, frustration, were what the Demo was about. Conceivably, power might have been momentarily outwitted by intelligence and daring, the natural guerrilla weapons of the weaker party. Home-made petrol bombs, even if Black Dwarfs had manufactured them in quantity, could not have blasted a way into the Embassy citadel. In any case, the point is not to imitate the violence of the enemy, which you are reprehending out of the other side of your mouth.

Such a demonstration is a mock war, which should culminate in a mock triumph. Peaceful means—protests, vigils, handing in petitions, letters to the editor—have long ago been exhausted, and everyone feels this. Everyone, that is, who cares about stopping the slaughter in Vietnam. But though English youth, accepting the challenge, has declared all-out war on the U.S., it does not have the weapons to wage it single-handed. As Mr. Manchanda said, "We are too few." Yet somewhere in between the old peaceful means and outright street battles or terrorism, there is an area worth study if your object is to harass and embarrass your enemy without terrifying the bulk of your own population, which in principle you are seeking to win over. The photograph which appeared in at least three London newspapers, of a demonstrator's boot kicking a policeman in the jaw while two other demonstrators held him down, is not really calculated to popularize the antiwar effort. No doubt that is why the newspapers used it with such unanimity, and no doubt too a photo might have been taken of the unique instance of police brutality attested by the National Council for Civil Liberties (reported in the *Guardian*), when an NCCL observer was kneed in the groin by one constable and then, when he objected and showed his accreditation card, he was beaten and kneed by "about" eight others. . . . The fact, however, is that no cameraman was around when that happened—only a young woman who gave supporting testimony—and most amateur observers in the square agree that police behavior where *they* happened to be was impeccable.

It was almost as if the bobbies, the more inactive ones, enjoyed it, were amused by the whole scene, especially since they were under orders *not* to intervene when they could avoid doing so. Cheerfully lacking authority, they could look on the crowd as equals. This absence of ill-feeling, on both sides, among those on the periphery of the sporadic actual fighting was much commented upon. Example: a young demonstrator standing with a cigarette between his lips, in the crush of bodies could not get his hands free to light it; a bobby, observing this, reached forward and politely struck flame from his lighter. The famous example, which many people could hardly credit, was the police joining the demonstrators in singing "Auld Lang Syne" as they all prepared to call it a night.

The high points of the afternoon were the magical escape of the young black man and the lowering of the Stars and Stripes at sundown. Both drew loud clapping and laughter. The slow hauling down of the U.S. colors was interpreted by the crowd as a symbolic surrender; it was what they *wished* to bring about, and they laughed as at an inadvertent pun. The low points were, first, the sudden apparition of the wounded, carried or assisted back from the front lines; second, the pushing and shoving and squeezing, which occurred whenever a charge of demonstrators was driven back into the square or into South Audley Street or when the police, having yielded ground, surged forward in a double wedge. At those moments I was conscious of a fear, for us all, of being crushed or trampled, but not, *pace* the sergeant, at any time of B.O.

So what did the demonstration accomplish, besides giving Whitehall the jitters? Any side-effects, such as heightening English national pride or training demonstrators in field maneuvers with the police, are beside the point, which is, did it give the U.S. a push toward withdrawal from Vietnam? I do not think it can be claimed with any assurance that it did. But there is another way of looking at the question. Try turning it upside down. What would *not* demonstrating have accomplished? And the answer is clear: nothing. So, given the choice between a problematical nothing and a certain nothing, maybe it was best to demonstrate after all.

It might also be asked whether the demonstration was counter-productive. That is, did it gain adherents for Harold Wilson's policy of loyal support to the U.S. State Department? Surely not, for people who were repelled by the march, by the rhythmic chants of "Ho, Ho, Ho Chi Minh" (the fee-fie-fo-fum of the youth ogre), by the slogans ("Smash the System," "We are all Foreign Scum"), by the flags, beards, and strange dress, do not make a connection between these phenomena and foreign policy. The fact that the main issue, Vietnam, was obscured by local issues, above all those of propriety and decorum ("Is this the right *way* to make your protest? Why don't you write a letter to the *Times?*") has its compensations.

Nobody who shuddered at the demonstration from his luxury-flat balcony would be moved to demand that the British immediately send troops to Vietnam or issue a statement of full confidence in the Pentagon. People like that might be moved in other ways, to demand a ban on all such marches or the exclusion of foreign troublemakers from the country or even to subscribe, out of curiosity, to the *Black Dwarf*, which they would not read after the first issue. One of their chief aims in life is to appear knowledgeable, like the party I listened to in the dining-room of my hotel the night after the march: an Englishman was explaining to a silvery blonde American woman that the "moderate" demonstrators who went to Downing Street and Hyde Park were O.K., in the best British tradition, whether you agreed with them or not, but that those who went to Grosvenor Square were quite another pair of gloves: "The thugs went to Grosvenor Square. Only the thugs." "I *see*," she said, thoughtfully nodding. "I see."

He spoke in tones of vindictive triumph. Yet the model behavior of the English police was not really a triumph for law and order. If anything, the reverse. The English bobby and his superiors rose to the occasion by disregarding the law. I do not know how many infractions were committed under my eyes—dozens, maybe a hundred—while the police stood by. Normally they would have reacted with the utmost severity to the *least* of those infractions. Indeed, there were times when the crowd, more alert to public safety than the see-no-evil, hear-no-evil guardians of order, began to protest. When a heavy object—a stone, I think—was thrown: "That's enough. What do you think you're doing, in a crowd like this? Somebody will get hurt." The crowd, in short, when authority did not move, *within itself* spontaneously created its own police force. In my opinion, the official policy was right and justified by the outcome. Nevertheless, it ought to be realized that the police, quite simply, were not enforcing the law. If they had started doing so, there would have been trouble.

This suggests two things. First, that in a tense situation leniency is a good idea—something everybody knows from private life while generally following the opposite principle in public affairs, as though our corporate persona were more "uptight" than our private natures. Second, that October 27

63

was a unique, improbable event, something to cherish in our memory book, for, short of Utopia, we shall not see it again. The police were submitted to a test and they passed it. They proved their endurance. But supposing, which seems likely, another and bigger demonstration is organized for Grosvenor Square, do you think they will stand by and again watch the law broken—a thing that is against their whole nature as policemen? A policeman unable to say "Move along, there. Step lively. Move along," as he sees a crowd collecting, is a broken man, whatever society he lives in and is employed by. Still more if he turns his back on an act of flagrant vandalism committed on private or state property. And what about danger to life and limb?

If there is anything more sinister than Mayor Daley's police, it is the police that stand by (as they did in pre-Hitler Germany, in Fascist Italy, in right-wing Karamanlis Greece, as in the American South now) while Jews, Communists, Socialists, liberals, Negroes, are roughed up, intimidated, killed, by hoodlums. A policeman is not a political expert; his job is to enforce the law impartially and not to be an accomplice in crime.

Granted that he does not always exercise even-handed justice: in capitalist countries, he is rougher on the poor than on the rich. Is it a coincidence or an illustration of this general rule that among those arrested during the Demo, there were *one* student and one "free-lance fashion model and writer"? The rest are listed as unemployed or belonging to the poorest category of workers—a bricklayer and a warehouseman—though many students were fighting, and I myself was carrying an umbrella, just as much of a weapon as a walking-stick or "a piece of wood."

A remedy for this regular diurnal injustice might be to reverse the practice and have a harsher code for the rich than for the poor—a quite reasonable idea when you come to think of it. But of course that will not happen under Harold Wilson's government. On the other hand, a permanent October 27 is unthinkable under any government: storefronts boarded up, horses rearing, broken glass and sticks and pennies flying, youths charging "the fuzz" while other fuzz stand by watching with folded arms. Such a policy would lead to the total demoralization of the police and its replacement by private bands of armed bravos. The American Embassy would be defended by the Marines, the Russian Embassy by the Red Army, and so on. In short, before reaching the future, we would detour via the Middle Ages, or through a state of universal civil war. It is possible that this is what is coming. In any case, it is clear that we witnessed in the Demo something like a medieval carnival in a modern setting, with everybody changing places, the fool becoming king for a day, Tariq Ali as Lord of Misrule, the police merging with the populace and even putting on false beards. But no more than a carnival did it "solve" anything. The sense of impotence felt most acutely by youth is still there, the system is still there, the war in Vietnam is still there, the cops have moved out of their dormitories, and the students have gone back to their classes.

Fall 1968

LECTURES

A Guide to Exiles, Expatriates, and Internal Emigrés

FIRST LET ME SAY what I think these terms signify in common speech. An expatriate is different from an exile. In early use an exile was a banished man, a wanderer or roamer: *exsul*. "For I must to the greenwood go, alone, a banished man." In ancient Greek times, a man with a price on his head unable to return home until he had ransomed his blood guilt. The Wandering Jew, I suppose, is the archetypal exile, sentenced to trail about the earth until the Second Coming. Or Dante, a *fuoruscito*, waiting for a Second Coming in the shape of the German emperor who would make it safe for him to return to Florence. Ovid, banished by Augustus and writing his *Tristia*.

The exile is essentially a political figure, though the offense he has committed may have been in the sphere of morals. He has incurred the displeasure of the state by some sort of levity of conduct or looseness of tongue—a political crime in a tyranny, ancient or modern. Or he is an unhealthy element sent to lonely quarantine in some remote spot, like Prometheus on his rock.

Though the term easily lends itself to metaphorical inflation—"I am in exile here, in this unsympathetic environment into which fate has cast me," as Mme Bovary might have sighed to the notary's clerk—it has not lost its primary, political sense. The exile waits for a change of government or the tyrant's death, which will allow him to come home. If he stops waiting and adapts to the new circumstances, then he is not an exile any more. This condition of waiting means that the exile's whole being is concentrated on the land he left behind, in memories and hopes. The more passive type, summed up in the banished poet, lives on memories, while the active type, summed up in the revolutionist, lives on hopes and schemes. There is something of both in every exile, an oscillation between melancholy and euphoria.

More than anybody (except lovers), exiles are dependent on mail. A Greek writer friend in Paris was the only person I knew to suffer real pain during the events of May 1968, when the mail was cut off. In the absence of news from Greece, i.e., political news, he was wasting away, somebody deprived of sustenance. They are also great readers of newspapers and collectors of clippings. The fact that the press of their country is censored (a corollary, evidently, of their exile) makes them more hungry for scraps of rumor and information which they can piece together.

Classically, exile was a punishment decreed from above, like the original sentence of banishment on Adam and Eve, which initiated human history. Today deportation of native-born citizens is illegal, so far as I know, in most Western countries, where the opposite punishment—refusal of a passport—is meted out to political undesirables, and assignment to forced residence, which is really a form of imprisonment, is practiced most notably by the colonels' regime in Greece and by the Soviet Union, as in the case of Solzhenitsyn. Today a man may be an exile from his homeland even though he left voluntarily—the Jews who managed to get out of Nazi Germany, defectors from the East, Cuban runaways, American draft-resisters and deserters.

A person who cannot return home without facing death or jail for acts committed against the government is an exile. Eldridge Cleaver in Algiers. Or for acts he may commit if he remains true to himself, a whole being. Or for no acts at all, if he belongs to a proscribed category owing to his race, class, or religion. But in recent times, it is worth noticing, a new word, "refugee," describes a person fleeing from persecution because of his category. Taken from *refugie*, it was first used in England in 1685 of the Huguenots seeking asylum after the Revocation of the Edict of Nantes.

The exile is a singular, whereas refugees tend to be thought of in the mass. Armenian refugees, Jewish refugees, refugees from Franco Spain. But a political leader or artistic figure is an exile: Thomas Mann yesterday, today Theodo- rakis. Exile is the noble and dignified term, while a refugee is more hapless. At one point in your flight you may be a refugee and later, covered with honors, turn into an exile. If a group of Greek writers draws up a manifesto, they are writ- ers-in-exile, but if we are trying to raise money to help them, they are refugees. The Vietnamese, Cambodian, and Lao peasants fleeing from the war zones are, of course, refugees; former Vietnamese politicians living in Paris are exiles.

What is implied in these nuances of social standing is the respect we pay to choice. The exile appears to have made a decision, while the refugee is the very image of helpless- ness, choicelessness, incomprehension, driven from his home by forces outside his understanding and control. We speak of flood refugees, earthquake refugees, persecuted by nature on account of the place they live in, war refugees harried by men for no other reason than that. Since refugees are seen as a mass the immediate thought is to process and resettle them. After first aid and minimal feeding. But no bureaucrat or so- cial worker would dream of resettling exiles. The whole point about them is their refusal to put down new roots.

They are more like birds than plants, perching wherever they are, ready for homeward flight. Even when they have funds to buy a little house, take a long lease on a flat, they prefer transient accommodations—bed-sitters or hotel rooms,

like Nabokov at the Hotel Montreux-Palace in Montreux. If
an exile buys a house or takes a long lease on a flat, it's a sign
that he's no longer a true exile.

An expatriate is almost the reverse. His main aim is never to
go back to his native land or, failing that, to stay away as long
as possible. His departure was wholly voluntary. An exile can
be of any nationality, but an expatriate is generally English
or American. The type was not seen in any numbers until
the Romantic period. His predecessor was the eighteenth-
century traveler, someone like Lady Mary Wortley Montagu,
but the true expatriate is not a gadabout. Nor a wanderer like
the exile. He tends to take up residence in some fixed spot
(which he may change definitively, as Henry James did when
he moved from France to England) and to buy property or
lease it. In fact, the acquisition of desirable property, also in
the form of furniture, paintings, statues, bibelots, seems to be
one of the motives for expatriation. This is clear enough in
James's novels.

The expatriate is a hedonist. He is usually an artist or a
person who thinks he is artistic. He has no politics or, if he
has any, like the Brownings he has acquired them from the
country he has adopted. The average expatriate thinks about
his own country rarely and with great unwillingness. He feels
he has escaped from it. The expatriate is a by-product of in-
dustrialism. The Industrial Revolution sent him abroad, in
headlong flight from ugliness. At the same time, of course,
he owes his presence abroad to the prosperity induced by the
factories and manufactures he is fleeing from. This too is
clearly, though somewhat coyly, stated by James.

The expatriate's need is to locate as far as possible from
the source of his capital and to be free of the disapprobation
of the administrators of the same. He is somewhat less compromised if he is "only" receiving checks, like Scott Fitzgerald, from the *Saturday Evening Post* or royalties from Scrib-

ner's, like Hemingway. Least compromising of all is to find work in the adopted country, like the poet Allen Tate acting as a janitor in a Paris basement, but the expatriate is seldom willing to work at a job, since the nine-to-five routine is part of the spiritual oppression he is escaping from. Dependence on money from a despised source tends to demoralize any but very young people. This demoralization is felt all through expatriate literature.

The exile too is dependent on money remitted from the homeland and other doubtful sources. The draft-resister's parents send checks; relations of the East European defector smuggle out icons and bits of jewelry which he can offer for sale. Without papers, the political refugee may have trouble finding work; if he is an author, he has exiled himself from his audience: at home his books are banned. But since he is not a hedonist money is not very important to him. As soon as he gets any, he is likely to share it with others or start a magazine.

Magazines are very important to exiles, and for literary expatriates they are morale-builders. To start a magazine— e.g., *transition*, *Blues*, *Broom*—is to start a sort of literary government-in-exile; up to then, you were just expatriates sitting in cafés. For the genuine exile, a magazine in the native language, like Herzen's *The Bell* or today's Polish *Kultura*, is almost as vital as mail. It is not only a forum for discussion but also a transmission belt to the home underground. Texts and news of secret trials, assassination attempts, purges, executions are smuggled out of the mother country, and copies of the magazine are then smuggled back in, to circulate in clandestinity.

The expatriate writers of the twenties and early thirties, mainly located in Paris, mainly rather poor or at any rate struggling, were also mainly American. Hemingway, Scott Fitzgerald, Henry Miller, Djuna Barnes, and so on. And of course Gertrude Stein and Edith Wharton, who were not poor. T. S. Eliot, Pound, and Conrad Aiken were living in England. The Irishmen Joyce and Beckett were living in Paris, Joyce having moved on from Trieste and Zurich. Norman Douglas and Percy Lubbock were in Italy. D. H. Lawrence and Katherine Mansfield had died in some awful combination of exile and expatriation, since their health forbade England to them. She was already an expatriate from New Zealand to England.

But when the dollar dropped in value during the thirties, after the crash, the Americans, by and large, went swiftly home, proving that even those who like Malcolm Cowley (author of a book called *Exile's Return*) had imagined themselves to be exiles were only expatriates. The few who stayed were driven back to the United States as refugees after the fall of France in 1940. Those few were the ones who returned when the war ended: the others had "refound their roots."

Today the expatriate writer is mainly a memory. In Paris, so far as I know, there are only Graham Greene, Beckett (unless he counts as French), James Jones, Nancy Mitford, Lesley Blanch, Italo Calvino, though there is a rumor that Lawrence Durrell is around. S. J. Perelman in England. A few live in Tangiers, a few still in Athens; in Rome, Gore Vidal and Muriel Spark. James Baldwin, in the south of France and before that in Turkey, is more of an exile than an expatriate. That is true of Burroughs too.

Expatriate writing, a potpourri of the avant-garde and the decadent, has almost faded away. In fiction, Henry James had set the themes once and for all. Everything that followed can be seen as a variation, however grotesque. *South Wind, The Sun Also Rises, Nightwood, The Alexandria Quartet, The Merry Month of May,* even *Tropic of Cancer.* From James on too, there is a certain Jackie-and-Ari color-supplement flavor to most of this fiction. The characters, from Isabel Archer to Henry Miller's hero, have come abroad to lead the beautiful life in one form or another. They are impersonating figures in a work of art—something few people dare to do at home.

The great exception is Joyce. But he considered himself an exile, not an expatriate. He proclaimed it in the title of his single play, *Exiles,* and in Stephen Dedalus's famous vow of silence, exile, and cunning. Of course, this was rhetoric: it was only in his own mind that Joyce was driven into exile by the tyranny at home. He could have come back without risk whenever he wanted and did several times. Yet he willed his rhetoric so fiercely that it commands belief, particularly since the difficulties of publication pitted him against the forces of order in the shape of censors wherever his native language was spoken. He was able to go home freely, but his books could not. In this, he differed from expatriates like Hemingway and Fitzgerald, who never had any problems with censors or customs.

Moreover, Joyce was no hedonist, though fond of white wine and song. He had come abroad with a purpose: "to forge in the smithy of my soul the uncreated conscience of my race." He was engaging himself in a conspiracy against the ruling forces of Ireland, and the infernal machine was to be his literary work. It was a plot, to be executed with the typical methods of the revolutionary: silence (i.e., secrecy) and cunning.

As an exile and a conspirator, he had no moral shrinking from accepting money from his hard-up brother, from his rich patron, Miss Weaver, from any available source. It was as impersonal as raising money to buy a mimeograph machine or material for making bombs. Unlike other exiles, he was a real loner, a conspiracy of one, yet he had great organizational talent and was always able to recruit a staff of collaborators: Herbert Gorman, Stuart Gilbert, the Jolases, Sylvia Beach, Samuel Beckett, Frank Budgen, Robert McAlmon,

Padraic Colum, not to mention typists, copiers, miscellaneous helpers. In London his chief agent, Pound, was active. In Paris there was a small cell of Frenchmen, headed by Valéry Larbaud. The expatriates who helped him fabricate the big bomb, first known as *Work in Progress*, became, as it were, honorary exiles, and the organization did not dissolve with his death.

He had the exile's characteristic restlessness: the Joyces were constantly moving. Yet he regarded his exile as permanent and definitive and was rather upset when the Irish finally got their freedom, which he feared might suggest that he no longer had any reason to stay away. He was making a *literary* revolution, whose strategy required his physical absence to foster mental concentration. True to form, he was nourishing himself on memories. Nothing could be farther from the expatriate "international novel" than his careful reconstruction of Bloomsday—June 16, 1904—with its remembered Dublin containing real streets and real people, like the scale model of some famous battle with all the generals, foot soldiers, and artillery pieces in place. *Finnegans Wake* is still set in Dublin with a cast of native characters, seemingly pre-World War I, who have become eternal.

Ada, you might say, is Nabokov's *Finnegans Wake*, polylingual, full of puns and linguistic jokes, placed in an imaginary future-past, where America and Russia have merged and annexed bits of France and Switzerland into their author's sovereign territory. The characters, like the Earwicker nuclear family, are closely related and prone to split and fuse; though not primordial or eternal, they attain patriarchal ages without taking leave of adolescence, as though playing naughty tricks on time. If the self-banished Joyce was making a one-man literary revolution, Nabokov, a genuine displaced person, has been trying throughout his career to make a one-man literary restoration, using his prodigious memory to undo the present. "Speak, Memory," he commands royally, in a title, and the masque begins.

Though he has the reputation of a modernist, his language is antique Mandarin, like his life style, and he is probably the greatest enemy of modernism extant. He is against psychoanalysis, every kind of "new" politics, atom bombs, avant-garde art. He is not just any White Guard exile but a dethroned monarch, like Charles the Beloved, in *Pale Fire*, traveling under the incognito of Kinbote-Botkin, a poor mad refugee. Nabokov's relations with English are often highly autocratic: witness his controversy with Edmund Wilson over his Pushkin translation—an international incident. He has written a long poem—and some shorter ones—to the Russian language, which he treats as a national treasure the usurper Bolsheviks appropriated from him, to turn over to the rabble.

Ada is his supreme revenge. There he at last reinstates himself in a supra-national, supercilious palace of culture, with a queen by his side; the mirror pair of children, like the Ptolemys, are brother and sister. "A Family Chronicle" is the subtitle; "Dynastic" would be better. Nothing could be more remote from the Family of Man or Here-Comes-Everybody of *Finnegans Wake*, which takes place in a pub.

Ada, in my view, is a failure, a misfired *coup d'état*, and this, I think, is not unrelated to the crows of triumph that shrill through it. The theme of need in all its sad and threadbare forms (Gogol's overcoat), so characteristic of the author, has here been cast aside or molted, like last year's set of feathers. But this theme and the allied one of insuperable distance, which everybody has experienced, if only when in love, have up to now supplied a human element, compensating for a great deal of extravagance and foppery in Nabokov's writing. We forgive the vanity and arrogance of the Pretender exile because, like Pnin, like Humbert Humbert, like Botkin, he is at least half a refugee. In *Ada*, there is no shared mass misery of furnished rooms, German boarding-houses and park benches, underpaid language lessons, *émigré* magazines and newspapers, sectarian bickering all leading on to American lectureships, missed trains, common-room snubs, motels. One of the chief interests, instead, is genealogy. It is as if the author, once a Russian exile in America, with all that implies of loss and grieving, had metamorphosed into an American expatriate living on a Swiss mountaintop "above it all."

Nabokov insists that he is indifferent to current Russian events, but that is only his way of snubbing the Soviet Union, just as his pose of being indifferent to politics is a snub to *engagé* literature. Actually, he is far from apolitical and continues to feud in books and interviews with left-wingers as a body and with Russian left-wingers in particular, including Chernyshevsky, author of *What is to be done?*, who died in 1889. More peculiar is his malice toward Pasternak, whom he half admired as a poet and who was dead too, and disgraced when *Ada* came out, in which Nabokov cites, among other repellent titles, *Les Amours du Docteur Mertvago*—i.e., *mertv* (death plus *merde*). This must be a case of novelist's jealousy. Nabokov, an exile, envied Pasternak, an "internal *émigré*"—a Soviet term of abuse often applied to Pasternak and meaning something like an internal expatriate, if that can be conceived.

As novelists, Nabokov and Pasternak were in rivalry for "the Russian land," a legacy they had from Tolstoy and Aksakov. They belonged to the same milieu, the old educated class—what the Soviets called "former persons," like ghosts—though Pasternak's family were lower on the tsarist social scale, artists and bohemians, city people and apartment-dwellers, rather than well-to-do landowners. And the external exile, despite his much greater worldly success, envied the internal exile—the man-in-possession.

Perhaps it was sometimes mutual. In *Dr. Zhivago* (page 312 of the English edition) Pasternak appears to be emitting a signal of some kind to the other writer. "Folding and un-folding like a scrap of coloured stuff, a brown speckled but-terfly" flies in and out of the story for the length of a para-graph, giving rise to some reflections on mimicry and protective coloring. Yury Zhivago, says Pasternak, has alluded to this subject in his medical publications. But Nabokov too, as a professional lepidopterist, has published on protective mim-icry—a fact probably known to Pasternak, who certainly was aware of him as a butterfly-hunter. Yet if the passage was in-tended as a fraternal greeting, it got a cold response.

The characters in *Dr. Zhivago*, many of them exiles from their former way of life, are swept up by the storm of the Revolution and become refugees. Sooner or later, everybody is in flight or hiding—refugees from war, from the Red ter-ror, from the White terror, peasants who have lost their homes, townspeople driven into the countryside by hunger. The long and beautiful train trip across the Russian land into the Ural Mountains, which recalls a trip in Aksakov's memoirs, is the great major sequence of the book, combining an idyl with an epic trek. The revolutionary storm spares nobody, not even the commissar Antipov, who is found toward the end hiding in a farmhouse encircled by wolves. With one big exception, the evil genius Komarovsky, Lara's seducer. He is last seen riding off in a *wagon-lit* to become, not an exile, for he has never been "political," but a true expatriate, doubtless smok-ing a cigar and heading for Manchuria. Another exception, another immune figure—who does not belong, though, to the naturalistic plane of the novel and who, like Komarovsky, is not even listed among the principal characters—is Yury's half-brother and miraculous protector, Yevgraf, the Angel of Death. According to Nadezhada Mandelstam, in her book *Hope against Hope*, the mysterious Yevgraf is simply some high-up bureaucrat whose miracles are worked by knowing "the right people," that is, by having a transmission belt to Stalin.

Pasternak's own situation varied between periods of internal exile and official favor and protection. With Solzhenitsyn, you get internal exile at its bleakest and in nearly all its forms and stages. Deportation, forced labor in a camp, forced residence, confinement in a cancer ward—in his novel of that name the sick are treated by the staff and people outside rather as if they were wilful exiles from a healthy society. His books take place in a climate so frozen and immobile that Pasternak's orphans in the storm, by comparison, are enjoying the wildest liberty. The revolution described by Pasternak still has something of a Tolstoyan natural force, awesome and fierce, but in Solzhenitsyn, the savage natural is replaced by the universal ordinary. He does not write about former people but about Soviet people and about Soviet society, almost as if there had never been any other kind. Nobody is homeless or buffeted by circumstance, since everyone must be registered. There are no outlaws hiding in the forest: Pasternak's red rowanberry trees have probably been leveled by a bulldozer to make a detention camp.

Nor is there any refuge in memory. For most writers-in-exile—e.g., Joyce, Nabokov, the internal exile Pasternak—recollections of childhood are a literary food source and have been hoarded, squirrel-wise, against the winter; it does not appear to matter whether the childhood was happy, like Nabokov's, or dingy, like Joyce's. Solzhenitsyn, a Soviet man (born in 1918), seems to have had no childhood to look back to for sustenance. That other dimension, the past, is seldom glimpsed in his books up to now, unless it is through the old peasant woman Matriona, who is herself a reminiscence, a piece of stout material left over from some prehistoric eon.

Unlike Pasternak, he has no influential connections, which would relate him to a sphere "higher up." At present he is being sheltered by the cellist Rostropovich, who is risking his passport by harboring him. His only "outlet" seems to have been teaching mathematics. One of the most interesting things about the drama of his getting the Nobel Prize award was the official threat not to let him back into the country if he went to Stockholm to receive it. They knew their man: Solzhenitsyn did not go to Stockholm. But he accepted the prize. He chose internal exile against the other kind—a decision some Westerners found mysterious since so many Soviet citizens are doing their best to get out. Solzhenitsyn insisted on his right to stay *and* to receive the prize.

The decision was typical of today's internal exiles in the Soviet Union, not only writers but scientists. Probably Mme Mandelstam, Sinyavsky, and Daniel would respond in the same way in the circumstances, and Akhmatova too, if she were alive. It is a question of politics and of pride—in fact, of national pride.* The internal exiles seem to have made it a principle to behave toward the Soviet Union as if it were a normal country, with an operative constitution. As though by their determination they could oblige the "as if" to come true. To go into exile, on the one hand, or conform, on the other, would be to give up any hope of that happening and to accept the Soviet Union as some sort of clinical monstrosity outside the norms of law. This notion they refuse. And they do not compare Soviet justice with U.S. justice or English justice or tsarist justice, but with articles in the Soviet constitution and laws in the statute books. Thus their frame of reference is Soviet reality, which they also occupy with their bodies rather like sit-in strikers.

This political determination is clear in Solzhenitsyn's books. He writes as coolly as if there were no censorship and no conceivable interference with publication. His books appear as simple statements of fact, without exaggeration or fantasy. That may be why memory of the distant kind ("the laundryman in the lavender flannels") has no place in them.

*In this connection, see A *Question of Madness* by Zhores and Roy Medvedev.

One of the few rhetorical reminders of anything "outside," of a larger frame, is the title of *The First Circle*, which refers to Dante's Hell. The prisoners there are relatively privileged spirits, like Dante's virtuous heathen, the First Circle being Limbo. Their punishment is light, compared to Ivan Denisovich's, and consists simply of exclusion, but it has the hellish characteristic of permanence. A better metaphor for internal exile might be Purgatory, a place where you wait, like exiles in a foreign land, to go home. Solzhenitsyn *is* home, and yet he declines to recognize the immediate political geography as permanent. This might be a definition of the internal exile: a man who has taught himself to behave as if he had already crossed a frontier while refusing to leave his house.

London, February 1972

Language and Politics

THE OTHER DAY a headline caught my attention in the financial pages of the *International Herald Tribune*. I normally don't look at the business section or the sports and avoid anything about astronauts. But that day—November 13—turning the pages I saw CHILEAN JUNTA WINS PRIVATE FINANCIAL AID. Then in smaller type: " 'Work spirit' Praised by American Banker." The news story related that private U.S. bank loans had suddenly become available for Chile—a dramatic turnabout following on the overthrow of the Allende government. The previous Friday, Manufacturers Hanover Trust had announced that it was extending a $24-million loan to a Chilean bank. According to unnamed banking sources, described as reliable, Manufacturers Hanover had lent an additional $20 million to the central bank of Santiago. In any case, the $24 million was the largest credit given to Chile by a U.S. bank since Salvador Allende took office three years ago. Altogether, eight to ten U.S. banks and two Canadian banks have offered Chile commercial loans amounting to about $150 million in the two months since Allende was overthrown.

You may wonder what all this has to do with language; the connection with politics is fairly clear. Well, toward the bottom of the page the writer quoted a vice-president of Manufacturers Hanover, James R. Greene, who on making the announcement spoke at length—I quote—"about the renewal of U.S. business faith in Chile." This is Greene talking: "The work spirit that I have seen in Chile leads me to fully trust that the international press will correct the negative image that is being spread about this country abroad." You will note one split infinitive, two superfluous "that"s, and two cliché phrases, "work spirit" and "negative image," that also seem to be circumlocutions. Aside from the question of whether an image can be spread, like butter or like a disease or like a rumor, one asks what the speaker can be alluding to by the blanket word "negative." It is indeed a blanket covering the summary executions of thousands of oppositionists, the countless illegal arrests, the setting-up of camps, the abolition of Parliament, the suppression of left-wing political parties, the suspension of all other political parties, press censorship, purges of the universities, factories, and state enterprises. This is what the colorless "negative image" translates into, and the selection of the word "image"—in its current PR definition, not yet, I see, admitted to my dictionary, copyright 1957—assigns a kind of deniability to all those public facts, as though they were bodiless, insubstantial, mere refractions of evanescent appearance, as opposed to reality.

By contrast to his handling of the negative, Greene eventually defines what he understands by the "work spirit." Something positive. Here he is again: "The fact that Chileans are working on Saturday is a very good antecedent, as far as my bank is concerned. This is very important in the financial world." So work spirit means that the forty-hour week has been abolished by the junta. He does not say, at least in the *Herald Tribune* quotes from him, that the junta has promised to return to private capital the "vast majority" of the more than three hundred foreign and domestic enterprises that were nationalized by the Allende government without compensation. Nor that it has announced that it is prepared to renew negotiations on compensation to the three U.S. companies whose copper mines were taken over—assets worth between $500 and

$700 million. That, the joyful undersong of the announce-
ment he had to make, possibly did not need to be put into
words. It was tacit. But what about the word "antecedent"?
Working on Saturday is a very good antecedent, he says, as
far as his bank is concerned. I have been asking myself what
word he was reaching for. "Precedent"? But "precedent,"
though slightly closer to the mark, does not make sense either.
Precedent for what, unless he means working on Sunday? The
thing he is trying to articulate, evidently, is that his bank takes
the extension of the work week as a good sign. Then why not
say so? Maybe, to his ear, sign was too commonplace a word
for a $24-million occasion. Or maybe, grope as he would, he
couldn't remember "sign." Not for the life of him. Was he
speaking off the cuff or reading a prepared statement? The news
story does not tell.

To get back, though, for a moment to Manufacturers
Hanover—no prior knowledge of the circumstances, of Allende's murder, U.S. investments, the blood bath, would be
required by a newspaper reader of Greene's quoted remarks
in order to understand that something was rotten in Chile.
His language inadvertently made that clear. In South Vietnam (when I was there in 1967), I noticed the same kind of
thing. If I had dropped straight from Mars, I thought, into
one of the daily press briefings, I would have known from the
periphrastic, circumspect way our spokesmen expressed
themselves that an indefensible action of some sort was going
on in that country. As with Greene, just about everything they
said, or, rather, "stated," was in a kind of bumbling code that
quickly translated itself into plain English: e.g., for "success,"
read "failure." The purpose of language, somebody—probably French—said, is to conceal thought. I don't agree with
the aphorism, yet the American language, as spoken today,
often bears it out with comical results: the attempt to conceal
an underlying thought or feeling produces almost total
transparence. As when Nixon, in his letter to Senator Sam

Ervin last summer about why he was not going to hand over the tapes to the Committee, said they might be subject to misinterpretation by persons "with other views"; he might as well have made an announcement that he had decided they were extremely damaging. That letter was the first confirmation of John Dean's testimony to come from what we could call a reliable independent source.

Of course there are people who have become so practiced in evasion, euphemism, circumlocution, and all the forms of lying that they would not know *how* to tell the truth if an occasion favoring truth-telling should arise. Their syntax, so twisted, crippled, and deformed by these habits, is incapable of directness, and the occasional forthright statement—"I love America," "I am not a crook"—though grammatically sound as a bell, has to be construed as meaning the opposite: "I hate America," "I am a crook."

But this is pathology, and though many or even perhaps most public officials and corporation heads are afflicted by it, I don't think it extends yet to the population at large. In the population at large, though, you find warning symptoms of a deteriorated faculty of expression: the inarticulateness of the very young and the long-winded prosiness of the middle-aged and old. On the one hand, "I went, like, to a party"; on the other, "Thursday evening I attended a function." The common speech of the people, on which Wordsworth hoped to base a new *ars poetica*, is riddled with such curious faults. Between the two examples I have just quoted there is only a generational gap; both seek to avoid direct statement. The continual "like . . . like"—"I went, like, to a party and we smoked, like, pot"—is the sidewise, slithering, crab-gaited, youth approach, whereas the elderly widow who "attended a function" is putting her own strange distance from "Thursday I went to a party."

Enough has been said—and for years—about "funeral director," "passed away," "senior citizen," "home" for "house," "wealthy" for "rich." Such linguistic vulgarities, contrary to what is thought, are not restricted to emotive fields, like death and old age, where fear is being held at a distance, or, like the home and money, where reverence is duly paid. "I got my car fixed"—not really a sentimental matter—now turns into "I took my car to be repaired." In rural areas, women talk of their "hose," and "what a lovely gown"; in cities there is "panty hose." Pedantic neologisms issuing from psychiatry are fuzzing up the atmosphere: "He is highly motivated." No matter how many times I hear that, I can never understand what it means. "He has high motives"? No. "He has a lot of drive"? Closer. Maybe "He likes the work he is doing." And "relate"—which is youth jargon: "I found I couldn't relate to Physics 1B." "He is an achiever" (or "an under-achiever") at least is clear. It means he does well (or badly) in school, including sports and "activities."

Take the still new adverb "hopefully." People who care for language, including myself, wince every time they hear it. It floats around in the sentence, attached to nothing in particular. "Hopefully the dollar will go up." There it certainly does not modify the verb, as a good adverb should unless there is an adjective somewhere to cling to. If it modified the verb, it would be "the dollar will go hopefully up." Yet it is not a grammatical howler, so far as I can see; it is a parenthesis thrown in, on the pattern of "incidentally," which is not a desirable form either, but, being useful, has got itself accepted. (I myself prefer "by the way" or simple parenthesis marks, as in this sentence.) It must have come to us from German "hoffentlich," normally translated as "it is to be hoped"; perhaps we are indebted to German businessmen, who introduced it along with Volkswagens and Mercedes. What is melancholy about the suddenly universal "hopefully" is that it seems to point to a contrary state of mind, that is, to an absence of hope. The speaker really fears the dollar will go down still further, and if you tell me "Hopefully we'll meet

87

in a better world," I can pretty well understand that we won't. Its free-floating position in the sentence emphasizes that insecurity, that lack of ground for hope. It is an irony that this pathetic invading adverb should be sweeping the country at what may be the lowest point in our history.

Our language, once homely and colloquial, seeks to aggrandize our meanest activities with polysyllabic terms or it retreats from frankness into a stammering verbosity. Americans are slow tedious talkers, and universal semi-education has made them worse. Only the poorer blacks and a few rural whites are still able to express themselves vividly and to find the word they want without too protracted a search. Maybe this is because they never finished school. Illiteracy at the poverty level (mainly a matter of bad grammar) does not alarm me nearly as much as the illiteracy of the well-to-do. In fact, it is almost a comfort and I could wish the poor might stay untaught forever, for their own sakes and for the preservation of the language, if the price did not include other kinds of deprivation. Poor blacks, some rural whites and a few gifted talkers are the only people I have heard in recent times use the language with relish. They are the only ones to enjoy talking artistically, for its own sake. Senator Sam Ervin's popularity on radio and television was based, I think, in large part, on his unabashed relish for the language; being old and rural, he sounded like a poor man. His relish for the language, sometimes positively syllabic ("eleemosynary," you could hear his tongue taste those vowels), seemed to be deeply related to his determination to get the truth of Watergate out and to his confidence that this could be done—slowly and painfully, like a tooth-extraction before the days of Novocain.

Senator Ervin was not always grammatical, but that enhanced the pleasure one had in him, because his grammar did not so much err as revert to older modes ("ain't," "it don't") and showed no disrespect for the forms of speech, that is, for the sinews of thought. By contrast, there was Jeb Stuart Ma-

gruder, a graduate of Williams College. Since I don't have
on hand a transcript of his testimony, I will construct a characteristic but imaginary sentence: "Mr. Haldeman indicated
to me that between he and I we had a problem." And here
is a real exchange between him and Senator Ervin. They were
talking about the "climate" prevailing in the White House.
Ervin: ". . . I just could not understand why people got so
fearful." Magruder: "I would characterize that at least my reaction was stronger after three years of working here than it
had been before." More genuine Magruder: "We agreed, Mr.
Liddy and I, that he would terminate from the committee all
activities." "In November of 1971 it was indicated to me that
the project was not going to get off the ground and subse-
quently G. Gordon Liddy came into the picture after that."
Finally, "I think from my own personal standpoint, I did lose
some respect for the legal process because I did not see it
working as I hoped it would when I came here."

I put the verb "indicate" in my imaginary sentence because it came up over and over in Magruder's testimony. The
choice of the word raised interesting questions. When he said
"he indicated to me" did he mean simply "he told me"? Let
us look at a few examples. "John Dean indicated to me that
I would not be indicted." "We indicated to Mr. Stans the
problem we had with money." [Haldeman] "indicated that I
should get back to Washington directly." "As I recall, we all
indicated that we should remove any documents that could
be damaging, whether they related at all to the Watergate or
not." Of Hugh Sloan and his perjured testimony to the grand
jury: "So I indicated at the meeting that I thought he had a
problem and might have to do something about it. He said,
you mean commit perjury? I said you might have to do
something like that to solve your problem and very honestly
was doing that in good faith to Mr. Sloan to assist him at that
time."

The last extract tells the story. "Indicate" means some-

thing less and more than "told." Sloan's "you mean commit
perjury?" points to the terrible difference between the two.
Sloan, an honest accountant (as his conduct before the Ervin
committee had already made clear), who insisted on having
things named by their names, and the devious operator Magruder, still posing to the Committee as a bashful penitent
freshman. Even when pressed by Sloan, he will not assent to
"perjury" as the right name for what he has in mind.
". . . something like that," he says. So must we conclude
that "indicate" in that crowd meant "tip off"? Possibly, but it
is hard to see how, in some of the circumstances, this was
done. When John Dean let Magruder know that he was not
going to be indicted, what form of words did he use? Or did
he wigwag the message? And when Haldeman indicated to
him, by long-distance telephone, that he should get back to
Washington right away, how did he put it, so that Magruder
would understand the order without being told it was one?
Did he say "The weather is beautiful in Washington at this
time of year, Jeb. The forecast for tomorrow is sunny and
mild"? From Magruder's parlance alone, you would get the
feeling of secretive men conscious of bugging devices everywhere. It was not surprising to learn that Liddy in California,
the morning after the break-in, warned Magruder to find a
safe phone. Nor, finally, that Nixon was tapping *himself*. And
if all essential communications were coded, in this involute
fashion, "indicated," never stated ("indicateur," in French, is
the common slang word for "informer," "police spy"), no
wonder there has been so much contradiction in the Watergate testimony as to who said what; they were all bent on not
saying anything to each other that could be pinned down to
a concrete meaning. Imprecision was the rule, and the cover-
up did not begin June 18 but had been practiced on a daily
basis in the ordinary transmission of messages. Indeed, what
we call talk for them consisted almost exclusively of messages. This was true no doubt even of banter.

John Mitchell had his own code, personalized, initialed JNM, like a monogram on a City Hall mobster's shirt sleeve. It was less bureaucratic than Magruder's, not so stamped by office routines. The expression "White House horror stories," for instance, was to be understood as an allusion to Charles Colson. Another favorite phrase, "in hindsight," mystified me. It cannot be code, but it is not English. What he means is "looking back," or, more starchy, "in the light of my present knowledge." You cannot say "in hindsight," any more than you can say "in foresight." For fun, I looked the noun up in the big *Oxford English Dictionary*. The original sense was the backsight of a rifle, and the word was first used by Mayne Reid in 1851 in a work called *Scalp Hunting*: "When you squint through her hindsights." The second reference for the word, still in the primary sense, is Farmer's *Americanisms*, 1889. The mystery is cleared up. You can see John Mitchell squinting through the backsight of his rifle at the Watergate affair, putting a bead on that wild Indian, Colson, on Jeb Magruder. That peculiar expression (not used by any other witness) is his enigmatic signature, hence, after all, a kind of code. Will it find its way into the *OED*?

Of course if he liked that word so much, if the picture gave him such dour satisfaction, he could have said "through hindsight." His lazy mind did not think it out. In lighting on the wrong preposition, he was a typical American of today. The breakdown of our language, evident in the misuse, i.e., the misunderstanding of nouns and adjectives, is most grave, though perhaps not so conspicuous, in the handling of prepositions, those modest little connectives that hold the parts of a phrase or a sentence together. They are the joints of any language, what make it, literally, articulate. As you know from experience in learning a foreign language, they are the hardest part to get right. You may have a pretty good vocabulary and have mastered the verb forms, the subjunctive, even genders, but you are still horribly uncertain about "de" and "à," "en" and "dans," "zu" and "nach," "aus" and "auf." Whether to say "Je pense de vous," or "Je pense à vous" (sometimes an almost imperceptible difference), "zu Hause," "nach Hause," "zu Bett," "im Bett"? They cannot be learned by mastering general rules; memorizing sentences containing them may be helpful but is no sure guide to a new sentence; the application of logic is useless, for their peculiarity is to defy logic, to be capricious. If you are like me, you will never really get hold of them in all their aberrant motion; even if you have spoken the language for fifteen years, doubt remains.

This means that they are the quintessential feature of a language; unlike nouns, verbs, and adjectives, they cannot be exchanged against their opposite numbers in a second or third language. In short, they are stubbornly idiomatic, from *idios* ("one's own, private, peculiar"). Though I said, just now, that logic is useless to a foreigner who is seeking to master them, they do express the inner logic of a particular language—a logic that is, precisely, different from the alien logic one is uselessly trying to apply. They are a birthright.

It is obvious that America, with its doors so long open to new citizens, would have a hard time maintaining the purity of those little particles of speech. Yet in fact our prepositions held out quite valiantly throughout the nineteenth century and through the first decades of the twentieth. I would date the deterioration from the forties; at least I first became aware of it in 1945–46 when I went to teach in a college and discovered from my students' papers that many of those young people did not have any idea what preposition was called for in a given circumstance. "Tolstoy in his progenitors and his disciples," one student wrote. To change "progenitors" to "predecessors" and "disciples" to "followers" only took a little practice in mind-reading—yes, the student agreed happily, that was what he had been trying to say, he guessed. But that "in"! Impossible to penetrate the thought process that had been working there. Some relation between Tolstoy and those who preceded him as well as those who followed him was adumbrated but remained inexpressible.

That prepositions point out relationships between members of a sentence is plain. In classical languages much of this work was done by declension of the noun. I have always liked the notion I came upon long ago in a Greek grammar that the declension was a visual thing for the Greeks. The noun was pictured as standing straight up (nominative), lying on its side (ablative), leaning (dative); I forget what the genitive position was. This innocent clarity of vision, an exercise of both the imaginative and the analytical faculties, has much to do with the beauty of Greek literature and also, I would guess, with the perspicuousness of Greek philosophy and Greek political thought. One thinks of Socrates: the fanciful stories and myths he invented, to lay bare, finally, a relation or sequence admitted by the hearer to be ineluctable. Also his idea that knowledge is an act of recovery from the storehouse of the mind; teaching was merely prompting the pupil to recognize something he had known all along, though he had not known he knew it, till Socrates showed him. The slave boy in the *Meno*. A thought, when fully grasped, should induce a feeling of recognition. This implies, of course, that our common universe, on close examination, makes sense, that there are connections, if only in the brain.

One reason for the loss of clarity in our current speaking and writing must be the fact that the classical languages are no longer taught in schools. In fact, the loss of control over prepositions—the articulate parts of speech—seems to have coincided with the disappearance of Latin as a "subject" in public high schools. Up through the war, at least in New England, in the mill towns (not just in Boston), Latin was still taught—Greek sometimes too—by vigorous unmarried old ladies. When they died or retired, it went. In New England, in former days, the teaching of Latin was considered indispensable to a truly civic education; it was thought to form

democratic habits of mind. Whether it did or not, the dropping of it from the program of free universal education certainly deepened the chasm between classes. And whatever it
did or did not do toward conserving democratic habits, Latin
surely promoted clear, analytic thinking and helped us in our
language to distinguish the relations between members of a
sentence.

Some of this training in logic and economy has been
delegated to mathematics. In the college I speak of, where I
taught literature back in the mid-forties, many of my best students were math and physics majors. They had no particular
gift for literature, but they knew how to follow a sequence of
thought, and if I had asked it of them, they could probably
have taken a sentence apart and put it back together. It was
usually a relief to read their papers. Unfortunately, today's
readers and writers cannot all be math and physics majors.

The disappearance of classics is obviously not the only
factor in the atrophying of the power to communicate. On
the grade-school level, there used to be parsing and diagramming of sentences. I wonder whether that still exists, and very
much doubt it. In my schools, we had to do it every day.
Some who were bored by parsing did not mind diagramming.
We also had to memorize poetry, but that too has gone, I
suppose.

Yet if Latin is no longer given and English is not taught
as rigorously as it once was, that is not enough to account for
the dimensions of what has happened. The public was startled and shocked by the language-murder committed before
television cameras during the Watergate hearings by White
House and Cabinet functionaries with college degrees. It is
true that the mixture of euphemism, circumlocution, and a
kind of insolent barbarity of phrasing gave an insight into a
new mentality that could take an ordinary citizen aback. But
the grammar, the clichés? Where had the public been during
the last few decades—in a cloister?—that it could have been

troubled by "at that point in time"? It cannot have been paying attention to its own speech or its neighbor's. Most people
sound like Jeb Magruder. Ninety percent of the letters I get
from Americans—strangers, I mean—are at best half-literate.
And these are from citizens who read books (that is why they
are writing to me), from sub-editors working on magazines
and in publisher's offices, from college professors who have
drafted questionnaires, from agents who want to sign me up
for lecture tours, who have an idea for a movie. If this sample of the population is a culture-conscious minority, what
must the majority write like?

I have plenty of evidence that it was not always so. I have
read logs kept by ship's captains describing the sea, the weather,
the ports and islands visited. These old skippers were not
Melvilles, but they could write clear and plain. Nor can I
conclude that most of them had had advantages, a superior
education. Maybe they had not even had parsing in their village schools. I have gone through a mass of papers found in
a barrel in a Massachusetts house. The family were store-
keepers, and many of the papers are commercial: inventories,
records of the dollar they "gave" for a pig, what five bolts of
calico cost this winter, what they paid the servant. But they
also kept letters. A member of the family would go to New
York on the steamboat and report back on the harbor, the
streets, the dwellings, the inhabitants, the strangers he met in
the boarding-house, the sermons he heard preached. In good
sober English, neat legible handwriting, and with a certain
power of description, especially where the sermons were concerned. I have read my great-great-uncle's journal, which he
started when he was a student at Dartmouth College before
the Civil War and continued into his old age, out in the
Middle West, where he went into the real-estate business. He
was certainly not an interesting man; in his youth he went
through a religious period that brought on paroxysms of conventional feelings; he too was a great church-attender and

carefully wrote down a description of each preacher—height, estimated weight, complexion, voice—a detailed account of the sermon and his own responses to it. When old, he was interested mainly in figures—the temperature outside, snow measurement, wind velocity, his wife's weight, which he recorded in the journal once a week. Yet, except for an occasional spelling lapse (he was a college drop-out), the journal is written in very acceptable, if colorless English. No clichés; he was a cliché himself, you could say, but his mild pen gave no offense. Today, one of his descendants cannot write a letter to the telephone company asking for service to be suspended without tying himself into knots so convolute that it would take a Houdini to arrange his escape from the opening clause.

Now it is possible that this breakdown in communication will soon be felt throughout the world. The Americans may only have pioneered it, as they have done with computers, the electrified kitchen, and pollution. If it is an effect of modern civilization which is being noticed first in America, then the causes must be larger than any merely local and parochial phenomena, such as the American character with its tendency to pomposity, the dropping of Latin, the permissive approach to the teaching of English. Indeed, those last may be more effects than causes of a world-wide revolution that will end in the dethronement or abdication of the word.

That of course is the gospel Marshall McLuhan has been preaching, although he speaks of the obsolescence of print rather than of the word itself. But if print is condemned, the word, it seems to me, will not survive long. It would be easier to reinstitute Latin in the schools and have everybody parsing and diagramming than to revert to an archaic age where words were carried by chant and gesture. Whatever can be said in favor of television as a "warm" or "hot" medium, it cannot reproduce the conditions of the Homeric world in your living-room. It cannot act as a preserver and transmitter of meaning. Far more than print, it lacks memory, and memory, of course, was a highly developed faculty in pre-literate civilizations, almost like an extra organ of the body. It still is among primitive peoples. Contemporary man's memory is not improving now that he looks at TV in the evening instead of reading a book or the newspaper. It is getting worse, and television itself is partly responsible for that. Not just the distraction caused by the intrusion of the commercials but also the flickering of the image, the mechanical failure obliging you to turn the dial, the necessity of concentrating on a small square area—all this makes nearly anything seen on television far more unmemorable than something seen on a movie screen, in a darkened house, surrounded by the silent presences of other movie-goers. And if certain pictures first seen on TV retain their peculiar ghostly black-and-white vividness, that is because usually you have seen them afterwards in the newspaper: Kent State, the shooting of Oswald. Nor will tape-recorders insure permanence; in the public domain we are seeing that demonstrated. Future generations may develop an aural memory, but the very popularity of taping today shows that modern people do *not* remember what they hear, and feel the need to have it played back. The same, in the visual field, can be said of the camera; few tourists today remember what they see.

The decay of language must be part of a whole syndrome in which formerly healthy human faculties—speech, sight, hearing, taste, locomotion, even touch—have been to some degree vitiated by technological advance. This is more evident with the eye, the ear, the feet, the tongue as an organ of taste, the fingers—who but a professional can feel a stone, a piece of material, or tell leather from plastic? Smell seems to be an exception; this sense may have *developed* with modern civilization, despite air pollution. In the Middle Ages people were less sensitive to bad smells, I think; nowadays Americans profess to have very delicate nostrils, which are offended, when abroad, by the stench of bad drains, Venetian canals, B.O. And the recent work of Saul Bellow shows the primacy he accords to his nose—what Mr. Sammler has against women, more than the way they talk, is the way they smell.

With speech, though, it is not clear how or why machines should have affected it; we have not yet invented a machine that will do our talking for us. And as for writing, have the typewriter, the ball-point, the felt pen really done more than lame our handwriting? True, thanks to the telephone, ordinary people write less than they did and those who write—or dictate—are mainly located in offices. Hence the householder, obliged to write a letter, copies the language of the business communications he receives or that of the social column of his local paper: "I attended a function," "I was present at the interment." Lack of practice in writing probably has as a side-effect an impairment or loss of control of speech.

Yet there must be something beyond that. I would guess that our incompetence with words had to do with consciousness-lowering. A reduced consciousness of what is happening, of sights and sounds and textures, is first of all imposed on us by present-day conditions: driving in a car you see less than when you walk; living in a city, in an air-conditioned apartment, you hear less than your ancestors did—no cock's crow, bird song, rustling of leaves, roar of waterfall. The chief noises you hear are sirens and the refrigerator. But aside from these deprivations (felt as such if felt at all) there are sights and noises you *will* not to see or hear, sensations you *will* not to notice—TV commercials, crowding, ugly bodies, ugly clothes, traffic jams, your neighbor's rock or his classical music. You simply turn them off, and this soon becomes an automatic matter. Your switch is always in the down position. If you want to change that, you find you have to sign up for consciousness-raising sessions or turn on with drugs.

But language is a consciousness-raiser. The problem there

is that the power of using and understanding language, like
all power, carries responsibilities with it. You consent to having it or you don't. And most people today would rather not
have it. You can't exactly blame them. If they agreed to use
and understand language clearly, this would only exacerbate
all those aches and pains of contemporary civilization by putting them into *words*. It is true that this can give relief but
not on a daily basis. Better the primal scream than intelligi-
ble words that lead nowhere. Better delegate language to experts and specialists, i.e., intellectuals.

Language on occasion may be a substitute for action (in
mourning, for instance) but in the long run if it is not linked
to action it becomes insupportable. "Don't just keep talking.
Do something!" This explains, I think, the current dislike felt
for intellectuals by the silent majority which Agnew knew how
to play on. They are grudged the power of articulate speech
which has been delegated to them in a world that has become unspeakable, where action is required, but none is
forthcoming. Of course our intellectuals are some of the worst
sinners against language; the fall-out in academic circles is
asphyxiating, and some of this must be the result of speciali-
zation, the loss of touch with common everyday utterance
implied by the delegation of powers. One of the amusing
sidelights of Watergate was the discovery that Haldeman,
Ehrlichman, Krogh, and a few others considered themselves
an intellectual elite. Haldeman was proud of his language skills,
and Ehrlichman showed an open intellectual contempt for the
workhorse politicians of the Senate. If the public came to understand, from their jargon, that these were brains-trusters, this
would help explain the absence of grief at their departure.

In any case, it is impossible to believe that the misuse
and abuse of English on the part of ninety percent of the
population are not to some extent voluntary. The numerous
handbooks on correct usage, though they sell, I believe, have
about as much "relevant impact" as Emily Post's or Amy

Vanderbilt's etiquette manuals, which sell too. I think people must read all these books for entertainment.

George Orwell foresaw the dangers for a free society of cant, jargon, and euphemism. He was thinking mainly of official and party hypocrisy, which a courageous writer could unmask while pointing to the right way by his own steadfast plain-spoken example. What he missed, I think—perhaps he came too early—was the element of consent in the public. A general will to confusion. He analyzed the phenomenon of double-think but saw it as something inculcated in the enslaved masses by training and repetition. That is not happening to us—unless you count the indoctrination practiced by advertising—and exposure (Orwell's remedy) of verbal manipulation and malpractice has no effect. How many times has Nixon been exposed as a liar? And nobody cared, except the exposers. Nixon, for most, is just a fact, and words, his own or anybody else's, do not affect him. What has brought him down, if he is brought down, is a delightful turn of technology—the tapes.

Unlike Orwell, I do not have a remedy. A few men and women in public life who spoke and wrote clearly might help, since people are imitative or, as the current phrase goes, need "role models." But I think any real improvement would have to be effected by the popular will.

A final comment. It is curious that the sciences of linguistics and semiology—both highly abstruse—should have come into vogue just at this time, when the structures they so learnedly analyze—sentences—are a gruesome mass of rubble. On the professorial level, this corresponds to the inroads of "hopefully" as denoting the utter absence of hope.

Philadelphia and Lawrence, Kansas, November 1973

Living with
Beautiful Things

IN THE LAST few years, art objects—primarily paintings and sculptures—have achieved an unusual prominence, almost notoriety, in the news. You have probably read in the papers about the furor caused in Japan by the arrival of the Mona Lisa from the Louvre. A young woman sprayed its glass case with red paint in order to protest the Tokyo National Museum's policy of excluding persons in wheelchairs from the exhibition. The museum then complied by setting aside a special day—May 10—for physically handicapped visitors to see the famous painting. To guard against frauds, those presenting themselves that day in wheelchairs were warned to carry medical certificates of disability, which would entitle them and their attendants to free entry; ordinary visitors and non-bona-fide invalids were banned. In a parallel demonstration, eight women's liberation activists passed out handbills in front of the museum denouncing the Japanese Cultural Affairs Agency's policy of "alienating the masses from the Mona Lisa," and some Japanese Air France stewardesses seized on the occasion to distribute handbills of their own protesting a management decision to transfer them from Tokyo to Paris. The women's liberation handbills maintained that the museum was practicing discrimination not only against cripples but also against working women, who were being denied the chance to view the painting. It was not clear how the museum had been able to do this discriminating—working women could hardly have been singled out and turned away at the door; perhaps the protest was against the museum hours, which, if they ran from nine to five, would automatically exclude most of the working population. Or maybe the price of admission was discriminatory. Still, if the hours were selective and the price of admission high, Japanese working men were being "alienated from the Mona Lisa" too. Why the rights of women to see the picture were regarded as more brutally violated than those of men was not explained in the news stories. Because the *Gioconda* is a woman?

The Mona Lisa, a disturbing work of art, has a kind of sorcery about it that provokes disturbances. People have been tempted to draw moustaches on it, to attack it with a knife; it was stolen by an Italian house painter in 1911—supposedly to protest Napoleon's looting of Italian art treasures a hundred years before; he took it back to Florence, where he repatriated it in his hotel room. It is always heavily guarded against the designs or sudden impulses of madmen. The confused storm that raged around it in Japan—while the painting itself remained still as the brooding eye of a hurricane—was almost predictable. You could say that it was in the painting's "character." Yet other paintings and sculptures with no international reputation as troublemakers or *agents provocateurs* have suddenly become eventful. A psychotic young man from Australia attacked the peaceful *Pietà* of Michelangelo in St. Peter's with a hammer and inflicted awful damage. While on exhibition in Belgium, a Vermeer from the Rijksmuseum in Amsterdam was savagely cut from its frame, and, despite careful restoration, will never be quite the same. From Colmar Cathedral, in Alsace, someone took the famous little Schongauer, the *Virgin of the Rose Garden*, and returned it more than a year later; so far as I know, the circumstances remain mysterious. In Poland, last May, a Breughel and a Van Dyck disappeared and were replaced by fakes. And in Florence, in

102

1958, a queer episode took place: someone went through the first three rooms of the Uffizi and pierced tiny holes in the eyes of the *trecento* saints with a sharp pointed object. In 1960 acid was thrown at a Rubens in the Pinakothek in Munich.

Last winter, another Vermeer, from Kenwood House in Hampstead, just outside London, was stolen and held for ransom, with dramatic threats to burn it if the ransom terms were not met. Several months later, acting on a tip, Scotland Yard men recovered it from a churchyard, propped up, wrapped in a newspaper, between gravestones. No ransom had been paid (the original demand had been for £500,000 worth of food to be distributed among the poor of a West Indian island); nor had the two Price sisters, held in English jails for car-bombing, been transferred to an Irish prison, as the ransom notes had ordered. In Ireland, a daring raid on Sir Alfred Beit's collection, which included a Vermeer, a Goya, a Velasquez, a Franz Hals, had striking similarities: a ransom price of £500,000 was demanded, plus the transfer of four jailed IRA terrorists from England to Ulster. Here again the pictures were recovered, unharmed. Bridget Rose Dugdale, who was caught wearing a wig in a cottage in Cork, turned out to be a second offender; she had been convicted last October of stealing £87,000 worth of art and silver from her father. Shortly afterwards, in June, the letters "IRA," two feet high, were found scratched across Rubens' *Adoration of the Magi* in King's College Chapel, Cambridge.

These sensational daring crimes and outrages against illustrious works of art should be seen against the background of the enormous publicity given in the press recently to art auctions and art sales generally. The prices fetched have had something scandalous about them, shocking to common sense and maybe even to common decency. And the publicity surrounding the sales has awakened public alarm for the national patrimony, particularly in England but also elsewhere in Europe. The flight of artistic capital to American museums and the homes of American millionaires has been viewed as a national calamity, similar to the "brain drain," and mass movements have been initiated to "save the Titian," "save the Leonardo," through voluntary contributions. This collective enthusiasm recalls old-time war efforts and historic sieges, when women heroically sacrificed their wedding-rings, their gold bracelets and earrings, to melt down to buy cannon and ammunition for the *patria*.

It was different in the days of Lord Duveen: when an English lord sold a Titian from his country seat, that was *his* business; what happened to locally owned works of art was of no interest to the common man. Today this whole sphere has been democratized.

Along with the shock or scandal of the inflation of art prices, other scandals in the art world have surfaced, some of a deflationary nature. The most famous instance, at least for Americans, is the case of the celebrated Etruscan warrior statues in the Metropolitan Museum, familiar to every visitor, to virtually every New York schoolchild, which were suddenly admitted to be early twentieth-century fakes. In Paris, last spring, there came the shock of the Picasso collection—a donation he had made to the Louvre. The big exhibition planned for it was hastily canceled when a number of the paintings he had owned for years were exposed as fakes. Shortly after this, in Italy, a gang of picture-forgers, picture-doctors, and their accomplices—two art critics—were seized by the police, along with the evidence: twenty-two paintings ascribed to masters ranging from Caravaggio to Modigliani.

Of course there have always been forgeries and hoaxes in the art world; Michelangelo was guilty of one, as a poor young artist, when he passed off as an antique a "Sleeping Cupid" he had carved, rubbing it with earth and scarring it to make it look as if it had been dug up. What is new is the fascination exercised on the public by art frauds and forgeries—all the more compelling because of the vast sums of money to be made in this field, though usually not by the counterfeiter himself, who turns them out by the dozen like a sweated laborer. New also, probably, is an element of pathology: the modern counterfeiter, unlike Michelangelo, does not do it primarily for money but for some kind of ego-satisfaction—the thought of his works passing, under an alias, through the marts of trade to mingle with the great in priceless collections. A forger turning out false Renoirs is making a protest against accepted art names and art values. He proves by demonstration that he is in the same class with the recognized master he simulates, all the while bitterly conscious that if he signed his own name to his products they would have no market at all.

In fact, pathology enters into most of the bizarre episodes I have been speaking of. The motive of gain, where present at all, is minimal, more a hope than an expectation. It is true that church robberies of an unsensational kind have been greatly on the increase—in rural France and Italy they are so common that you do not even read about most of them—but the art objects stolen, not being famous, are marketable, and unguarded country churches offer a natural temptation. Such thefts can be plotted on the graph of a general increase in lawlessness and hence belong to normal criminality. In the current epidemic of sensational art snatches, though, as in the bodily attacks on defenseless works of art, there are signs of some new and contagious social malady. The fact that every one of those world-renowned paintings has been returned or recovered by the police shows that the thieves were not acting according to a well-thought-out rational plan, unless the plan was to seek publicity. And indeed all those acts, taken as an ensemble, of burglary and vandalism can be best seen as advertisements; the main achievement has been free space in the newspapers. Advertisements for a cause, as in the huge letters "IRA" scratched on the Rubens, or else pathetic commercials for an unrecognized individual, like the

Michangelo *Pietà*'s assailant. Yet even when the grievance crying for remedy seems to be clear and specific, one can sense, underneath, a murkier umbrage. That Japanese woman with her spray-can—was she merely protesting museum traffic-regulations that denied the Mona Lisa to an already disfavored category in the population, those unable to walk? Or was her protest also directed at its enigmatic target, the Mona Lisa herself, and at the disproportionate attention, the tribute, paid her, that is, paid art with a capital A, by society? The exclusion of society's weakest and most infirm members from the spectacle may have been only the last straw, the final determinant for an assault on art and art values as that protestor conceived them.

Certainly the group that seized the Kenwood House Vermeer in an armed raid was proclaiming a state of war against bourgeois values and specifically against the value bourgeois society appears to set on art. "You transfer our freedom fighters out of your bloody prisons or we will kill your precious picture." That was the tone of the ransom messages—a tone of furious contempt for prevailing English standards, which rate an inanimate object, a piece of property, higher than two lives. And the hijackers were right in their perception of the English value scale; it took the theft of the Vermeer to advertise the worth of the Price sisters' lives, which up to then nobody but fellow terrorists had thought to weigh or appraise. As the appointed Sunday drew near when the death sentence pronounced on the Vermeer was to be carried out, the general feverish concern over its fate proved—no doubt to the hijackers' satisfaction—where the public's sympathies lay. With the picture, obviously.

I am not going to condemn that attitude. I shared it. And the equation as posed by the revolutionaries was not exactly a fair one: the poor Vermeer had not "done anything," whereas the two girls had committed a capital crime. On the other hand, mixed with the agonized sense of the hostage's total innocence and helplessness, there was probably another feeling that reflected less credit on humanity—the feeling that the Vermeer was irreplaceable, the corollary being, of course, that the Price sisters were not. Nor is that idea, though repugnant, utterly false. We like to say that each human life is unique and therefore sacred, but we *know* that Vermeers are very rare and that there will never be any more. While violence-prone girl terrorists are, by comparison, common, and, it would seem, quite easily and quickly manufactured—look at Patty Hearst. And if, as a private person, each Price sister is unique, as revolutionaries they must hold themselves to be as interchangeable as standard parts of a machine: if one militant is struck down, another will spring into her place.

In the end, the hostage was not sacrificed. Maybe, as with Iphigenia at Aulis, some Olympian god intervened. Or, more factually, the people that took it did not have the heart to make good their threat, so they gave it back. Like a frightened airplane stewardess, held at gunpoint, the Vermeer had a terrible ordeal but survived, much to everybody's relief. The picture was luckier than some of the businessmen and diplomats who have been held for ransom during these last years, and its escape suggests that the group that hijacked it were less contemptuous of art values than the ransom messages implied. Or else that they did not consider the picture "worth" destroying and instead just dumped it where the cops could pick it up.

In any case, what we have here and in the Dugdale heist is a novel guerrilla tactic. Art objects are kidnapped and held for ransom just as though they were South American Exxon representatives or USIA foreign-service officers or millionaires' grandchildren, like Patricia Hearst and the Getty boy. A little strip had been cut off the back of the captive Vermeer and mailed to a newspaper to show that the kidnappers meant business—just like the Getty boy's ear. And on the public the effect was very much the same: we winced with sympathetic pain, as though the picture were sentient, as though it were alive and bleeding. The Vermeer's captors evidently aimed at striking terror into the English public through the newspapers, perhaps seeing this as a means of having their demands met by the authorities. With the Vermeer, this tactic (borrowed from the Mafia or from the Getty boy's kidnappers) did not work. The effect of terror on a mesmerized community is to convince the community that the assailants will strike again, and the sense of an omnipresent threat may induce resistance as well as compliance. Had the demands for the return of the Vermeer been met, no painting or sculpture in England would have been safe or so the public reasoned and no doubt the authorities too. Mr. Getty, in refusing to pay Paul Getty's ransom, thought along the same lines. "I have many grandchildren," he declared, meaning (I hope) that if he paid the price set on Paul, he would be putting the others in danger.

Such decisions, of course, are hard to make. What is interesting, though, is the fact that with any other costly material object but a work of art little anguish would have been felt either way. A decision *not* to pay ransom for a yacht or an airplane ("let them blow it up, then") would not call for any agonizing reappraisals. Only a work of art, in such endangered circumstances, appears equivalent to a life, so that the decision to sacrifice it or risk it, in the interest of safeguarding other works of art, becomes political—a matter of common concern. "Do we stand firm and let them execute the Vermeer?" The old excruciating choice between the One and the Many.

With the nineteen pictures in the Beit collection, less emotion seems to have been felt. Housed on Irish soil and acquired with the proceeds of South African mines, the collection itself, in the newspaper accounts, made an impression of loot or booty stashed in a pirate's haven and in that sense fair game for another set of hijackers, differently motivated.

Of course many, perhaps most, art treasures have been looted from somewhere, usually a poorer country, but they are not such fresh loot as the Beit swag seemed to be; like the Mona Lisa in the Louvre or Cleopatra's Needle in New York's Central Park, they have had time to grow a few roots. If the same paintings had been seized by three armed men and a woman from the Dublin National Gallery, much more outrage would have been experienced.

In the news stories of her capture, Bridget Rose Dugdale was described as an heiress "obsessed by inequalities." If her police record can be taken as evidence, this obsession of hers centered on collections of art, and she is not the only one to feel that ownership of beauty in material form confers a kind of privilege not inherent in the possession of cars, stocks and bonds, furs, even diamonds. A mysterious moral privilege that is different from mere wealth though generally associated with it. Mere wealth, in fact, we often feel, should not entitle a person to a privy association with beauty. Comparing the owner with the Rembrandt on his walls, one is conscious of an awful discrepancy, an injustice of fate that has brought these two together like an ill-assorted couple. The owner, alas, is not worthy of his possession. Yet we would not feel that about a magnificent Rolls-Royce, though we might faintly envy its possession, or about one of Mr. Onassis's yachts. Or Jackie's clothes and jewelry. One may despise all those things or half-wish one had them, at least to try on, but there is no virtue in them, no magical property that we sense as communicable, no aura beyond that of wealth, of which they are the outward signs.

Most of us like to think that beauty is not only a good in itself but also that it is good *for* something. We envy those who are in a position to surround themselves with beautiful things—in the form of paintings and statuary but also china, antique furniture, well-laid-out gardens—not merely for the sensory pleasure that must derive from looking at them and handling them or for the status they bestow but because we are sure that if *we* lived with them we would become beautiful too. As though some of the beauty inherent in these objects would be bound to rub off on their possessor and *a fortiori* on the children exposed to them from birth. In our wistful imagination, the wonderful contagion extends even to those charged with their care and maintenance, if it is only a daily cleaning woman, who is lucky beyond her fellows, people like to say, to be in contact with *objets de virtù*, each in its ordered place, that she dusts and polishes. No doubt there is some truth in this: to serve a god, beauty, indwelling in beautiful things, feels more rewarding than to slave for some member of one's own species. The daily service of beautiful things conduces to decorum; it is a rite, a kind of communion, as we notice whenever we wash a fine wine glass as opposed, say, to a jelly jar. Nearly everybody, even the most insensitive, has had some hair-raising encounter with the aesthetic present in man-made things, just as nearly everybody, even the most irreligious, can attest to some brush with the supernatural, if only in the form of thought-transference.

And yet museum attendants seem to be immune to contagion from the god; mysteriously, no magic rubs off on them. Maybe constant exposure to beauty has made them coarsely indifferent or is it constant exposure to crowds? To spend a working day watching over beautiful things is evidently not enough to turn you into a lover of beauty.

For the visitor to commune with works of art, it seems essential to be alone with them or relatively alone, and the mere presence of a crowd, the sound of other voices, in a museum or art gallery, is felt as a sacrilegious intrusion, just as in a forest or on a mountain peak. The purely visual experience of beauty is peculiar in this respect, distinct from other aesthetic forms such as concerts, operas, plays, which are enjoyed democratically. I do not think anybody would like being the only spectator at a play. True, reading demands solitude or at least freedom from distractions, but that does not apply, obviously, to listening to a novel or poem being read aloud or declaimed, which was our original experience of literature and still is for children, who relive phylogenetically the experience of the race: "Tell us a story." By contrast to the ear, the eye is a jealous, concupiscent organ, and some idea of ownership or exclusion enters into our relation with visual beauty. The eye is a natural collector, acquisitive, undemocratic, loath to share. Possession, appropriation, may be purely cerebral. I "collect" a painting or a statue or a passage of landscape when I stand before it in contemplation. I am storing it away—or trying to—in my mental treasure-house. Nobody could feel covetous at a concert, but who, going through a museum or a stately home, has not had an itch to possess some object (generally a small, portable one) on display?

The idea of taking his art collection with him into the next world does not occur to a modern millionaire. Yet for older materialistic cultures—the Egyptian, the Etruscan, the Mycenean, with its famous beehive tombs—those who had the good fortune to live with beautiful things could count on their companionship throughout eternity. The dead man in his tomb was equipped for the after-life with what he had enjoyed most in his sensual life: vases, cups, jars, painting, statuary, food and drink, slaves in simulacrum, bracelets, necklaces. The Etruscans buried a dead child with his toys around him. These pagan burial customs have a whiff of suttee about them—a sacrifice of the living (if art can be thought to be living) to comfort the dead. Such piety appears to us barbarous. We would not bury an oil man with his favorite Giorgione or Titian or even his Francis Bacon. What a waste, we would think. They should go to a museum, of course, together with his signed French furniture, and his estate will benefit from a tax write-off. To bury a piece of property of world-recognized value would strike most modern people as nothing short of criminal, and a will containing such a proviso would be taken, probably, as prima facie evidence of unsound mind.

Yet is the museum as the last resting-place for "priceless" works of art really the solution that socialists and civic-minded millionaires like to fancy for the disposal of this unique category of property once jealously kept in the family, in papal and episcopal palaces and the gold-encrusted chapels of high-born cloistered nuns? Socialists think that art ought to belong to everybody and not to a favored few. This sounds right in theory, but in practice there is no way that that particular pie can be cut and distributed fairly. Once a work of art enters a museum, instead of belonging to everybody, it belongs to nobody. Shares in it, that is in the physical space in front of it, are disputed between touristic groups with their guides, individual visitors, artists with sketch pads, copyists sitting at easels. As public interest in art mounts, the situation worsens. The inflation of art values encourages a kind of voyeurism, which in turn stimulates unbalanced persons and others with private or social grievances to commit acts of violence within the sacred precincts, and these acts of violence, in their turn, draw bigger crowds. The Kenwood House Vermeer, before last February, was probably one of the few Vermeers outside private collections that you could look at in peace; no more—once it is restored and put back in place, it will surely be mobbed, as happened with the Michelangelo *Pietà*, already a crowd-collector. I was not in Florence when that madman (never identified) pierced tiny holes in the eyes of the fourteenth-century female saints, but I can imagine that those first rooms in the Uffizi, normally quite deserted, were thronged that summer with curiosity-seekers trying to make out where the holes had been and closely querying the guards.

What happened with the Mona Lisa in Tokyo is a perfect illustration of the problem. In excluding handicapped people in wheelchairs, the Japanese Cultural Affairs Agency had made a democratic decision. Estimating the crowds that would queue up to see the picture, they allotted thirty seconds per visitor for viewing: obviously people in wheelchairs would slow up the flow of traffic and deprive others still waiting of the chance to see the Mona Lisa. In fact, as I read somewhere, because the crowds were even bigger than had been estimated, or because the demonstrations and their aftermath created bureaucratic confusion, the allotted viewing time was eventually cut to ten seconds. But nobody can "see" the Mona Lisa in ten seconds *or* thirty. The whole idea is an absurdity. When you think of the dilemma—and things are not much better around the painting when it is at home in the Louvre—you wonder whether a better solution might not have been to resort to the Etruscan expedient of burying the Mona Lisa with her first owner, François I, back in the sixteenth century.

For today, I see no solution. There is no way of persuading people, democratically, by television appeals, to stay away from museums if they are not urgently interested in art. The nineteenth-century philanthropists, endowers of provincial universities and schools of art and design, had a good idea: to present casts and copies of famous works of art to small cities and towns, for students to work from and citizens to look at, to improve their general culture. One American, a relation of Harriet Beecher Stowe, commissioned the painter Fantin Latour to copy *all* the paintings in the Louvre. Andrew Carnegie, in Pittsburgh, made a collection of replicas (now the Carnegie Institute) of the standard art repertory—not just statuary and paintings but also familiar masterpieces of architecture—portals, façades, porticos. The cream-colored big room housing them still stands as he left it and has an eerie, haunting or haunted, beauty, but today it must be unique. Today originals are demanded. Every town, every college must have originals for its museum. The old plaster casts of the Laocoön, of the Hermes of Praxiteles, Venus of Milo, that stocked the provincial museums of my childhood have vanished without a trace. Are they stored in museum basements or have they simply been junked, like the copies of Rembrandt's *Old Woman Cutting Her Nails* and the *Blue Boy* that Americans used to hang in their living-rooms? The scurry for originals of any and every description naturally helps to send up prices, and at the same time it is these very prices, which they have read about in news magazines, that make people curious to see the most famous and costly originals of all and, if not prevented, to touch them wonderingly, as if to make sure they are real. Tourists who have been given to understand that paintings and sculptures are the only kind of currency that is not going to depreciate will naturally not be satisfied by copies, as their grandparents were, but must file in person past the Mona Lisa, the Birth of Venus, the Night Watch, gaze up at the Winged Victory and Michelangelo's David. Yet this is not the whole story.

In addition there is the belief, which I spoke of just now, that direct contact with visual beauty is, in Berenson's phrase, life-enhancing and hence that deprivation of it or the acceptance of substitutes—reproductions and plaster casts—amounts to spiritual starvation. That is why any program, however rational, for limiting access to famous works of art known to contain large quantities of that essential element would have as little chance of gaining approval in a modern society as a zero-growth program designed to take away milk from school-children.

But is there any empirical foundation for such a body of beliefs? What does beauty do, exactly, for those people we consider fortunate in comparison with ourselves, in that they are exposed to it regularly while we are not?

Let us look at art dealers, to start with. Well, as a class, they are not morally better than butchers or dentists; certainly they have a worse reputation. They are not more enlightened or refined than most other groups in the population; in fact, in my experience, they tend to be rather vulgar. They have a

114

certain amount of specialized knowledge, most of it highly technical but nonetheless more interesting to the rest of us, since we *are* interested in art, than what is contained in a dental journal. As a class, that is about all you can say for them. But you could argue that art dealers are not a fair example to choose, since their relation to art is commercial; they are buyers and sellers of produce.

Let us turn, then, to museum curators. Again, no moral effect of the regular exposure to beauty is perceptible. As a group, they are probably more upright than stock speculators or used-car dealers. They are better educated than the average person, but that is not an effect of being a curator so much as a cause. Having studied art history in a liberal-arts curriculum and done some post-graduate work, they qualified to become curators. It is not a job you work up to by starting as a guard. In general, they are better dressed than the national average and have better manners. The job requires them to be fairly presentable and to have a fund of lively or informative conversation. They are rather good at gossip. In every other respect, I would say, they are timid and mediocre creatures, though I can think of a few shining exceptions, mostly women. Association with beauty has not given the mass of curators large hearts or soaring minds; in extenuation, it must be said, that they have been obliged to associate not just with Assyrian cylinder seals and Coptic portraits but also with art patrons and donors: they have learned to flatter and suck up for the museum's sake and to do quite a little lying and glossing over, in justification of museum policies. Once more, as with art dealers, their relation to beauty is impure. A good part of the job, on the higher levels, is promotion and public relations, and the professional concern they must have with wills, the fierce competition between museums for legacies and bequests, brings out a suggestion of the tactfully hovering vulture.

When I go on to art historians and critics, some slight

115

improvement will be noticeable. A rare critic or art historian appears to be divinely inspired, an enraptured angel with fire-tipped wings as in some Florentine painting; beauty *has* been infectious. It has cast a glow over those eager features; he stands at the lectern with a pointer, happily calling for a new slide: he himself an Annunciation. Yet such unusual figures are found not only in the field of art history but in science, mathematics, theology, philosophy, Shakespeare studies. And one curious point is worth noticing: quite a few of those illumined art historians have spent their home lives in ugly, utilitarian, or generally tasteless surroundings. Their communion with the beautiful did not endow them with the faculty known as taste and help them in the selection of furniture or even in the modest acquisition of works of art. Art historians, in general, astonish their students and acquaintances by having quite hideous little personal collections, of which they are often proud. Lack of money cannot be the explanation for this blind spot. You do not need to be rich to collect. Bernard Berenson, who became a rich man and was famous for his eye, was criticized by his younger friends for having a "dowdy" or "tacky" house and a third-rate (with some exceptions) lot of pictures.

In any case, art critics and historians, on the average, are in no way superior, morally and aesthetically, to judges and doctors; from the samplings I have taken, I would rate them considerably below. Again, it is the same story as with curators and art dealers. Their relation with the beautiful is compromised by quasi-commercial factors. The calling is highly competitive and productive of jealousy and vicious backbiting. There is continuous rivalry in expertise. That is true for most academics—economists and sociologists and professors of literature. But the historian or critic of art is in a special position: the beautiful is a commodity with a market value. A professor of poetry who is underwriting Yeats, say, while his rival is committed to Eliot, does not stand to lose anything material—nor to lose anybody else anything—if Yeats's stock goes down and Eliot's rises; only his infallibility is at stake. But the art critic or art historian utters opinions that are expressible to others in terms of currency. His judgments affect the real market, sending prices up or down.

If his field is old art, he must pronounce on the genuineness of past works; his attribution of a drawing to Raphael rather than to some obscure follower is of immense interest to a dealer and to the eventual buyer. He is paid, of course, by the dealer for his authentication, which will be quoted and eventually turn up in a catalogue. If other art historians, when the drawing is shown, deny that it is a Raphael, the suspicion may arise that he has taken a cut of the sale price. Maybe he hasn't, maybe he was only stating his honest conviction, but there are more subtle forms of bribery and more subtle ways of cheating on an attribution.

If, on the other hand, our friend's field is contemporary art, he soon discovers that he can "make" an artist by favorable reviews. The artist or his grateful dealer will want to reward him with gifts of paintings—payments in kind whose market value will accrue over the years. There is nothing wrong here necessarily. An artist, naturally, will feel friendship for the critic who "discovered" him, and if the poor artist comes around with a painting or a sketchbook, how can the critic refuse? In contrast to the appraisers of old art, he may feel like a pure, non-commercial spirit. But he too is part of the art business. Where the old-master specialist authenticates a drawing as being by Raphael, he authenticates new work as being art.

For both the old-master specialist and the critic or advocate of contemporary art, friendship may be a corrupting element. The contemporary critic has multiple friendships with artists and dealers, where the historian tends to be close to curators and buyers. But anybody who is involved with the appraisal of art is courted by rich people who need guidance in forming their collections. The historian is wined and dined and brandied, taken in private planes to view the Hermitage collection in Leningrad, met by chauffeurs when he arrives in a strange city, whisked out to villas and châteaux and elaborate country houses. His path is smoothed; he becomes familiar with butlers; wherever he goes, in this company, it is as though a silencer had been set down before him, like the pad you put under the cloth on a dining-room table or, in those circles, under the Aubusson rug. The contemporary critic is "hosted" by a different type of rich person, the informal type, as with "informal" art, and the itinerary is different— the Kroller-Müller museum in Holland, the Ludwig collection in Aachen may be opened at off-hours for him, he will be emplaned for the Venice Biennale and the exposition at Kassel—but he too grows familiar with prodigality. The introduction into the life of wealth, even semi-servantless American wealth, is almost bound to uglify the uneasy recipient of its favors.

Either he becomes intensely snobbish or he turns cynical and jeering, often both at the same time or in abrupt alternation. He mocks the well-disposed people who entertain him as soon as they are out of earshot and sometimes before. When he is back with his real friends—bohemians or professors—he boasts of the houses and collections he has visited while disparaging their owners. The trouble with the beautiful is that either it belongs, as I have said, to nobody, which means museums and crowds, or it belongs to somebody. There is always some sort of fence around it, and scaling that fence, for the outsider, involves unbecoming acrobatics, acrobatics that leave the art historian and his younger, brasher brother, the discoverer-critic, with an occupational deformity.

Let us turn finally to the owners, ignoring restorers and framers. If we stopped to examine them, it would be the same as with dealers, curators, and critics: beneficial effect of association with art nil or practically nil. With owners, we might

expect it to be a little different, especially if we leave out fash-
ion-followers (for whom the beautiful will not stay still but
keeps dizzily changing its locus) and brutalized speculators who
buy pictures because they have been assured it is an investment, "like money in the bank." But if we stay with real
ownership, based on love or infatuation or family ties (inheritance), we seem to be on familiar territory. Most of us have
owned or lived for a time with small particles of beauty and
have found that a source of security, like any close rapport.
Yet we must admit to something else: the longer we live with
some object or objects we think beautiful, the more we cease
to be aware of them, as with a long-married couple. There
are pictures on my walls and little objects on my mantelpiece
that I do not "see" for weeks, maybe months, at a time just
as you cease to hear a clock ticking in a room. Possibly that
is not true if you live with a great painting—a Rembrandt, a
Vermeer, a Goya—I have not had the experience but I imagine that the command on the attention-span in those cases
would be more powerful, and it would be days rather than
weeks or months during which they hung unnoticed, mere
vague presences. I suppose that if for a whole year you do not
"see" a Dutch drawing or a little Greek vase you own, it is
time to give it away, on the principle that if you find you
have not worn a dress for a year, you ought to get rid of it,
although it is still "good." But nobody is willing to do that:
with the dress, yes, but with the vase or drawing, no, decidedly not. And if some moralist insisted, we might argue that
there is another kind of seeing different from conscious looking: how can we measure the influences beautiful objects have
been exercising on us, subliminally, all the time we thought
we were not noticing them?

But, accepting that argument—the only defense really that
can be offered for living with more than our senses can absorb—what is the influence and how does it work? Instead of
scrutinizing ourselves in relation to our small treasures, let us

119

look at big collectors, who should be subject to more influences. I am afraid we are no better off than we were with art
dealers and museum custodians, at least in the moral sphere.
Think of Goering. I have known gentle art collectors, mild
and philanthropic where the arts are concerned, glad to lend
and serve on boards, even one or two who are liberals (in the
American sense, i.e., slightly to the left) in politics and devoted to human rights—this is a very rare species. But the
majority, I must say, are not very nice people. Living with
beautiful things, inherited or acquired, has not enlarged them;
one could almost think the opposite. It would be interesting
to study the evolution of a collector of art. Was he small,
narrow, selfish, and deeply reactionary to start with or did de-
votion to his *things* bring those traits out in him? Or put it
this way: is the owner of choice furniture and superb paintings better or worse than the ordinary rich philistine? My guess
would be worse, though he may be a little easier to talk to,
at least at the start.

Quite poisonous people, on the whole, are attracted by
the visual arts and can become very knowledgeable about them.
This is much less true of literature: a bookish rich man or
country gentleman is likely to be a quite humane and responsive individual (I do not mean a bibliophile, who is just an
art collector with a slightly different field of activity). A bookish man will be an omnivorous reader, obviously, but he will
not be greedy: by consuming more reading matter than is
customary he does not deprive anyone else of his share, and
this is probably an important difference. The same could be
said of music.

But to return to the question of the influence that we
think ought to be exercised by daily exposure to works of art.
Is there any rub-off at all? Well, in the case of the collector,
I think one is discernible. He inherits or acquires taste. Not
always but often. Sooner or later, those who are covetous of
beauty, whether they are Renaissance popes or tyrants or

120

modern collectors, generally develop a faculty of discriminating that often extends to other departments of life, particularly to the table. Though not to the moral or intellectual
sphere. So that it comes down to this: the taste one develops
from association with beautiful things equips one to select more
of them. That is all: a rather vicious circle. Yet the idea of
taste (something, by the way, that artists themselves often lack)
as the sole increment or residue of days and nights spent in
company with Botticellis, Rembrandts, Titians, African masks,
Meissen, pre-Columbian totems, is not what we meant when
we thought wistfully of the privilege of living with beautiful
things. There must be something more. Perhaps the mistake
we have been making is to consider the matter in terms of
individual ownership and private enjoyment (important as that
is for quiet communion with the visual), rather than in terms
of whole cultures. A city of spacious parks, communally owned
statuary erected in public squares and looking down from the
façades and rooftops of public buildings, a city of handsome
residences and noble civic structures, must be better, we feel
sure, to live in than a shanty-town, and not just because it is
more hygienic, and more pleasurable to the eye. Such a city
ought to inculcate virtue.

Certainly that belief was widely held in the ancient world.
The city was pictured as a teacher, and the more beautiful
and stately the city, the better the civic lesson. Machiavelli
thought so: of the love of liberty characteristic of small free
republics, he wrote in his *History* that "the public buildings,
the halls of the magistracy, and the insignia of free institutions" would remind the citizens of their liberty even after it
had been lost for generations. Nothing in these old concep-
tions had anything to do with forming the *taste* of the citi-
zenry—only a taste for virtue. Architecture and sculptured
ornament, as well as free-standing statuary, daily visible to
everyone, imprinted a coded message, as in genetics, or so it
was assumed, and the first act of an invading enemy was to

raze the city and all its monuments, so that no memory of civic life would remain. Similarly with church building and decoration; the component of beauty and splendor in the stone fabric was part of the edifying element, although opinions differed among the monastic orders as to how large a part the sensuous ought to play—the Cistercians thought that the rounded apse was sinful (curves were more wicked than right angles), and their churches have a flat east end. The modern notion of sparing beauty in warfare—hit the railway yards, men, not the cathedral—was undreamed of, since beauty was, in those days, inseparable from the messages it carried to the people.

As cities became bigger and more ugly, with the advance of the Industrial Revolution, the faith in architecture and sculpture (painting to a much lesser extent) as nurturers of virtue was replaced by faith in Nature. Natural beauty was seen as a character-former; a child brought up under its influences was regarded as particularly fortunate. The Romantic, Wordsworthian belief in Nature's beneficent powers is still with us, but we now think of it in terms of vacations, camp, pack trips, sailing.

All these sets of belief in the ennobling power of beauty are justified by subjective experience. Beauty communicates an instant sense of joy that arrives like a revelation. Seeing a spring apple orchard, a field of wild flowers, a Greek temple, a Renaissance fresco, a Henry Moore makes us feel not only good but "good." Since we know this, empirically, since the experience of instant well-being is unfailing, how can we doubt that civilizations that provide such experiences on a daily basis are "better" than those that don't? Otherwise a child, considered as a spirit, would be just as well off being brought up in a trailer camp or a Holiday Inn. Of course you don't believe that; neither do I. Nothing could *make* me believe it. Yet the evidence, such as there is, is rather shaking. Let us take Germany. The most beautiful parts of the country, everyone agrees, are Bavaria and the Rhineland. Nature is far more beautiful there, in the Black Forest, along the Rhine and the Moselle, in the Bavarian Alps, and man's works are too—cathedrals, churches, palaces, bridges, town architecture. The Rhenish towns and cities, and Munich, Nürnberg, Würzburg, Bamberg, Regensburg are the treasure-houses of Germany—they also had the best artists. Yet Bavaria and the Rhineland had much the worst Nazis, and Bavaria is still a neo-Nazi stronghold; I am not sure about the Rhineland. In Italy, you found something similar; the worst Fascists, the most irreducible, were in Machiavelli's city of Florence, with its halls of civic virtue still standing. The analogies can be carried to my own country. The prettiest parts, I understand, contain some of the most vicious people: unreconstructed mountainous sections of the South, Carmel Valley in California.

There may be special explanations for each of these cases or there may be one general explanation: the most beautiful parts of the world tend to be the most retarded, the most passed by in the course of modern development. That is why nobody has yet torn down their quaint main streets to make a shopping mall or bulldozed their apple orchards for a plastics factory. Their inhabitants, having been passed by, would be the most resentful and bitter. Maybe. But the facts remain alarming, any way you look at them.

If beauty is good *for* something, then it is a mysterious something that we today cannot put our finger on. Or else it is good for nothing. It is useless. That may be why we are letting it disappear with so little regret. It is an enigma, a perplexity, impossible to fit into the social scheme, tending to gravitate toward people with ugly souls or inviting people with ugly souls to gravitate toward it. The only thing we can think of to do with it, once it is prized from their grasp by taxation, is to install it in museums, thus rendering it, as I have been saying, in many notable instances all but inaccessible, except to those same few who already possess more than their share of it and who are let in to rejoice their eyes during hours when the public is excluded.

When he was Minister of Culture, during de Gaulle's regime, André Malraux had a nice inspiration. He took some of the Louvre's twentieth-century statuary and put it in the Tuileries Garden, where every bus rider or motorist or passing pedestrian can look at it, without standing in line or paying admission. Some days, riding or walking by, you notice it. Some days you don't. It is just as if it belonged to you, in your own apartment, sometimes asking for your complete attention, sometimes not bothering you. A good idea, to get art out of museums, but it would not work with paintings, and has any other Minister of Culture or mere mayor followed it up? Maybe it would make no difference. The link between beauty and civic life has been lost, and Malraux's statues, not being garden statuary, at first looked pathetic and absurd plumped down on the grass.

As for private ownership, perhaps the modest collections of the last generation are as far as we can decently go. A china tea service, a fine clock, water colors, slag obelisks, some pretty and old chairs. Those things at least did not do Mother or Grandmother any harm, and they may have bettered her, indefinably, like a poor Cretan peasant's icons or the Roman's lares and penates. If beauty is a god, and I still think he is, he requires some private service and domestic rituals. The objects we own—I am speaking of people like myself—are generally commemorative. Of an occasion—the day we bought them—or of the friend who brought them back to us, from a trip to Greece, pre-colonel. They are objects of piety, and the little bit of beauty that is in them is valued both for itself and as a souvenir, for the memories that attach. Well, that is how English tourists in the nineteenth century bought Canalettos and Guardis, the way, almost, that we would buy a postcard—as a reminder of mornings or afternoons spent in the city of Venice. We own, my husband and I, a Greek, or, rather, Greco-Sicilian, stone bull and a little Egyptian hawk, both bought in Palermo, one rainy afternoon from an old crippled Yugoslav woman, who had a shop upstairs in her big flat that was three-quarters junkshop and one-quarter museum. I cannot say what they represent to us, beyond themselves, but certainly the temple at Segesta, a wild iris my husband picked for me there, in January, a hawk we saw flying, maybe the local wine Corvo, which means hawk, the biggest rainbow we ever saw, driving through the rain near Enna, like a rainbow in a myth, the lake where Persephone was snatched off to hell, the Emperor Frederick the Second, known as Stupor Mundi, the limping Yugoslav woman, *her* history. . . . Well, I am not going to give you my autobiography, but there are bits of it and of our joint history clinging like lichens to the broad-necked stone bull and the little ivory hawk, which always stay together on our library table, placed just so, as a pair. In the particles of beauty we keep around us, that are *ours*, by gift, purchase, or inheritance, as well as in the deposits of memory left by visits to museums and galleries, by walks in the woods or fields, there are rights of ownership, claims; our "collections" belong together, are interconnected, by virtue of their relation with us, and amount to the story of our lives. When we die, the collection they constitute will fall apart; they will go their separate ways, be dispersed, like our bodies.

The perplexities, I think, surrounding works of art, the injustice of their uneven distribution among the population, arise from the fact that they are both body and spirit, and whereas with music and poetry, one could say that the spirit predominated, with paintings and sculptures, the corporeal, material form not only predominates but cannot be separated from the spirit, just as with a human creature. To try to di-

vide up fairly is like the Judgment of Solomon. But we have
no Solomon, and in the end the true mother, whoever she
is, will have to yield up the baby to the false mother and sadly
go away.

Aberdeen, Scotland, Spring 1974

Novel, Tale, Romance

I WANT to distinguish at the outset three types of prose narrative—novel, tale, romance— which are currently thought to be indistinguishable. The only difference most people now recognize among types of fiction is one of length, which can help us tell a short story from a novel and helped (once upon a time) to tell a short story from a short-short story. But I am not going to be dealing in these remarks with short stories as a separate class. Most of them fall under the headings I have just named. They can be divided into 1) abbreviated novels, 2) brief tales, 3) fragmentary romances. If the form has a definite character of its own, I have been unable to determine it.

Nor will I be dealing with the "novella," which to me is only an affected name for a shortish novel or a longish short story. Originally, in Italian, it was applied to stories or "histories" like those in Boccaccio's *Decameron*. In French, it became *nouvelle*, as in *Cent nouvelles nouvelles*, where, as in the *Decameron* (though not in the *Heptaméron* of Marguerite de Navarre), the little narratives tended to be licentious. In German, the *Novelle*, thanks to the Romantics, became a genuine form, with naturalization papers; in our time it was favored by Thomas Mann. But in English the word for short novel is "novelette," which quickly became pejorative, meaning a rather cheap love story and giving rise to the damning adjective "novelettish" before passing out of use altogether. Nobody talks of novelettes any more.

Another class of prose fiction is fable—from the Latin *fabula*, which in turn goes back to an ancient term, *fari*, meaning simply "to speak"—the root, incidentally, of *fatum*, or "fate," i.e., "what has been spoken." I shall not be discussing fables either, though they did not go out with Aesop. The obvious contemporary example is *Animal Farm*, but I think *1984*, a cautionary tale, must be a fable too, and William Golding's *Lord of the Flies*, most of Golding, probably, also *Brave New World*, *A Clockwork Orange*, and quite a lot of science fiction.

Fables, with or without talking animals, are allegories—*allegoria*, the description of one thing under the image of another—and, whatever a novel may be, it is not an allegory. It lives in its own right; its characters are not personifications; their names do not refer to abstract conditions or qualities such as "Pilgrim," "Everyman," "Zeal-of-the-Land-Busy," "Patience." If a character in a novel is named "Krook," as in Dickens's *Bleak House*, this is not shorthand for a dishonest person—never. Mr. Krook with his rag-and-bone shop and his weird cat Lady Jane is something much queerer and more complex than that. And the statement I have just made—"A novel is not an allegory"—can be developed syllogistically, like this: "No novel is an allegory," "X is an allegory," "X is not a novel." Apply it to a specific case: "*1984* is a parable for our times. A parable is a form of allegory. No novel is an allegory. Therefore *1984* is not a novel." Such little tests can be useful.

Adding to the confusion in this sphere is a tendency of reviewers to read no matter what novel as "a parable for our time"—at best an unctuous pronouncement, evoking the laying on of hands. But to try to read a true novel as an allegory does not deepen the meanings in it; rather the contrary. It leaches out any meaning that is not didactic.

Novel, tale, romance—these are the classes of prose narrative I shall be alluding to, and, before I can comment on some mutations in their current behavior, I shall have to make clear what those classes are or were. Of all these forms the tale is the oldest and maybe the most persistent. Unlike the novel and the romance, it is pre-literate in its beginnings, and something oral still clings to it, however sophisticated it becomes. A tale always has a teller and, around him, an implied circle of listeners, with the suggestion of a campfire. The teller is the guarantor of the tale's authenticity, which is why he remains present even in late developments of the form such as Conrad's "Marlow" stories, where the veteran ship's officer spinning his yarn is more a traditional accessory than a necessity for validating a far-fetched account. We would believe *Lord Jim*, I think, without Marlow's attestation to the truth of it. But it is Marlow's voice that reminds us that the story of the young, untried first mate and his instant of cowardice is not a novel but a tale.

The teller, I must add, now and then creeps into the novel, where he does not belong, but he functions there as a sort of Master of Ceremonies (*Don Quixote*) and quickly drops from sight. Whenever he creeps in (and it is important that you note this), even though he invariably appears as an "I," a first-person singular, he is not the same as the "I" of an autobiographical novel like *David Copperfield* or even of a pseudo-autobiographical romance like *Great Expectations*, whose hero, Pip, though he writes in the first person, is not Dickens himself when younger. The same could be said of *Jane Eyre*, another pseudo-autobiography: the lucky heroine ("Reader, I married him"), despite some points in common, is someone different from Charlotte Brontë, who had no Mr. Rochester in her life. The "I" of the tale, as opposed to the "I" of novel or romance, is never a participant; he is an observer, a witness who comes forward to testify to an event in itself unusual or even unlikely on the face of it. In Conrad's tales, he may double or even triple, as though to give auditory perspective, like an echo: the author, Joseph Conrad ("I" Number One), hears a story from his old acquaintance Marlow ("I" Number Two), a trustworthy commentator, and it may happen that Marlow, lacking first-hand knowledge of some part of the tale, relates what he has heard from still a third narrator. In principle, you could go on indefinitely, with infinite regression, as in the picture on the old Quaker Oats box.

A strange light on the secret nature of the tale is cast by etymology. "Tale" in French is *conte*, in Italian *conto*, in Spanish *cuento*; in German it is *Erzählung*; in Dutch, *vertelling*. It is clear, to start with, that the Germanic words have a different linguistic root from the Romance-language words. And in most of these Western languages there is a separate word, often a more common one, for a narrative other than a tale: our own "story," deriving from the Latin for "history"; the French *récit*, German *Bericht*, Dutch *verhaal*, meaning literally "a report." Now all the words for tale, even though they stem from two independent roots, have to do with counting, with adding up, or directly with the word for number. I will illustrate it in Italian: *conto* = "tale" and also = "bill" ("*Il conto, per favore*" in a restaurant); *contare* is "to count" and also "to relate." Here it is in German: *erzählen* (to tell), *Erzählung* (tale), *Zahl* (number). And Dutch: *vertelling* (to tell), *getal* (number). There is the same thought buried in the English "recount" ("He recounted me a tale"). The teller of a tale, then, is indistinguishable from the teller behind the counter in a bank, who *tells* out your money, rapidly adding.

I find this deeply mysterious. What is it trying to say to us? Conceivably, it only points to a metrical origin of all formal narration: "Tell me not in mournful numbers." "Meter" / "measure." Verse, like cloth, is measured in feet. Yet that does not satisfy my curiosity, partly because human speech (the "telling" and "*erzählen*") cannot have started out as verse but, rather, in grunts related to gestures—of pointing, for example. Perhaps the telling refers, rather, to a need for listing in orderly sequence evident in early narratives, intent on documenting a tradition. "These are the generations of Shem: Shem was an hundred years old, and begat Arphaxad two years after the flood: and Shem lived after he begat Arphaxad five hundred years, and begat sons and daughters. And Arphaxad lived five and thirty years and begat Salah. . . ." Or the Homeric catalogues.

In any case it seems to me that the counting, the addition of particulars, implicit in those words for tale in so many different tongues must refer to the piling up of incident, the "And then . . . And then?" that E. M. Forster speaks of in *Aspects of the Novel* but that applies in any narration. It applies, I feel, with particular force in the tale, where the anticipation of the listeners is keyed to a spoken narrative in which incidents are doled out, as it were, one after another, like haricot beans, each having equal weight, without the increasing pressure of "building" toward one or more climaxes that is typical of the novel. In a tale we wait to hear what will come next, but the waiting is less suspenseful than it tends to be in the novel; from long practice in listening, we can afford to be patient while our teller counts out the bills that are our due reward.

Cervantes, often cited as the inventor of the novel, had a wonderful understanding of every form of narrative and exemplified it in *Don Quixote*. That he appreciated the effect of counting, of simple accumulation, so profoundly rooted in the tale is shown in Chapter 20 of Part One, where the knight orders Sancho Panza to tell him a tale to help them both pass a wakeful night in the outdoors. Sancho Panza obliges, bidding his master, as the condition of his story-telling, that he keep mum and not interrupt.

"I say then," recounts Sancho, "that in a village of Estremadura there was once a goatish shepherd (I mean that he tended goats), and this shepherd, or goatherd, as my story goes, was called Lope Ruiz, and this Lope Ruiz fell in love with a shepherdess, who was called Torralba, which shepherdess called Torralba was the daughter of a rich flock master, and this rich flock master—" "If you tell your story, Sancho, that way," interrupts Don Quixote, "and repeat everything you have to say twice over, you will not finish in two days." "My way of telling it," replies Sancho, "is the way they tell all stories in my country, and I don't know any other way of telling it." "Tell it as you please then," answers Don Quixote, "and since it is Fate's will that I can't help listening, go on."

Thereupon Sancho continues his story, till he gets the goatherd to the bank of a river (duly named) with his flock of goats, which he wants to take across. But, instead of a ferry, he can find only one fisherman, with a boat so small that it will hold only a man and a goat. "All the same," says Sancho Panza, "he spoke to him and arranged with him to carry himself and his three hundred goats across. The fisherman got into the boat and carried one goat across, returned and carried another, and came back again and carried over another— Now keep an account, sir, of the goats the fisherman is carrying over, for if one should slip from your memory, the story will end and it will be impossible for me to tell you another word of it. I'll go on, then, and say that the landing place on the other side was very muddy and slippery, which delayed the fisherman a good deal on his ferrying back and forth; all the same he came back for another goat, and another, and another—"

"Reckon that he has ferried them all over," interrupts Don Quixote, "and stop coming and going in that manner or you will not finish getting them over in a year." "How many have gone over so far?" inquires Sancho. "How the devil do I know?" says Don Quixote. "There you are!" comments Sancho. "Didn't I tell you to keep a good count? Well, the tale is ended,

thanks be to God, for there's no use in going any further."
There in fact the tale ends. Like somebody in a fairy story,
Don Quixote, heedless of Sancho's warning, has broken a spell.
It is like the legend of Cupid and Psyche. As Sancho remarks, philosophically, "As far as my tale is concerned there's
nothing more to add, for it ends where the mistake in the
counting of the goats begins." In short, being a true tale, it
is endless and can only be stopped.

Don Quixote, needless to say, is a reader of romances—
a higher class of narrative. The romance is to the tale as Don
Quixote is to Sancho Panza. His impatience with Sancho's
patient adding of one goat to another is a literary criticism:
he misses the foreshortening ("Reckon that he has ferried them
all over") familiar to him in his beloved romances of chiv-
alry. In this sharp difference of tastes, Cervantes himself does
not take sides. Don Quixote, after all, addled reader of romances, and Sancho Panza, methodical teller of primitive
tales, are both characters in still another literary genre—the
newborn novel. And in one sense, certainly this *Don Quixote*, ancestor of a whole new tribe of fictions, is something
more than a "straight" fiction. It is an extended piece of technical commentary, studded like a ham with piquant samples
of every known type of literary composition. Such various-
ness and amplitude are characteristic of the novel. You will
not find the like in tales or even in romances, despite their
habit, or vice, of digression.

Both the tale and the romance deal with the marvelous, with
faraway, fabled lands ("Heart of Darkness," *Invisible Cities*),
with forests, jungle (*Green Mansions*), remote, barely navi-
gable rivers, and especially islands (*Robinson Crusoe*, *The Swiss
Family Robinson*, *Vendredi ou les limbes du Pacifique*, *Lord
of the Flies*), desert by preference. Both are close relations of
the literature of voyages and exploration (Hakluyt, *The Oregon Trail*, *Two Years Before the Mast*, *The Green Hills of Af-*

rica), and it may be hard to separate, within a single author, e.g., the Melville of *Typee,* travel report from Polynesian romance.

The tale's distance from its listeners, when not geographical, may be an effect of inhabitual weather: tempests, floods, extremes of heat or cold. Poe's "Descent into the Maelstrom," an almost clinical description of the sucking motion of a giant whirlpool, is a classic account of the malevolence that natural forces when irritable seem to possess. But the necromancy practiced on an ordinary and familiar environment can produce an effect of strangeness to a frightening degree. Whereas romances are rarely fearsome, even when teeming with dragons, tales quite often are. The fear that must underlie even our most cordial relation with the elements has an established place in them. I think of "Rock Crystal" ("*Bergkristalle*") in the wonderful collection *Colored Stones (Bunte Steine, 1853)* of the Austrian Adalbert Stifter; it tells of two children, brother and sister, lost in a mountain snowstorm at Christmas-time while returning from a custom-honored three-hour walk to their grandmother's house down the valley. The quite ordinary and familiar two-horned alp traversed by the shoemaker's children becomes a mountain more magic than any of Thomas Mann's imagining.

All the tales of *Colored Stones* have minerals for titles— "Granite," "Chalkstone," "Tourmaline"—and the central fable in each has to do with the rescue of children from some menace jutting out of the everyday—the folkish model, I suppose, would be "Hansel and Gretel." Yet even in his longer works, which are not so deep in enigmatic Nature, Stifter has the faculty of "making it strange." His long novel or tale or romance—I hardly know what to call *Der Nachsommer,* the book every German-speaker remembers from schooldays— centers on a fairy-tale house behind a trellised gate, *das Rosenhaus,* every inch covered with roses, as though it were made of petals; there is a bird-feeding station at every window and,

134

inside the simple and practical but delectably wealthy dwelling, are a great marble staircase, to mount which one must
don felt slippers, a marble hall, a sculpture gallery, a picture
gallery, a scholar's library, inlaid furniture of rare and curious woods, a collection of musical instruments, drawers upon
drawers of prints and drawings. Attached to the estate are farm
buildings, dairies, a cabinet-making shop, a grotto, cold frames,
hothouses, watering devices; the whole ingenious paradise,
which runs like a Swiss watch, has proceeded from the brain
of a mysterious, white-haired, plainly dressed owner whose
aristocratic name we do not learn till we are more than halfway through the story.

Like a novel, it has a young narrator who doubles as hero
and like a novel it is compendious and extremely instructive,
giving lessons in mineralogy, gem-cutting, castle restoration,
furniture restoration, church architecture, soil irrigation,
agronomy, ornithology, meteorology, botany, landscape architecture, the growing of cactuses in greenhouses, in particular the *Cereus Peruvianus*—I cannot begin to tell you everything that is in that book. Like a romance, it has high-born
characters (with the exception of the "I" and his friends) and
the complications, misunderstandings, false-seemings, endless journeying typical of the genre.

What decides me, finally, that it must be a tale (yes, a
protracted fairy-tale) are the relatively low birth of the hero
("Mein Vater war ein Kaufmann" is the first sentence, and
"die Mutter," he is quick to tell us, "war eine freundliche
Frau") and the fact that despite his adventures in learning to
know the world and every single thing in it, he is never an
active agent, as the hero of a novel or a romance should be,
but even in love always passive, docile, wondering, wonder-
struck, like someone in a dream. It has a queer, troubling
likeness to a *Bildungsroman* in that the hero, whose full name
we never know, is constantly *acquiring*—as is proper maybe
for a merchant's son—knowledge that is sensed as tangible

property while he himself, like a Tom Thumb, does not grow or age.

The novel is set in society, whether of country folk, thieves, or worldlings. The tale is set in Nature or the crannies of History; the romance is set in a Nowhere, without a capital city or foundation myth but generally endowed with a name, be it Graustark or Amazonia. A novel, with all due allowances, lays claim to being true; that is why plausibility is one of the main criteria by which its events and characters are judged. In the tale (as I have indicated) the presence of a living narrator is proof of veraciousness, as though the fellow appeared before a notary public ("Before me personally came . . .") to affirm that in some far-off place or time such-and-such events happened, wonderful as it may seem. While the reverse of veraciousness *and* of plausibility is the romance's stock in trade.

Emma is believable; *Middlemarch* is believable—there were and still are quantities of Lydgates and Rosamonds and a fair share of Mr. Casaubons. *Madame Bovary* is believable. All of Balzac is believable; no oath is needed to certify that things like those described happen with due regularity. You can say that of any true novel. It *reminds* you of what you know. *Anna Karenina*, they say, originated in the suicide of a lady who lived near the Tolstoys; several smart social arbiters, we learn, "sat" to Proust for the Duchess of Guermantes. But the force of a tale derives from the sense that it is scarcely believable but true, both at once. Very different from the sensations of the reader of a novel: you are willing to credit it because someone who was there—a fictional someone—is telling you.

That is the situation with *Wuthering Heights*, a highly improbable story. So much so that it needs *two* narrators to convince us: Mr. Lockwood, the new tenant of a nearby house, succeeded by his housekeeper, Nelly Dean, who in her youth

136

was in service at Wuthering Heights. If a non-participating narrator is a fairly sure sign that the story we are reading is a tale, the multiplication of such narrators suggests that something "smells fishy" in the whole case, perhaps because of an uncertainty of genre. Moreover, there can be two different sorts of first-person narrator in one and the same book. For example, *Lolita*, which purports to be a "found" manuscript, is introduced by Narrator A, who explains that he has merely edited a text written in prison by a certain Humbert Humbert (Narrator B) shortly before his trial. This framing device lets the reader know in advance how the story will end, with its teller's death. An unromantic, even anti-romantic piece of information that informs us, also, that we are on the frontier of novel-land.

To repeat, a romance is improbable on the face of it. Nobody but Don Quixote would confuse romances with real life. Look at "romance," sense 3, in the big Oxford dictionary: "A fictitious narrative in prose of which the scene and incidents are very remote from those of ordinary life; *esp.* one of the class prevalent in the 16th and 17th centuries, in which the story is often overlaid with long disquisitions and digressions." By its very nature, the romance is unhistorical, the antithesis of recorded history. Sidney's *Arcadia*, written for the entertainment of the Countess of Pembroke, his sister, is a good example in English of the genre: the king of Arcady, Basilius, has two shepherdess daughters, Pamela and Philoclea, who enlace destinies with two shipwrecked princes to engender a typical vine-like, branching plot, which has no more to do with the annals of antiquity than the decorative patterns of twining garlands and vegetable motifs on a pillar of the day.

Curiously enough, this is not the case with the tale, which is embedded in history like ore in a mountain fissure. In his beautiful essay "The Storyteller," Walter Benjamin speaks of a tale by Johann Peter Hebel that tells of a young miner entombed in the bottom of his tunnel on the eve of his wedding. The bride never marries, and one day many years later, when she has turned into a wizened old woman, a body is brought up from the abandoned tunnel that she recognizes as her betrothed, preserved by the action of iron vitriol from the normal processes of decay. To show how Hebel was able to make graphic the lapse of a long period of years, Benjamin quotes the following sentences.

> In the meantime the city of Lisbon was destroyed by an earthquake, and the Seven Years' War came and went, and Emperor Francis I died, and the Jesuit Order was abolished, and Poland was partitioned, and Empress Maria Theresa died, and Struensee was executed. America became independent, and the united French and Spanish forces were unable to capture Gibraltar. The Turks locked up General Stein in the Veteraner Cave in Hungary, and Emperor Joseph died also. King Gustavus of Sweden conquered Russian Finland, and the French Revolution and the long war began, and Emperor Leopold II went to his grave too. Napoleon captured Prussia, and the English bombarded Copenhagen, and the peasants sowed and harvested. The millers ground, the smiths hammered, and the miners dug for veins of ore in their underground workshops. But when in 1809 the miners at Falun . . .

And, speaking in his own voice, Benjamin adds:

> Never has a storyteller embedded his report deeper in natural history than Hebel manages to do in this chronology. Read it carefully. Death appears in it with the same regularity as the Reaper does in the processions that pass around the cathedral clock at noon.

138

Likewise the tales of Kleist set the marvelous in a historical frame: "The Betrothal in Santo Domingo," "The Earthquake in Chile," "Michael Kohlhaas" (which tells about a merchant and horse trader, a real popular leader or rabble-rouser of Luther's time). Then there is the stranger-than-fiction "The Marquise of O——," taking a queer old story already known to Montaigne but placing it in the campaign of the French Revolutionary armies in northern Italy, where the Russian Suvorov won a series of initial victories for the allied side and was rewarded with the title "Prince Italysky"—pure musical comedy—by the mad tsar.

In Kleist's tale, a contested Lombard fort falls to the Russians in a night attack, during the course of which the commandant's daughter, the widowed Marquise, is saved by a Russian officer from rape by his men and gratefully loses consciousness, but then, nine months later, inexplicably gives birth to a child. She advertises in the newspaper for the father to come forward, and he proves to be none other than her savior, Lt.-Col. Count F——. The tale has a miraculous ring to it on more than one score; not only is a child conceived, as it were, immaculately, in the fury of battle, but Suvorov's Russians let loose in Italy appear supernatural, outside the order of things, like visitants from space. The uncanniness of the pivotal event is enhanced by the circumstantiality of the narration, which seems dipped in "magic realism" as the logistics of the campaign, the aristocratic command structure, the postings of Count F—— (to Constantinople, to Naples, to what is evidently Milan) are duly set forth, like colored pins on a military map.

It was Suvorov who in his younger days, in Russia, in Catherine's time, had put down the Pugachev revolt, which, twenty-eight years after "The Marquise of O——," was to figure as the real subject of Pushkin's tale, or story, *The Captain's Daughter*. Indeed, the Cossack pretender Pugachev, who called himself Peter III, had some of the characteristics of a Russian Michael Kohlhaas, the protagonist of Kleist's tale. If Kleist's tale is deeper, with something in it of a primeval contest, this may reflect the fact that the stubborn Lutheran horse dealer has a grudge against the way the real world is organized.

Both Kleist and Pushkin, insofar as they were Romantics, responded to upheaval, revolt, and counter-revolt, contemporary or "historical," and to the attendant wandering of peoples. In this literature, it is as though the uprooting, the turning upside down, created by the victories of the French Revolution and the Napoleonic campaigns—whose tremors were felt as far away as the black Haitian empire of Dessalines—had revived a climate of fear similar to that of primitive times, when tales were told in the firelight. No Romantic tale-teller was exactly a revolutionary, but many were drawn by the *infernal* quality of rebellion, by the ferocity, as of devils incarnate, so well evoked by Kleist in "The Betrothal in Santo Domingo," and even in "The Earthquake in Chile," where wickedness unbridled is released in the "higher classes" by a natural, non-political disaster.

The Romantic period in northern Europe, following the "time of troubles" brought by Napoleon's armies, was the highest point of achievement of the modern tale. It may mean something that England, untouched by Napoleonic invasion, has no tales to show from this period—Stevenson came later, and Scott, an antiquarian, cannily used the Border ballad material and the inspiration of the German Romantics to invent a sure-fire genre—the historical novel. In America, possibly in the wake of our own revolution and internal migrations, we had the tales of Hawthorne; we had Melville; we had Poe. *Evangeline*, had Longfellow turned it into prose, might have been an ideal tale: the wanderings of the Acadians, like a Biblical people under sentence of eternal exile, across the face of a new continent—virgin early-American forest scenery. But Longfellow's hexameters are unsuited to the telling of a tale. Verse in general lacks the requisite flatness of tone, suggestive of the annals of a reign or a parish register, indicated by Kleist's "(Aus einer alten Chronik)" prefacing "Michael Kohlhaas."

It is worth noticing that tales flourish in northern countries. The romance, on the other hand, seems to have thrived on the Mediterranean littoral, where its forebears were the epic (above all, the *Odyssey*) and the pastoral. It may be that the deep northern forests and wooden cottage architecture are a reason for the difference—the same difference observable in the linguistic fact that there are no equivalent words in Romance languages for "uncanny," "weird," "fell," "grim," "grisly," and so on. The only translations that I have ever seen for any or all of them into French are *étrange, inquiétant, mystérieux, bizarre.*

Walter Benjamin found an affinity between the teller of a tale and the craftsman or artisan: "If one wants to picture these two groups [of story-tellers] through their archaic representatives, one is embodied in the resident tiller of the soil, and the other in the trading seaman." Then, as he tells it, in the Middle Ages an interpenetration of these two archaic types took place through the trade structure. The resident master craftsman and the traveling journeyman worked together in the same room: "If peasants and seamen were past masters of storytelling, the artisan class was its university."

There is surely some truth here, especially as the telling of a tale responded to a rhythm of work—weaving or spinning. It may be more than chance that *Silas Marner*, by that archetypal novelist George Eliot, has the atmosphere of a tale about it: the miser's heap of gold in the workman's lonely cottage, the turning bobbin and shuttle, the sinister forest quarry and the skeleton it secretes. The hero, after all, is a hand-loom weaver (like Stifter's father), solitary and half-demented, toiling at an already archaic craft. There are tale-like elements too, like a fitting under-music, in *The Mill on the Floss*, noticeable in the part played by the river that turns the wheels that grind the grain that nurtures the miller's family— the familiar River Floss that, slowly becoming unrecognizable, claims the lives of the miller's children, Maggie and Tom, in a great climactic flood.

If the tale is native to northern countries—I think not only of the German-language Romantics sprung from *Des Knaben Wunderhorn* but of the Danish Isak Dinesen in our own day and her predecessor J. P. Jacobsen, originally a botanist—the novel, on the contrary, is a foreigner. It is remarkable how few German examples there were in the nineteenth century—the great period of the novel elsewhere. A single one is inevitably mentioned: Fontane's *Effi Briest*. But what else? Not Stifter's *Der Nachsommer*. Certainly not *The Sorrows of Young Werther*, even though it shares an epistolary form with *Clarissa Harlowe*, twenty-five years its senior. *Werther*, rich in sentiment, is weak in character. Yet psychology, as it used to be called, is the strong suit of the true novel, which has room to show the growth of relationships between people, just as it has room to show children growing up (*David Copperfield*) and the growth of a tendency in a single human soul (*The Mayor of Casterbridge*). There is no psychology in *Werther*, no observation of a remotely "clinical" kind; if there had been anything resembling detached observation, the book would not have produced a rash of sympathetic suicides.

When the German tale expands, it is likely to turn into a romance, or into what we in English like to call the Gothic novel, though there is nothing Gothic or novelistic about it. Even in the present century, the true novel is rare in the German language. *Buddenbrooks* is the best example but also, more modernist, *The Man Without Qualities*. I find *The Magic Mountain* hard to classify: on its medical, sanatorium side, it is a novel, but then it drifts off into parable and loses its novelistic bearings. The rest of Mann is mostly tales: *Felix Krull*,

Tonio Kröger, Death in Venice, "Mario and the Magician." His best work, in my view (apart from *Lotte in Weimar,* a delightful novelette), is *Doctor Faustus,* a "big" book that draws on nearly all the varieties of fiction, while avoiding the heavy archness he was inclined to when self-important (think of the Joseph books), to isolate and define the nature of German-ness—a problem posed to him by the National Socialist triumphs, on the one hand, and by the Apollonian figure of Goethe on the other. For his Faustus, Mann found clues and analogies not only in Goethe's drama and in the magus of legend but also in Martin Luther, in the émigré Anabaptists, in the history of music, the twelve-tone scale, and in the spi-rochete of syphilis, all but omnipresent in the life histories of Germanic artists. One clue that escaped Mann's notice in this congeries of early symptoms of the disease of National So-cialism was the fact that I have just alluded to—the strange paucity of novels in the Germanic tongue, a paucity manifest in his own output.

The novel, after all, is the literary form dedicated to the rep-resentation of our common world, i.e., not merely the com-mon ordinary world but the world we have in common. The faculty for apprehending it—this world conterminous with each of our separate life experiences and independent sensibilities, this world that lies between us—is, of course, common sense, the faculty we need to serve on juries, assess job offers, judge the character of strangers. . . . Common sense, also known as the reality principle, rules the novel, commanding the reader to recognize only events and personalities that do not defy it. A person like Heathcliff flies in the face of common sense, which declares that there are no persons like Heathcliff, no Mr. Rochesters either, whatever authors would fain believe.

Common sense (Sancho Panza) may be the same as tra-ditional wisdom, the wisdom of the species. This faculty in-heres in all of us, just as the golden theorem of Pythagoras, once demonstrated, is ineluctable for every brain; it was greatly valued by Tolstoy as a moral dowsing rod within everybody's reach. It is how a mere child, like Natasha, is able to distinguish good from evil, just as well as, in fact better than, men and women of the world. Common sense tells you the way things *are*, rather than the way your covetous ego or prehensile will would like them to be. And the sparsity of novels, the great carriers of the reality principle, may help to explain German defenselessness in the face of National Socialism, which—to us, incredibly—was not recognized by most Germans as a monstrosity until Hitler had perished in his bunker.

Even today German writers of fiction persist in the traditions of the tale and the romance. Günter Grass is the clearest case. *The Tin Drum* is too prolix to be a tale, though it has some earmarks of the type—the dwarf hero and his magic drum, for instance—but the general effect, it strikes me, is of something more like a plebeian romance, with multiple adventures though without love interest. Some of his later fictions—*The Flounder*, for instance—are closer to the pure tale. The German tale, unlike those of other languages, has found it hard to separate from the fairy story, especially the *Märchen* with animals in the place of characters: I think of Mann's *The Holy Sinner*, in which the hero, an early Christian saint, turns into a hedgehog.

It is obvious that these categories of mine cannot be hard and fast. And it may be that there are some fictions that will not fit into any of them, even with some letting out of the seams or determined squeezing. Leaving aside the hopeless conundrum of *Gulliver*, what is one to say of the picaresque novel— *Moll Flanders* or Nashe's *The Unfortunate Traveler*? Is there any reason in these cases, beyond habit, to have recourse to the term "novel" at all? The best reason, I suppose, is the extensive, all-but-encyclopedic accounts they contain of social types and class shadings. And along with that you find an extraordinary, non-poetical language, a prose that is the quintessence of the prosaic. Without the picaresque, the classic novel ran the risk of being "gentrified."

Even when fictions resist being classified in these traditional drawers marked "Novel," "Romance," "Tale," the effort to see them typologically is productive. It is more enlightening to look on *Dr. Zhivago* as a prolonged tale of journeys and transformations, death and resurrection, forests and bandit-like figures, than to treat it as a novel and expect it to make novelistic sense, like all those earnest reviewers who complained that it was implausible and had too many coincidences. . . . It is not a novelist's assessment of the Bolshevik Revolution (Solzhenitsyn's *August 1914* and its sequels, by contrast, are precisely that); it is a terrifying and beautiful tale set in the still pioneer geography of the vast Russian terrain against the wild and shifting scenery of revolt and revolution. Reviewers sought to "relate" it to Tolstoy, but the vital relation (as often happens with the tale) is to nonfiction, above all, to Aksakov and his exquisite recollections in *Family Chronicle* and *Years of Childhood*, of the Orenburg region in the Urals (Pugachev territory, by the way) and of an arduous pioneer railroad trip of the whole family to Siberia.

The least useful procedure is to assume that any fiction of a certain length is a novel or that a novelist of standing, say Hardy—exception made for the occasional short story— could sire only novels. Or that a habitual teller of tales—say Conrad—could sire only tales. In fact, as I see it, *Nostromo* and *Under Western Eyes* do not belong to the same family as *Lord Jim*, "The Secret Sharer" or "Heart of Darkness." Similarly for Hardy: *The Mayor of Casterbridge* and *Jude the Obscure* (novels), ought to be distinguished from *The Return of the Native* and *Far From the Madding Crowd* (tales). The problem is where to put *Tess*. The important role played by Nature, Tess's insistent misfortunes, the cruel tricks of coincidence, her wanderings and execution suggest a tale; yet arguing against that are the social pretensions of the Durbeyfields, the "psychology," so finely analyzed, of Angel Clare, not to mention the implicit critique of the industrialization process as it touches English agriculture.

Like *Tess*, some of the most arresting fictions of modern times are puzzles to classify, and it may even be that an inherent anomaly contributes to a disquiet that they engender. I am thinking of Joyce's "The Dead," a very long story, which would be a full member of the novel family were it not for the ending. At the outset "The Dead" looks like an intensely social narrative firmly set in the mundane (classically novelistic) world of professions, politics, careers. Like *War and Peace*, it starts at a party.

In the first sentence, as if on the threshold, we meet the servant who is helping the guests off with their outdoor things: "Lily, the caretaker's daughter, was literally run off her feet." This is everybody and nobody talking—the collective voice of the party. It is a dance, an annual Christmas event put on by Gabriel Conroy's aunts, and, as in a real novel, we are told what refreshments the guests are served, given samples of the speech Conroy, a middle-aged literary man, must deliver to honor the old ladies, his thoughts during the music and the dancing, his passage-at-arms with a partner who is a strong Irish nationalist, and finally the lust he begins to feel for his wife, as they make their way home to their hotel through the snowy streets. There is even the un-tale-like suspicion that Gabriel Conroy and his wife Gretta must be something like Joyce and Nora. But a song, "The Lass of Aughrim," sung at the party has reminded Gretta sorrowfully of a young lad in Galway who died for love of her when she was a girl living with her grandmother. Gabriel's designs on her body are thwarted; in their room she cries herself to sleep, remembering Michael Furey. And Gabriel goes to the window. At that

146

moment the short novel is transformed by incantation into a tale:

> His soul swooned slowly as he heard the snow falling faintly through the universe and faintly falling, like the descent of their last end, upon all the living and the dead.

Note the echoic effects of "soul swooned slowly . . . snow falling faintly" and, again, in inversion "falling faintly . . . faintly falling," none of which would "go" in a novel, any more than would a lad dying for love of a girl, both being offensive to the robust spirit of prose.

The mutation, I think, in this exquisite early story is an eerie premonition of *Ulysses*, published eight years later. Here an essence or, one might say, concentrate of novel is changing form as we listen and watch the process of transformation. It was a crucial moment. The surface shifting of genre, like a sex change, was testifying to a deep disturbance in the underground structures of the novel. After this, the novel would never be the same again, though the unsettling of its clear and stable identity did not become noticeable to the public or even to other writers until *Ulysses* revealed the whole truth.

To account for what had happened I am going to come back to the first sentence of "The Dead." But before doing that I want to note, very summarily, signs of a decomposition of narrative that became evident soon after the appearance of *Ulysses* and was surely to some extent its result. An outstanding case is Faulkner, who responded to the Joycean example in various and quite contradictory ways. On the one hand, he constrained the novel to revert to the tale in works like *As I Lay Dying*, *Light in August*, "Old Man" (from *The Wild Palms*), or to outright saga, as in "The Bear" and parts of *The Hamlet*, and, at the end of his life, to allegory (*A Fable*)—a romance, somewhat unconvincing, called *Sartoris* was designed for the *Saturday Evening Post*.

On the other hand, and at the same time, he sought to reconstitute the traditional, pre-Joycean novel; his enterprise, taken as a whole, clearly has Balzacian aspirations: Yoknapatawpha County lays claim to being a microcosm of the *comédie humaine*. Yet the individual pieces of that broad jigsaw are far from resembling the historical realism of nineteenth-century practice. Take *The Sound and the Fury*, a stream-of-consciousness narrative that has obviously felt the effect of European modernism and is therefore regarded, justly, as the most experimental and difficult of Faulkner's fictions—the opposite of what we think of as Balzacian.

In fact, though, the situation of the stream-of-consciousness narrative was not so simple, even for Joyce himself or Virginia Woolf, its leading practitioners. The interest, for them and for their followers and imitators, was in narrowing the narrative focus to the perceptual screen of a single consciousness or (more commonly) several consciousnesses, multiple fields of vision. We were allowed to see only what would appear on such a screen, often a half-shuttered or impaired one; evidently, once you started on this kind of experiment, you would soon be trying out various types of distorting lenses to see how the world looks through them—the artist's eye (Lily Briscoe), the madman's eye (Septimus Smith), the idiot's (Benjy in *The Sound and the Fury*).

Strangely (as it may seem now, given the long-term results), the aim of the new techniques was a greater exactitude—the distortions being conceived as truer to the laws of perception than old-fashioned straight narration. Moreover, the introduction of multiple consciousness (in *Ulysses*, *The Sound and the Fury*, *Mrs. Dalloway*, and in USA, *Les Thibault*, *Les Chemins de la liberté*, right up through *The Naked and the Dead*) was also aiming at realism, in the sense of a wider representativeness, inspired by the social sciences. A democratization of the novel seemed to have been decreed, as specimens of every category of human being demanded equal treatment; the hero was demoted or sent into exile, and each human unit was allotted an eye of its own. Between the two wars, thanks to multiplicity and stream of consciousness—separately or in combination—the novel, though fractured, retained its ascendancy.

Few tales were published in this period, narrators had all but vanished, and romances had been sentenced to best-sellerdom—*So Red the Rose, Anthony Adverse, Gone With the Wind*. The novel's besetting problem—credibility—seemed to have been bypassed, since multiple viewpoints ("Einsteinian relativity") denied the possibility of establishing objective truth. In painting and sculpture, a similar development had occurred, and there too the process had begun (with the Impressionists) in a search for a greater realism and fidelity to the laws of perception that entailed the resolute junking of perspective.

The Second War and what it uncovered made drastic demands on the public's power of belief, and the effect on the novel, though slow to be felt, has been radical and long-lasting. The old problem of credibility, with Auschwitz and Hiroshima, affected not travel tales but real central events, whose dominant trait had become unreality, utter unlikelihood encroaching on the stable and familiar and rapidly expanding its empire to include space, the gulag, nuclear terror. It was up to the novel, as custodian of the reality principle, to react. But, though the expectation was widely felt, there was no prompt response, unless one counts the parable of *1984*. The only indication that the novel was preparing to buckle down and help us believe the unbelievable was the return of the narrator—first noted, if I remember right, in *Lolita*. Not so long afterward came works dealing, not yet with the death camps but, more modestly, with such questions as the making of a fascist: Moravia's *The Conformist* and *The Tin Drum*

149

of Günter Grass, which showed the Nazi era, appropriately, from the "low" viewpoint of a grocer's household in Danzig, with a dwarf child banging a toy drum as the focal consciousness. *Mr. Sammler's Planet, Sophie's Choice, The White Hotel* followed, each portraying, in one way or another, a survivor of the death camps whose individual experience is meant to relay, through letters, journals, flashbacks, interior monologue, a "found" manuscript—fiction's familiar devices—"the central experience of our time." All were best sellers, but none succeeded in carrying literary conviction; it is maybe not a good idea to reduce the incredible to a state of fictional believability. A persuader figure like Mr. Sammler makes the horrors still impinging on his consciousness seem considerably more unlikely than they were in factual reports.

There are some kinds of material with which the novel in its governing common sense is unequipped to cope. The trench experiences of World War I were at the very limit of the novel's powers. In the matter of "the novelist's responsibility," silence would be preferable to the musings of a narrator like Stingo in *Sophie's Choice*. Possibly it is a matter of tact.

In contrast with these efforts, I want to return to the first sentence of Joyce's "The Dead," which shows what the novel *can* deal with and what, more and more in our time, it has been condemned to deal with, like Sisyphus pushing his stone up the hill. I refer to the phenomenon of banality and repetition—Flaubert's curse.

"Lily, the caretaker's daughter, was literally run off her feet." Now maybe that does not strike anyone but me as worthy of notice. "What is new in it?" the reader may well ask. Or, rather, what *was* new in it when Joyce put it down? Fortunately, the question is easily answered. What is new is in the word "literally," which of course is not to be taken literally—nobody is literally run off her feet. This should lead us to ask who is saying this silly, exaggerated thing. Not Joyce, clearly, not the narrator (there is no narrator), not Gabriel Conroy, the protagonist—he would not use a commonplace expression like that. If you listen carefully, you will overhear (as I have suggested) everybody talking, or nobody talking, which amounts to the same. And this new, strange *vox populi* was Flaubert's invention (contemporary with early versions of the phonograph); you would not find it in Jane Austen or Balzac or George Eliot or Tolstoy though all of them were much concerned with the quality of ordinariness and its pervasive expressions, the noise that Heidegger called "chatter."

This sound of echoing clichés, further amplified today by the new means of mass communication, must have a large responsibility in what is called the "death of the novel," which depends on social intercourse for its characteristic life, on parties like Anna Pavlovna Schérer's at the opening of *War and Peace,* on public meetings and every kind of get-to-gether—think of the *comices agricoles* in *Madame Bovary,* think of the fete for needy governesses in *The Possessed,* think of Proust. The discovery Joyce made in "The Dead," surely, was the seedy, moribund state of all this human commerce, once full of life and variety, now good for nothing (he must have concluded), serving no purpose that could be considered "creative," not even the ends, always rather questionable, of satire. The reversion to myth and incantation, as Gabriel at the end stands at the window, is a judgment on the world of the novel.

The mechanization (by now automation) of the social in the modern world has affected not only public events. It has penetrated the inner life of the modern person, so that it was bound to become apparent in the stream of consciousness like a pollutant in a river from the dumping of factory waste. Joyce, particularly sensitized to these effluents, would soon be noting the internalizing of triteness in *Ulysses*—in Molly Bloom's monologue and the occasional riot, as in the Oxen of the Sun episode, of parody and pastiche. And it became the entire subject of *Finnegans Wake*, which is an encyclopedia not of knowledge but of the trash collected in the human consciousness jointly by Everybody-Nobody. (Nothing is totally new. The *Wake* had been anticipated, albeit mildly, by Bouvard and Pécuchet's "Dictionary of Received Ideas.")

Yet the lint in the recesses of our gray matter, as in the inside of our pockets, could not fail to be inartistic, and I doubt that *Finnegans Wake*, for all its musicality, its spiraling form, and so on, was designed to give pleasure, as works of art do. Rather, it seems almost designed to give offense, as though Joyce fully accepted the price to be paid by the man who *would* write a novel in the present age. It is hard to guess whether he foresaw that he would be exchanging readers of the customary kind for scholars and specialists, whose pleasures in the act of reading are perverse to a repellent degree. Probably he did, being a churlish spirit, trained to sour amusement. His contempt is open: anybody not caring for his "trashy" masterpiece is free to turn to tales and romances; we see the author indicate with his stick the scraps of them strewn about his vast dust heap. But for anyone still desirous of that baggy thing called a "novel," *Finnegans Wake*, he can assure the world, is the only choice left.

I do not disagree. If there was ever a theme set, like a fairy-tale task, for the modern novel, it was not the horrors ("Heart of Darkness"), not the incredible or the apocalypse, but the universal ordinary, which presents no believability problem, except to the higher reason. As has often been said, *Finnegans Wake* was a dead end; it led nowhere for those who came after. The letter scratched up by the chicken in Earwicker's back yard incriminating the householder with its nonsensical banality may well have been the novel's suicide note.

Montreal, Oakland, Poughkeepsie, 1981–82

REVIEWS
AND CRITICISM

The Tolstoy
Connection

FOR WESTERN READERS Alexander Solzhenitsyn's *August 1914* is a difficult book. The geography is unfamiliar; the logistics are bewildering to anybody but a military specialist; and the chronology is not easy to follow since the scene keeps shifting and many events overlap. Here the author has, in fact, been helpful, taking pains to scatter unobtrusive dates in each of the episodes (there are sixty-four chapters, which comprise fifty-five episodes told in direct narration, two flashbacks, four summaries, three montages of newspaper clippings) as they unroll, sometimes simultaneously, sometimes in sequence, during the fatal month of August 1914.

In the first chapter, laid in the remote steppes of the southern Caucasus, a young volunteer waiting for his train on the station platform buys newspapers reporting the Russian victory of Gumbinnen, which, as we later learn, took place August 7 in far-off East Prussia. Therefore the book must begin on August 8 or, more likely, 9. In Chapter 4, the following morning, a young woman on an estate in the northern Caucasus by which the volunteer's train has just passed has received "such a happy letter" from a lieutenant in the field who has not yet seen battle; this letter—as we discover 510 pages later, in Chapter 59—was postmarked August 5, at Ostrolenka, in eastern Poland. Even if the passage of the volunteer's train had not told us what day it was, we would know

that it was some time during the week before August 15, because the young woman's parents are keeping the fast preceding the Assumption of the Virgin, and there is no meat or
milk on the breakfast table. On the previous Friday there has
been an eclipse of the sun, which, for students of astronomy,
will place the chapter celestially. Throughout the novel holy
days and saints' days are imprinted in the characters' awareness, marking the calendar dates. The peak of the action is
reached on the Day of the Assumption, August 15, which saw
the disaster—for the Russians—of the battle of Tannenberg,
recorded in history as the German Cannae (Hannibal's encirclement and annihilation of the Romans) but here shown less
as a clear-cut battle than as a diffuse series of groping movements toward and away from the enemy on the part of Russian troops lost in a sandy forest and playing a nightmare game
of blindman's buff.

The beautiful dovetailing of Solzhenitsyn's timetable, with
its inlaid and often barely visible, almost watermark-like pattern, is clear enough to those who take the trouble to trace
it. But the reader seeking light from Western sources will only
become more confused unless he is warned that the author is
using the old Julian calendar, in force in Russia until 1918.
If, as I did, he tries consulting Winston Churchill's *The Unknown War* (1931), to make events tally, he should subtract
thirteen days from Churchill's time-calculation or add thirteen to Solzhenitsyn's. The same for the *Britannica*, twelfth
and thirteenth editions.

As for geography, the publisher has supplied a map in
the form of end papers, but this is inadequate to the needs of
a lay Western reader who really wants to understand what is
going on in the novel. I am told that even for a Russian who
was alive in 1914 the text is hard to follow, not because of
any stylistic obscurity, but because of the dense thicket of
military tactics and strategy he must work his way through. If
ever a novel called for visual aids, this is it. What are wanted

are military maps and diagrams showing troop positions and movements throughout the crucial days of mid-August, how the four and a half corps of the Second (Samsonov's) Army were deployed, the placement of the cavalry divisions on the flanks, plus a table of the names of the five commanding generals, of the generals who served under them, and of those who commanded cavalry divisions. Footnotes or an explicatory preface describing the structure of a tsarist division, regiment, battalion, right down to company, would also be useful, and perhaps some identification of the historical persons in the novel.

I admit that at the beginning I took General Samsonov (partly because of his name) for a fictional character, a bemused, broad-browed, overweight, asthmatic Samson among the Philistines of his staff and Army Group Headquarters. Of course, no Russian would make that mistake, any more than we would about Generals Pershing or Joffre. But I should still like to be sure that Colonel Vorotyntsev, the novel's other hero and its searchlight intelligence, is imaginary (as the translator, Michael Glenny, declared in a *Life* article) and not partly real. In the Grünfliess Forest, wounded and leading a small group of men to find a way out of the enchanted German ring of encirclement, Vorotyntsev abruptly tells one of them that he knows he will come out alive because an old Chinaman told his fortune when he was serving in Manchuria: he will not be killed in any war but will die a soldier's death at the age of sixty-nine—that is, in 1945. Does this riddle mean that we might find his name among those of officers shot by Stalin in that year—the date of Solzhenitsyn's own arrest? Such a gently dropped clue, a pebble in the forest, would be characteristic of this author's way of working. The reader might also like to know (a fact I found in the *Britannica*) that General Rennenkampf, commander of the First Army and one of the book's many high-placed villains, was shot by the Bolsheviks in 1918.

There is double reason to regret that the publisher (Farrar, Straus & Giroux) has done almost nothing—beyond printing it in English—to make the book accessible to the ordinary American reader. It is in need of a pathfinder or friendly scout, because in other ways, having nothing to do with what corps the Kaluga regiment served in or who was General Sirelius, *August 1914* is going to be disorienting to current Western sensibility. It is likely to be put down in anger or dismissed as dated in its techniques (which is true, especially of the streamlined, "modernistic," silver-screen inserts when the author switches to film scenario), corny (true, too, sometimes: "mounted, as always, on his powerful stallion," "moving freely now at his full, magnificent height"), and, anyway, impossible to finish. To be fair to the book will not be easy for many readers, particularly those who like an author to conform to their own notions of political good manners. Solzhenitsyn himself, to say it straight out, is rude and unfair in his novel to a whole category of society: the "liberals" and "advanced circles" of 1914, those who opposed the war and patriotic sentiments, who yearned, they thought, for revolution, despised religion, authority, tradition, anything respected and handed down. He has it in for those people, just as he would have it in for you and me, if he could overhear us talking. His standards are harsh and simple. There is one test he applies to each and all of his characters: what is their attitude to military service? Among men of draft age the bad are readily identifiable: they avoid conscription, they serve unwillingly, they have contempt for the colors and/or run away under fire. Among regular officers they are the ones who serve from ambition to get good marks in the rating book and promote their careers. Among the rest—mostly women and girls— the bad, who are more silly than wicked, reveal their trivial natures by denouncing patriotic demonstrations and doing everything in their power to deter their sons and schoolmates from joining up. The good serve their country, sometimes even at the cost of sacrificing principle—like the volunteer of the first chapter, who has been a practicing Tolstoyan, forgoing meat and sensuality—or, if too old to serve, defend it with their sympathy even when they are Jews and members of a liberal milieu deeply opposed to the pogromistic tendencies of the government.

It is not a question of *approving* of the war; few of the good do, and to the more educated and wiser among them the war is a tragedy that will set progressive forces in Russia back ten years, twenty, a generation. Rather, it is a question of being willing to take one's part in the tragedy or not. The central ethic of the novel is one of sharing, and the characters are judged by whether, in their souls, they are sharers or hoarders. The prosperous draft-dodger on his "economy" in the Kuban hoards his worthless life; the enlightened liberal hoards his little store of second-hand ideas, which he regards as principles too valuable to sacrifice. From the author's point of view, they are both looking out for Number One, like the cowardly, self-serving generals; the difference is that the liberals and "advanced people" do not know it.

None of this can sit very well with American liberals, who have consistently sought to dissuade young men from sharing in the Vietnamese tragedy. Does the shoe fit or not? Well, let's try it on. Russia, after all, was fighting a powerful neighbor far better equipped technologically than itself and capable of overrunning its territories—not a tiny "backward" country at the other end of the world. We can breathe easier: Solzhenitsyn would not want us to support Nixon's bombers; surely not.

A better parallel might be with World War II, which was opposed by a splinter of American radicals (including myself) with many of the same arguments advanced in *August 1914* by that highly unpleasant character Ensign Lenartovich, and a chorus of two Rostov students shrilly maintaining that the real enemy is capitalism.

But this parallel is not right either, for, as I now believe, the war against Hitler was necessary (no other means has ever been suggested for closing the gas ovens), and Solzhenitsyn is not talking about necessary wars or justified wars but about a war that, unjustified on either side, was nevertheless endured and suffered by the masses, from whose blood sacrifice, in his opinion, nobody, once it began, should have held himself aloof. He also seems to be saying that the Russian defeat, in which defeatist liberals played a part, led to the avoidable catastrophe of Bolshevism—a debatable proposition, since it is based not simply on an ethic but on a cause-and-effect sequence. Was October 1917 avoidable, in the long run, and was it inevitably and by definition a catastrophe? Did the Lenartoviches "cause" Stalin?

It is hard to read this volume without an eye nervously straying to current events and one's own responsibility in them. The temptation to do so has been put there by Solzhenitsyn himself, who clearly intends his reader to draw inferences from what he describes and apply the lesson to present-day life. Unlike the usual historical novel, far from offering escape into scenes of antique battle and undisturbed folkways, this book constantly, insistently brings one back to the present, as if the errors, sins, and follies of 1914 were still corrigible if one would only take them to heart.

Occasionally, on the strategic and tactical plane, the book seems merely to be refighting the Masurian Lakes campaign, and this time winning it—thanks to the clear-eyed Colonel Vorotyntsev, promoted in our imagination to full general. But the underlying engagement is for our contemporary hearts and minds. The author is urging us to turn away from the terrible encircling trap of revolutionary ideology and take the safer course of gradualism and inch-by-inch social progress. Yet to trust in progress today, when no cure for the body politic but surgery is visible, seems old-fashioned, almost simple-minded. It would take a Rip Van Winkle still to hope for gradual betterment through reforms. Solzhenitsyn must be aware of this and aware also that "reformist" is a term of vilification in the Soviet Union and not a banner to fight under anywhere, unless perhaps in some crusade for simplified spelling or an intramural church struggle. It is as if his book had been designed to offend "advanced people" wherever they are to be found—revolutionaries, real and false, all those who wish, at least in thought, to be ahead of their time rather than behind it or in the middle of it.

Bravery is one of the highest values in *August 1914*, and the author exemplifies it in his own person to an almost alarming degree. He takes no protective measures whatever against the criticism he must have foreseen from Soviet literary officialdom and from many independent leftist writers in the outside world who have supported him up to now. Take, for instance, the question of class origins. The two principal figures, both deeply sympathetic, are a general and a colonel: Samsonov and Vorotyntsev. The great majority of the characters we come to admire or like belong to the gentry or the property-owning kulak class: Colonel Pervushin, Colonel Kabanov, General Nechvolodov, General Martos, Colonel Khakovskoy, the two Colonels Smylovsky, Lieutenant Kharitonov, Colonel Krymov, the volunteer Isaakii and his friend Kolya, both students. A giant peasant, Arsenii, whom Vorotynstev takes as his orderly, is simple, good, brave, and extremely capable. An artillery sergeant-major, Terenty Chernega, a rough diamond, ranks high for competence and dauntless resolution. The peasant conscripts in the mass, "those trusting bearded men, those friendly eyes, those placid, selfless faces," are proved to have immense courage and endurance when put to the test—in particular the men of the Vyborg, Estland, Neva, and Dorogobuzh regiments—but few individuals stand out among them. On the negative side, there are scenes of Russian peasants looting the German towns, and the fact that their officers are looting too, in a genteel way that makes it look more like a leisurely shopping tour, does not equalize the picture, not at any rate to Soviet-style critics, who measure with a ruler. From a Soviet point of view, the amount of favorable space allotted to individuals of the officer class is utterly disproportionate. And why, these critics will ask, does Solzhenitsyn not show us a single proletarian?

Of course, in such a story, which is a story of leadership and its collapse, the chief actors will inevitably be officers. But hostile reviewers are unlikely to find the explanation there, in the most natural and obvious place; rather, they will look for it in Solzhenitsyn's "psychology." A frequent slur cast on him is that he comes from the officer class, which is both false and true. Solzhenitsyn's father was a lieutenant in the tsarist army and a Tolstoyan (like the boy Isaakii, who is evidently drawn from him—his last name is Lazhenitsyn); the family were well-to-do peasants forcibly settled by Peter the Great in Cossack territory. Yet, even if Solzhenitsyn is excused by his censors for extending sympathy to men like Samsonov, Vorotyntsev, and the various gallant colonels— who, after all, were patriots and have long ago passed into history—what about his unconcealed approval of "military" ideas of discipline, duty, command? Soviet Russians may not find much to object to here. But American liberals? And their children?

The generals in the book who send lying dispatches, disobey orders, cover up, and run away are held up to scorn, not for being militarists, but for being bad militarists who fail in their duty. Samsonov, who is no genius but honest and duteous, offers a touching contrast in his respect for the code of honor.

Still, courage, discipline, a high sense of duty to those

both above and below, are not the unique property of men in the regular army who feel honor-bound by its rules. These qualities are also found in revolutionaries. And the bias of this opening volume of Solzhenitsyn's chronicle (the next will be *October 1916*) appears in the fact that the only so-called revolutionary we really get to know (and that one must say "so-called" tells a lot) is the despicable Ensign Lenartovich, who has not the slightest sense of duty and deserts his unit at a crucial moment with the excuse that his skin is too valuable to the workers to be left on the field. His cowardly desertion and striking out for himself (he wants to go over to the Germans and explain to them that he is a socialist) is a betrayal of the sole examples he knows of the oppressed masses he claims to be for—the men serving under him. He does not waste a thought on what will happen to them. Such a character is not basically implausible; there may have been many of him in the Tsar's army. Yet he is rather thinly realized and uninteresting. The shallowness of Lenartovich (even granting that he is conceived as a shallow person) shows a failure of justice on the author's part—understandable, God knows, humanly, after what he has suffered and seen others suffer because of the "ideas" of such embryo theorists, but in the author-as-novelist a shortcoming nonetheless. Tolstoy, one feels, would have gone deeper into Lenartovich, as he did with such a worldling as Vronsky, whose whole way of life he held in contempt and loathing. He would have probed, overcoming distaste, holding his broad nose if necessary, till he found a wretched fellow creature in the weak, complacent, sloganized young man. In Tolstoy's universe, cowardice in war is not so damning, i.e., so "revealing."

Nevertheless, when this is said, I have to remember that the scene of Lenartovich in the forest, with all its one-sidedness, is magnificent. He has been found, sitting on a tree stump, by Vorotyntsev and his party, which at this point consists of only two—the giant peasant, Arsenii, and the young lieutenant from Rostov, Lieutenant Kharitonov, who has been released from a hospital with concussion and is trying to rejoin his unit. The opposite of Lenartovich, who does not have a scratch on him and is blubbering about having "nearly been killed" in a potato field by Germans. Lenartovich lies to Vorotyntsev about why he is not with his regiment, and Vorotyntsev sizes him up correctly as a deserter. Yet he takes him on as a responsibility. Lenartovich, sizing *him* up, decides to play along: Maybe this smart colonel can outwit the Germans and get the party through the line. Next they come upon a group of peasant soldiers from the Dorogobuzh regiment carrying two stretchers, one with the body of their dead colonel, which they are taking home for burial, and the other with a wounded lieutenant who is wrapped in the regimental colors. Carrying those heavy stretchers, these last survivors of a regiment that was cut to pieces covering the retreat of others in a heroic rear-guard action have traveled more than twenty-five miles along forest paths, up and down hill, through the German lines. The opposite of Lenartovich.

At Vorotyntsev's invitation the two groups join up. Lenartovich is horror-struck. Is Vorotyntsev going to risk their own safety by taking on a dead body and a stretcher case? He cannot understand why "this clear-headed colonel was giving in to the ridiculous obscurantist notions of these peasant reservists from the darkest corners of Russia." He revises his opinion of Vorotyntsev sharply downward and becomes even more impatient and resentful when Vorotyntsev obliges him to take a front pole of the dead man's stretcher, he himself shouldering the other. Lenartovich has figured out that the wounded lieutenant, obviously a reactionary, has wrapped himself in the colors as a ruse to make those superstitious fools carry him: The whole procession is a disgusting, dangerous farce. But Vorotyntsev, when they come at last to a resting place, turns out to have a plan. He finds a sunny burial spot on a little hill and explains to the men that they are going to bury Colonel Kabanov now. They accept (the more willingly, Lenartovich perceives, because he and the colonel have been sharing the burden of the body), and the grave is dug. There follows a funeral service, with Arsenii—who, it comes out, has sung in his church choir—intoning the prayers for the dead "in his strong diaconal voice" and leading the responses.

Lenartovich stands aside, with a twisted smile of condescension, not adding his voice to the responses, but his head is bared. Once the body is buried, there is still the problem of the wounded lieutenant they are carrying. Vorotyntsev makes no allusion to this, and they go forward with the stretcher till they are near the spot he has selected for them to try to cross the German-held main road. They wait for night. Then the reactionary lieutenant shows that he "knows his duty." Volunteering to stay behind, he invites the men to unwind the colors from his body, which they do; a peasant is wrapped in them. But, at the last minute, colors or not, they decline to accept his sacrifice. The strongest of the reservists, as they start to cross the road under machine-gun fire, picks up the lieutenant and hoists him onto his shoulder. The stretcher is left behind in the wood.

Now if you subtract Lenartovich from these happenings, which occupy three separate chapters, you see that the narrative is not the same without him—less forceful, less strangely moving. He, the deserter, is essential to that motley group in the woods, by no means all "good" men but sharing some natural wisdom he lacks. The ensign's very apartness from the others, his quality of onlooker, his coldness and self-satisfaction, his indifference to the colors, his irreligion, complete and sharpen the picture like the introduction of a shadow. If all this is a lesson, there must be someone present whom the lesson is aimed at—a heathen, in fact. Though perhaps not entirely irredeemable. Vorotyntsev thinks he has the makings of an officer in him—an estimate Lenartovich would angrily reject if he could see the thought running through the colonel's head. But if the potential for good in Lenartovich had been explored for the reader, in other words, if his creator had treated him more fairly, shown him to us "in the round," the very chiaroscuro of the effect I have just tried to describe would vanish. This novel is *not* the work of a liberal imagination, and its strong alternations of light and shade are essential to its particular vision, which is less close to the optics of *War and Peace* than to moralized myth whose beginning is the Separation of Light from Darkness.

The Masurian Lakes campaign is taken by Solzhenitsyn as the text for a sermon interspersed with cautionary tales and deriving much of its force from the natural setting of wilderness, menacing lakes, isthmuses, deep pine and oak woods. The failure of leadership to guide the men through the uneven, broken terrain, moral as well as topographical, is ascribed— and this is a surprise—more to plain stupidity than to any of the more familiar vices. The stupid generals of Army Group Headquarters, ignorantly directing the movements of Samsonov's and Rennenkampf's armies, issuing idiotic orders and insane counter-orders, neglecting the most elementary details of supply and transport, so that the men march five days beside a railroad track when they might have been sent by train and go into the attack hungry having received no bread rations and often not even hardtack; the stupid, lethargic corps commanders who order a retreat when their men are winning a battle, fail to send up reinforcements in a tight squeeze, do not notice a large gap in the defense perimeter, mistake two columns of advancing Germans for a Russian relief force and do not dispatch scouts to investigate, send out uncoded wireless messages, so that the amazed Germans are informed of their orders of the day and troop dispositions; and behind all these fools, the jackasses of the General Staff under the Tsar's uncle, the Grand Duke Nikolai, himself rather intelligent and alert but too fearful of court intrigues to use seriously his power as commander-in-chief to fire his incompetent and well-connected subordinates. All this massed and beribboned stupidity is seen as a kind of opaqueness, density, darkness of mind into which no thought can penetrate, no ray of truth or reason.

The primordial night of these men's minds is, in fact, the source of their cunning, lies, and incessant evasions, their adroitness in bureaucratic in-fighting, and avoidance of responsibility—an adroitness of maneuver and power of anticipation that they pitifully lack on the field. Stupidity is the mother of calculation; the task of covering up their incompetence stimulates their brain-power to an unremitting and feverish activity.

In contrast to the prevailing idiocy of the Russian command (an exception is General Martos, commander of XV Corps, a lively, intelligent man and brave as well), Solzhenitsyn sets the efficiency, good organization, and technical competence of the Germans. He admires German management, which he sees as progressive and enlightened, an example the Russians ought to have taken to heart. Yet, among the German generals he notes degrees and shadings of mental capacity. On the German side the outstanding brain is Hermann von François, too conceited to be respected as a man by Solzhenitsyn but, as a general, brave, brilliant, agile, resourceful. Solzhenitsyn attributes the victory of Tannenberg entirely to von François, and Churchill concurs, although, at the time Churchill wrote, Ludendorff had been assigning himself the credit. Von François was successful because (although, like Martos, he was a mere corps commander) he was not afraid to go over the heads of the cautious and pedantic Ludendorff, his wooden superior, Hindenburg and the General Staff itself to complain directly to the Kaiser when his projects were being thwarted. Nor did the Kaiser let protocol stop him from telephoning to von François in the field to hear his opinion on the correct deployment of his corps. That such a relation is possible is proof in itself of German superiority. Among the more pathetic documents cited by Solzhenitsyn are two Russian soldiers' jingles, one mocking the Kaiser, who is represented on a postcard as a miserable tomcat—"So who leads the German army? Willy Whiskers—stupid cat!"—the other mocking von François—"O Hermann the German, you're wicked and silly! Almost as bad as that fool Kaiser Willy!" Von François also had the sense, when he did not get the orders he liked, to disobey the orders he got; in an intelligent man Solzhenitsyn excuses and even applauds this.

As further contrast to the ponderous stupidity at the top of the Russian command, which was also top-heavy (there were too many generals in the Tsar's army), the author lets us see the intelligence and skill of many field officers, ranking down from colonel to captain, and the quick apprehension and perceptiveness of common soldiers like Arsenii, who cannot read and takes a German grand piano for a funny kind of black billiard table. The human resources and learning skills of the Russian people never cease to delight and astonish Vorotyntsev whenever he comes upon them. And whenever he meets intelligence, it goes hand and hand with bravery. In Solzhenitsyn's mind these qualities appear to be linked, as if in a holy marriage. No brave man can be wholly stupid, and no darkened mind venturesome. Whether this is true or not (which may depend on your definition of intelligence and of bravery), Solzhenitsyn, I think, loves intelligence because for him this faculty or its free exercise comes as much from the heart as from the brain. Lenartovich, whose judgments are almost infallibly wrong, illustrates the fact that nobody can be more stupid than a highly trained intellectual.

In any case there can be no doubt that in the present novel intelligence, whenever it shows itself, produces an effect of sheer joy comparable to the sensation of coming into a clearing in the woods. The circumstances of war, testing responses at every turn and with unexpected results in terms of rank and education, isolate this faculty and render it more valuable, more indispensable for survival than it is in ordinary life. At the same time, absence of it or momentary failures of it are much more conspicuous, taking the form of colossal blunders, for which somebody is going to be blamed.

In *August 1914* Colonel Vorotyntsev is the carrier of the precious quality. He has been sent as a sort of divine messenger by the Grand Duke, and his function is precisely to gather intelligence and report back to his commander-in-chief. Arriving on a Sunday (August 11), he finds Samsonov still in eastern Poland, comfortably installed in his headquarters and enjoying a pre-dinner rest. He has in fact been lying down, in his stocking feet, with his military tunic off, the picture of unruffled tranquillity, though his mind is uneasy because his superior, General Zhilinsky, at Army Group Headquarters, back in Bialystok, has been sending him impossible orders to keep pushing his troops ahead, though they have been nine days on the march already without the regulation day's rest, and they need a halt anyway for supplies to catch up with them; their rations are running out. Besides, it worries him that he has had no information about the enemy's whereabouts, nor about that of the First Army, to his right; nothing has come in from cavalry reconnaissance or from Army Group Headquarters. It is five days since his troops crossed the East Prussian frontier; the worn-out men have been advancing through an eerie, deserted countryside. For three days they did not see a German or hear a shot fired. Another irritation: Zhilinsky has taken two of his corps away from him, leaving him with three and a half, while the invisible and, as it turns out, inactive Rennenkampf somewhere to the northeast has seven. Army Group Headquarters is confident that the German forces are up there facing Rennenkampf in the north, where they can be cornered and destroyed. Samsonov's instinct tells him that they are somewhere on his left, to the southwest of Rennenkampf: Why, after being defeated at Gumbinnen, would they just stand still in that marshy lake region waiting to be trapped? Zhilinsky will not listen and every day orders him to move his army farther right (i.e., to the northeast), while Samsonov, pursuing his instinct, is edging his forces left, where he is sure the Germans are. Sure enough, that day he has had confirmation. Contact has finally been made; yesterday a unit of General Martos's XV Corps, on the *left* of the left center, has wheeled *left* and caught the enemy, defeated him, and forced him back. This has been the battle of Orlau, August 10.

The sudden appearance of Vorotyntsev in his peaceful head-quarters, on top of the news of this victory, galvanizes the corpulent Samsonov, who quickly orders his boots and tunic and places himself behind a desk. Soon he and the staff col-onel are standing before a big wall map as he excitedly argues his case, pointing to the pins denoting troop positions, which Vorotyntsev has understood at a glance, and plunging the flag of XV Corps even more firmly into its place. Recognizing from Vorotyntsev's questions that here at last is an intelligence, even if a not uncritical one, Samsonov realizes that "in this man God had sent him the very person he lacked on his staff—someone he could talk to." Despite their disparities of en-dowment, visible in their bodily structures (Mercury to a somewhat out-of-training Hercules), it is a meeting of minds.

Samsonov is by no means a brilliant intellect; his mind works slowly, even heavily, unlike that of the fleet messen-ger, but they have understood each other at once. Here at Ostrolenka, surrounded by fools and human wolves, hurried on and reprimanded by those other fools and wolves at Bi-alystok, Samsonov has had one great yearning, which is to have time to *think*; there is an unpleasant buzzing in his head that disturbs his concentration, and he is aware that there is some vital factor in the situation that eludes him. And yet he is *right*, and Zhilinsky is wrong, and, behold, Vorotyntsev *agrees*. What is more, Vorotyntsev shows him where he is making a mistake; using his fingers as a compass, he indicates to the general that his headquarters are now six days' march from the front line—much too far away. Samsonov immediately feels himself blush; he had not noticed. Tomorrow he will move his headquarters to Neidenburg. Yes, God has sent this man. Moreover, the wonder-worker has brought an incredible message: Samsonov's prayers have been heard, and they are going to give him back I Corps, which has been immobilized at Soldau, when it ought to have been moving up to make liaison with Martos in the center. Vorotyntsev will personally carry the order to General Artamonov so that there will be no chance of its miscarrying or being slyly ignored.

Thus at his first appearance the "clear-sighted" Vorotyntsev is placed for the reader squatting before a map and measuring with the compass of his spread fingers the distance between two points, i.e., using his body as a tool for understanding and instruction. From then on, he will rarely be separated from a map. The nadir of the action is reached when he awakes, with Arsenii, in the Grünfliess Forest in a condition of total despair, having lost his horse and his map case: "Arsenii was the only one left. Vorotyntsev had striven to help an entire army, and this single soldier was all that remained to him." Help arrives in the form of the dazed Lieutenant Kharitonov, who has with him a set of maps he has pinched from the German barracks at Hohenstein, while his men, turned loose like a force of nature on the products of German craft and industry, were grabbing macaroni, preserved veal, beer, sugar biscuits, cocoa, and his fellow officers were grabbing haberdashery, perfume, a child's bicycle, rugs, and ladies' coats. That is, only Kharitonov, one of the book's secondary heroes, has, by a sort of divination and hardly knowing why he does so, looted German property that has real value and is not just an article of consumption. His appearance in the woods is providential, the supply coming to meet the demand, and the superiority of the German maps to the Russian ones points the lesson once again. The map of the forest paths, glued together by Kharitonov in the hospital, is spread out on the ground by Vorotyntsev, who "hovered over it like a falcon over its prey." Thanks to the intelligence drawn from it, the party and the stretcher-bearers who will soon join them are saved.

Maps, an improvised compass, binoculars, a Japanese flashlight—these attributes, denoting vision, belong to the half-mythic figure of Vorotyntsev as much as the caduceus and the winged sandals to Mercury. Science and the intelligent use of it are indispensable to practical wisdom. Before they meet Kharitonov, Arsenii proposes that, rather than try to break through, he and the colonel build a hut in the forest and hide in it till winter, staying alive on roots and berries. Hermits, he argues, have done it in the desert. "But we're not monks, we're soldiers!" succinctly retorts Vorotyntsev. General Nechvolodov, a somewhat senior but parallel figure to Vorotyntsev (is he historical or a fiction?), with the same idea of usefulness, is repeatedly shown gazing through binoculars, and he makes use of a German flashlight, a trophy presented to him by a sergeant; he knows astronomy and astonishes an artillery colonel by being able to tell the time by the stars.

The application of science to the immediate problem of survival is not, though, the ultimate wisdom. The decisive moment in *August 1914* comes when Samsonov, having determined to share the fate of his army, moves his headquarters a second time, from the occupied town of Neidenburg up to Martos's advance post in the field, and disconnects the Hughes teletype. He wants relief from this chattering instrument carrying senseless orders from Zhilinsky and messages that demand reply. The move from civilization into the wilderness allows him to cut it off. Now, ignoring his staff, who are obliged by the rule book, and against their inclination, to stick with him, he can be alone with his thoughts. As he rides out at a trot from Neidenburg on that "red-letter day" of August 15, his mind is suddenly clear and confident. Yet, as the reader senses, he has taken his first direct step toward suicide. The decision to cut himself off has a double meaning that he is not yet aware of. The Hughes teletype has been bringing him only useless babble—static—because on the other end there is a group of idiots; so clarity is achieved by silencing it. Yet the gesture also means that he has put himself beyond communication: when Vorotyntsev, who has sent him an urgent letter by a dispatch rider telling him how he can still save the situation, comes to meet him in a field, to say that remnants of the Estland regiment are still holding out, Samsonov seems no longer to recognize him. The colonel too has become part of what is now a general irrelevant noise, like that buzzing in his head that has accompanied him from Ostrolenka and prevented him from thinking.

Has this mental activity, disconnected from any purpose, a significance or value of its own? Perhaps a higher value? Samsonov is a religious man, and the night before his fateful decision, on Assumption Eve ("die höchste Zeit," he has been murmuring to himself, "the highest time"), we have seen him at prayer. The notion of a peak of time has come to him as a clear thought piercing the darkness. A phrase from a German school-book, "es war die Höchste Zeit sich zu retten" ("it was high time to escape"), referring to Napoleon in burning Moscow, has floated back into his memory and fused, we suppose, with a holy image of the Virgin mounting upward borne by angels. There is a message for him in it, he feels; it is high time for him to do something, if he could only make out what. During the night he has waked up sweating, with the word "assume" in his ears: "Assume command"? "I assume thee into my keeping"? In fact, his time is accomplished. The next morning, having disconnected the teletype, he will be with Martos, near Nadrau.

When Vorotyntsev hurriedly rides up on August 16, the Feast of the Uncreated Image of Christ, he finds Samsonov in a field near Orlau, saying farewell to the remnants of his army, taking off his cap and thanking them. He has moved his headquarters again during the night to get away from the advancing Germans; except for a few disciplined units, his troops are fleeing everywhere. Something might still have been salvaged, since the German encirclement is not yet complete. But Samsonov, to all intents and purposes, is no longer in command. That afternoon, he moves once more, or, rather, is moved, like a bulky, powerless idol, jostling in a cart with his chief of staff, whom he can no longer even bother to despise. He is in a trance, buried in thought, which he emerges from to declare suddenly that he is going back, alone, to find XV Corps. His staff dissuades him. Next they are on foot; he is letting those men tear off his epaulets and bury them. Early the next morning, August 17, he slips away from them and hides in the woods. When they are gone, he kneels down in a clearing, and, begging God's forgiveness, he shoots himself.

These scenes of Samsonov mounting to his destiny while descending the staircase of power and authority are truly Shakespearean. There is nothing that I know of in Russian literature to compare them with. The closest is perhaps Mussorgsky's *Boris Godunov*; it is as if the slowly toppling Boris were merged with the fool in the snowstorm. But Boris has been a wicked man, and Samsonov is a good man, if not a very good general, who has done his best, given the circumstances, which are largely out of his control. His awareness of that, of a dimension in experience (not just in generalship) that evades him and yet whose presence he senses, is what makes him a larger and even, yes, wiser being than Vorotyntsev, who so clearly sees what should be done at every juncture, how all may yet be saved if a hole in the line is plugged, how if I Corps can only be joined up to XV Corps, von François's encirclement can be smashed and the enemy, in turn, caught in a Russian pincers. . . . This precise, long-range vision, surveying all contingencies like a pair of binoculars sweeping over a distant slope, is limited by its own perceptions. It does not sense, as Samsonov dimly does, uncontrollable factors, i.e., the will of God, which has made everything just as it is and not otherwise: the fatal lakes, himself with all his shortcomings and oversights, the Grand Duke, General Zhilinsky.

Throughout the novel Solzhenitsyn is engaged in a polemic with Tolstoy. He disagrees with Tolstoy's contention in *War and Peace* that "great men" cannot influence the course of events but at best can only swim along with it and await a counter-current or the turning of the tide. Solzhenitsyn holds that leadership is determining in war and uses examples from the tragic Eastern campaign to prove it. He is also angry with Tolstoy, or so it seems, because of the effect Tolstoy's doctrine of love and non-violence had on young men of the war generation, persuading them that it was wrong to accept military service. In the first chapter Isaakii meets another Tolstoyan in the railroad station, a rather homely girl whom he has known in school and corresponded with. She reproaches him when she guesses that he is on his way to volunteer and, seeing that her words are making no impression, brings out her final argument: "What about Tolstoy? What would Lev Tolstoy say about it, have you thought of that?" Isaakii has. "I feel sorry for Russia" is his answer. In a more sarcastic vein the author portrays Roman Tomchak, the rich and useless draft-dodger of several early chapters, as a great admirer of Lev Nikolaevich: he has had several oil paintings made of him by an artist in Rostov—Tolstoy scything, Tolstoy holding a plow, Tolstoy standing on his front steps—and has explained to his ignorant father that "to admire Tolstoy was the thing to do among educated people, that he was a count and great national figure. . . ."

Such rather low blows aimed at an author who had died in 1910 (and who would not have reciprocated Tomchak's admiration) seem puzzling, especially in view of the many Tolstoyan elements in Solzhenitsyn's own writing and general outlook, even if a desire to make clear his *differences* with Tolstoy may help explain his sharpness. The real explanation, though, lies probably in the nature of these differences, which on examination turn out to be basic—something Solzhenitsyn himself may have discovered in the course of writing this novel. If there is a Solzhenitsyn faith unmistakably expressed here, it is opposed at every point to the doctrines preached by Tolstoy—on history, the role of leaders, technology and progress (Tolstoy held that in itself technology was morally neutral but that in a bad society machines only multiplied the existing potential for evil), the Orthodox Church, war. Assuming that the semi-mythic Colonel Vorotyntsev is a prototype or model, Vorotyntsev's idea of *usefulness*, the principle that guides him through the book, with his map case, binoculars, and torch, is in direct contradiction to the Tolstoyan view of the *uselessness* of any attempt to direct the movement of events. There can be no accommodation between these views. It has to be one or the other, for, if Tolstoy is right, then the keen, bright-eyed colonel is just wasting his time galloping from point to point, measuring and asking questions.

But Vorotyntsev *is* just wasting his time and getting a lot of people needlessly killed. That is what the plot demonstrates from start to finish. When at the end he arrives at the Grand Duke's headquarters determined to report the *truth* of what has happened, he gradually discovers that he is making a useless expenditure of breath: nothing will be changed. Vorotyntsev is only effective or useful when dealing with small, relatively humble matters, the kind that do not get recorded in history: sending some men to hold, for a few hours mistakenly thought to be precious, a thin line of defense, heartening the men during an artillery barrage, burying Colonel Kabanov, finding his way in the forest. . . . And it is only in this domain, of the small, "low," humble event, that Tolstoy saw individual action as useful, capable of inducing change. Far from refuting Tolstoy, the novel confirms him. As Solzhenitsyn himself points out, General Martos's repeated victories not only accomplish nothing but even confuse matters further. Only on the level of colonel or below do we see leadership exercising a positive influence; but these brave, self-sacrificing officers are leading the pathetic remnants of a regiment or artillery brigade—not more than a handful of men. True, *August 1914* shows us a wealth of examples of *bad* leadership, mostly located at the top; and, on the German side, General von François's character and personality do seem to have been determining. Yet there was also the factor of luck, in which the Russian bungling and incompetence was a large component. We see the same thing, though, with Kutuzov in *War and Peace* taking advantage of the enemy's folly.

Yet, whoever is right—Solzhenitsyn or Tolstoy—about the course of history and the sense or lack of sense it makes does not matter so much here as the fact that the novel, as opposed to the novelist, seems to be so often on Tolstoy's side. On the plane of drama Samsonov achieves a grandeur of which Vorotyntsev, a model leader, is incapable. Samsonov's capacity for suffering and endurance, his eventual passiveness, as of a massive natural object, all of which show him as the opposite of a "great man," seem to be moving him to a supreme wisdom—the full acceptance of his fate. He bows to it, just as he takes off his cap to each of his demoralized soldiers, some of whom have served him badly. The marvelous realization of this character, though not in any way Tolstoyan (Tolstoy detested theatre), nevertheless supports Tolstoy's view of what is important, finally, and what not. In creating Samsonov on the scale he does, Solzhenitsyn denies the ultimate interest of those cause-and-effect sequences he has been elaborating in order to pinpoint blame. It would be strange if he were not aware of this. Is the fact that Lenartovich is one of the men Samsonov lifts his cap to intended merely as an irony?

In using Vorotyntsev to draw the lesson of what ought to have been done to avert the Tannenberg disaster, it seems as though Solzhenitsyn has walked into a trap. To make this intelligent colonel effective he would have to write a different ending to the tale than the one history has provided. But if the colonel is not effective, then intelligence turns out to be a rather useless quality unless it is combined with power, which historically it rarely is—so that Vorotyntsev emerges more as a fantasy or dreamy wish fulfilment than an actual living possibility. We are left with the fleshly reality of Samsonov, one of the contributing causes, it could be said, of the Bolshevik Revolution. And whatever the novelist thinks about that, the novel disagrees. All the novel finds is the essential *Hercules furens* sitting on a tree-stump "throne" deep in reflection.

September 16, 1972

On Rereading
a Favorite Book

REOPENING *Anna Karenina* after more than thirty years, I find that I know it virtually by heart. Every episode, just about every incident, every observation is as I remember it and *where* I remember it. Other favorite books suffer alteration during an interval of being unread. Coming back to them, you see that you have totally forgotten a whole sub-plot; secondary characters have become complete strangers—does the name Raffles in *Middlemarch* ring a bell? Or else episodes that have stuck in the memory do not seem to be there at all or have shrunk to a phrase or a paragraph—needles in a haystack. One's feelings toward the main characters may have altered with the onset of "maturity": now we prefer Pierre to Prince Andrei and Hector to Achilles. Recently I had the mortifying experience of meeting once again the wise youth Adrian (*The Ordeal of Richard Feverel*), like a childhood crush grown unrecognizable—what could have been the attraction? The return to a favorite novel is generally tied up with changes in oneself that must be counted as improvements but have the feel of losses. It is like going back to a favorite house, country, person; nothing is where it belongs, including one's heart.

But in *Anna Karenina*, oddly, the only big thing I have forgotten is one I would expect to remember: that Levin's older brother, the consumptive, is a Communist. Add to that a little thing: that Vronsky has whiskers and a moustache with tips

that he twirls. Otherwise all is in its place: Anna's swift resolute step, Karenin's ears, Vronsky's white, strong, even teeth,
which, when we have our last sight of him near the end of
the novel, after Anna has killed herself, are making his jaw
twitch impatiently with an incessant gnawing toothache. Yes,
it is in a train station, like Anna's death and their first meeting, and he is going off to fight as a volunteer in the Serbian
war against the Turks (taking along a whole squadron at his
own expense), and there are ladies with bouquets to see the
brave volunteers off. And whom does he meet at the first stop,
on the platform, but Levin's other brother, the writer, who
commends him for his public spirit. And Vronsky tersely answers. " 'Yes, as a weapon I may be of some use. But as a
man, I'm a wreck,' he jerked out. He could hardly speak for
the throbbing ache in his strong teeth, that were like rows of
ivory in his mouth." Then, on the station platform, a different sensation, "that set his whole being in anguish," causes
him for an instant to forget his toothache; the sight of a tender
gliding smoothly along the rails has reminded him of Anna's
still-warm mangled body and lovely intact head as he had
found her laid out on a table in the railway shed. Remorse
overwhelms him, and his face works with sobs.

The somatology, the harsh reduction to bedrock, is pure
Tolstoy. Yet it would be wrong to sense a sarcasm and think
that Vronsky is "shown up" by having a toothache—the most
untragical, because most everyday, of human ills—at such an
inappropriate moment. Rather, the "lowly" origin of the ag-
ony he suffers raises him, as if on a cross. In that moment he
is redeemed from his creator's scorn. The reproach of Anna's
memory has been powerful enough to anesthetize the ache
"for an instant," which is as much as can be expected of a
man. A bite of remorse that is sharper than the gnawing of a
toothache is the mark of a strong nature. Indeed, as a man of
feeling, Vronsky has passed a final exam here that many or
most of us would fail. Tolstoy has judged him, ultimately, as

a human animal, and, measured by that standard, Vronsky's "points" stand out.

The inappropriate, in fact, the utterly inconsonant, is Tolstoy's peculiar stamping-ground: Pierre's white hat and green swallow-tail coat at the battle of Borodino; Levin's search for a dress shirt on his wedding morning. The story of Levin and Kitty—and of Vronsky and Anna—has begun on that note, with the foolish, totally unsuitable smile on Anna's brother's face when his wife confronts him with proof of his adultery. Since that unforgivable smile Dolly has refused to see Stiva, which is why Anna has had to come from Petersburg to reconcile them. Stiva's smile is both a dreadful giveaway and it is not. As with Vronsky's aching big tooth, Stiva is not diminished by an irrepressible surfacing of his animal nature. On the contrary, that involuntary movement of the lips, a reflex as he tells himself, somehow bestows credit on him, where the appropriate gestures—denying everything, justifying himself, begging forgiveness—would not have. The smile is proof of both his "bestial" guilt and his bestial innocence, i.e., his simplicity. His inconsequence is a sign of the good in him, as, I think, it always is for Tolstoy. It is of the same family as Levin's absurd remark—utterly out of keeping with his feelings, which are wholly bent on Kitty—toward the beginning of the novel when Stiva, who has invited him to lunch, asks him whether he likes turbot: "What? . . . Turbot? Yes, I am *awfully* fond of turbot." No doubt Levin, hearing himself, could have bitten off his tongue, and this too is a sign of election.

The two men—one in the raptures of undeclared love, one (when he remembers) in a state of marital apprehensiveness—lunch on three dozen oysters, champagne, Parmesan, soup, turbot, chablis, roast of beef, capons, finishing off with a fruit salad. Even Levin, who would have preferred cabbage soup and *kasha*, does not lack appetite. This is a book of the body, and Stiva, though he is a procurer only of nourishment (perch brought live to the kitchen, asparagus, and a joint are what he gives Karenin for dinner), is a sort of Pandarus-by-example. Like Criseyde's uncle, he is a joyful advertisement for the flesh and its claims—a sympathetic figure, more sympathetic, certainly, than he ought to be, given Tolstoy's morality. Those three dozen oysters stick to him like a classical attribute or like the manner of his martyrdom (St. Lawrence's gridiron, St. Apollonia's teeth) to a pictured saint.

Meanwhile his incongruous friend and boyhood comrade, Constantine Levin, is trying to live for his soul, but his soul, having become incarnate in Kitty (Stiva's wife's sister), turns out to be obstinately practical, boiling raspberry jam on a charcoal stove on the terrace in the Shcherbatsky way (no water), matchmaking, knowing how to make people comfortable. The thing that astonishes him in Kitty, who is barely grown up, is her tranquil power of handling death, that strange, unnatural rupture with the body.

Sacramental moments, where the spiritual infuses the physical with an overpowering sweetness, are rare in this novel; I think chiefly of the Sunday scene where Dolly's children, having taken Communion at the peasant church in their freshly washed and let-out best clothes, are then, as if to be cleansed a second time, piled into the wagonette to go mushrooming and have a bathing party naked in the river. Here, by a miracle, body and soul are not pulling apart, like an ill-matched team of horses. They can hardly be separated, and when the smallest child, after taking the sacrament, says in English "Please, some more," she of course is right to ask for seconds, as though the Eucharist were a particularly nice dinner.

All this materiality helps account, no doubt, for the fact that *Anna* stays so unchanged in the memory. There is little in it that could be subject to erosion or blurring. Each scene *says* something clearly and distinctly, like an illustration to a child's alphabet book; each figure has its emblem or emblems, which acts as a fixative. We get something of the kind

182

in *War and Peace* (the Princess Marya's heavy tread, Prince Andrei's small white hands) but haphazardly by comparison with *Anna*, where not a sparrow can fall without a special providence. Karenin's protruding ears, his habit of cracking his knuckles, and high shrill voice are truly damning details, condemning him in perpetuity.

No matter how old one gets, if one lives to be a hundred, one's preferences among the people in this novel will never alter. Impossible to like Karenin, and, between honest-hearted Dolly and her unfaithful husband, one still cannot help siding with him, perhaps for being so incorrigible. This trait, seldom endearing in real life, is a prime virtue in a fictional character—Falstaff, Mr. Micawber. Like them, the delinquent Stiva wears well. He surprises in a predictable way, reminding you at once of himself. Of course there is another side to such figures: the pleasure we take in them is somebody else's pain. Dolly's children's patched and gusseted clothes point a telling finger at their father's wayward habits. And yet we do not mind too much on their behalf. Those let-out seams and pieced childish dresses are intrinsic (naturally!) to his spendthrift make-up; we are not judges in Children's Court. As readers, we have other standards. Is it proof of false values if we prefer life-enhancing people (Stiva, the old Prince Shcherbatsky, Anna, Vronsky) to life-diminishing ones (Karenin, the Countess Lidia Ivanovna and her pious circle, Mme Stahl, even Kitty's sacrificial friend, Varenka)? At any rate Tolstoy agrees. The most unpleasant characters in the novel are the paragons; in comparison, the triflers and worldlings are unoffending—they merely are what they are.

In fact, none of the characters in *Anna Karenina* is corrigible. The changes they go through, sometimes quite surprising, "utterly out of character," like the metamorphosis of Karenin at Anna's sickbed, in the end do not change anything. True, they bear witness to a capacity for change in human nature, and the glimpses we are given of that capacity make the pessimistic *Anna* far more exhilarating than the optimistic *Resurrection*, which succeeded it. Karenin *is* reborn at what he takes to be Anna's deathbed; in the act of pardon he rises from the bureaucratic death-in-life that is his normal state of being. But these wonderful changes do not last. The character reverts to its previous "set." There is no place in the world for a metamorphosed Karenin. Vronsky turned painter is still Vronsky in an artist's hat and cloak. That is a fact; that is the way it is, and not exactly anybody's fault. An inborn capacity for change is, as it were, corrected by the contrary force of inertia.

Nor does that always work out so badly. Take the chapter where Vronsky adds up his debts—does his *lessive*, as he calls it. The normal fictional expectation is that he will never be able to pay all those bills, especially with Anna on his hands (which we are sure she soon will be). Here is the gun hanging on the wall that must go off in the last chapter; only ruin can lie ahead for him. Yet to our relief and bewilderment this is the last we hear of the subject. Since he and Anna are soon traveling in Italy and then back in Russia living in great style while he plunges into costly farming experiments, we might assume that someone (his mother doubtless) has died and resolved his difficulties. But nothing of the sort; after Anna is dead, his mother is again in the station, to see him off for the Serbian war and ride part of the way in the compartment with him. In short (as happens with countries), his monetary crisis, which seemed so desperate, somehow does not come to a head. Life goes on as before. That is the way it is: we add up our debts, shove the heaps of bills we have no way of paying back into the drawer, and worry along pretty much as before. "Ruin" is just a word. The gun on the wall shoots blanks.

It is terrible that it should be so, almost as terrible as that Karenin is unable to taste for long the pure joy of forgiveness. Anna would seem to be the exception to that bleak rule; she is punished for her "sin," and at least this *looks* like something decisive. It is clear that she kills herself to be free of the force of inertia at work in her circumstance. Nothing so very dreadful has happened: Vronsky has not left her; he has not even ceased to love her despite the provocation she gives him. The cruel alteration is not in him but in herself: the gradual coarsening of her face and body—allegoric, as always in Tolstoy. "She had broadened out all over." Suicide for her is an act of rebellion against the indeterminateness, lack of clarity, imposed on her like a privation of freedom. By throwing herself at an oncoming train, shaking off the encumbering little red handbag, surely a symbol of her worldly position, she violently writes *Finis*—at last a definition.

For me, *Anna Karenina* is terribly true, almost truer than any novel ought to be. No illusions are permitted to survive in its rigorous climate; *War and Peace* is softer, more clement. Levin ends *Anna* with the admission of his own incorrigibility; he has not changed, as he always dreamed he would, and now he knows that he never will be different. Still that is not quite the end; he tells himself at once that there *is* a difference, even though it is imperceptible—an *inner* difference that he owes to the rediscovery of the Christian truths he has known as a child. True, nothing outwardly will change, but he has lost the inner feeling of meaninglessness. Now every minute of his life has a "positive meaning of goodness with which I have the power to invest it." These are the last words of the novel and a kind of consolation. But since, precisely, by Tolstoyan standards the proof should be visible and palpable, there is no reason to believe that this too is not an illusion, of a very common kind, created by need.

Everyone needs the good, hankers for it, as Plato says, because of the lack of it in the self. This greatly craved goodness is meaning, which is absent from the world, outside the chain of cause and effect and incommensurable with reason.

Yet Levin's intimations of it owe a great deal, surely, to Kitty, to the unaccustomed delights of fatherhood and new-married life, i.e., to material factors, so that the conviction we are left with as we close the novel may be just as time-determined as Vronsky's feeling of pureness on leaving the Shcherbatskys', which is partly due to his not having smoked for several hours. The hero of *Anna* is Anna, after all, not Levin. She is the tragic sacrifice, and if the novel is a tragedy, of temple-like Greek logic (the only novel in history to achieve this stature), it is because the power of suffering in Anna imposes meaning by the drastic act of auto-destruction. The excruciating ache of Vronsky's strong, even teeth, the twitching of his jaw are a restatement of the theme in his limited corporeal language.

[March 22, 1981]

Acts of Love

CALVINO IS A WIZARD. His last work of fiction, *The Castle of Crossed Destinies*, was inspired by two packs of tarot cards. The hero of the latest, *If on a winter's night a traveler*, is "the new Calvino"—in other words, itself. The novel the reader has opened is the same novel a Reader inside the cover has gone to a bookstore to procure, having seen an item in a newspaper announcing that a book by this author, the first in several years, has appeared. Everything fairly normal so far. Calvino's Reader—the one inside the story—is a reasonable updating of the "dear reader" of the old fictioneers. As we might expect, relations with him have become more informal, positively familiar: right away the author is calling him "you" (*"tu," "ti," "te,"* in the original), which is like getting on a first-name basis at the first handshake. "Calvino," a hospitable figure, is concerned that the new owner of his book should have optimum conditions for the enjoyment of it: good light, a comfortable position, no distractions ("No, I don't want to watch TV!"), cigarettes and an ash-tray if he smokes.

What may strike the reader (small *r*, you or me, not Him) as possibly a bit odd is the insistence on the Reader's anticipation, as though this were an *ars amoris* and the whole first chapter, in which we meet author and reader but not yet the book, were the foreplay, stimulation of erectile tissue prior to the act of reading as recommended by a rather permissive sex

manual. The Reader is instructed to "Relax," "Concentrate";
we watch him, alone at last with the desired object, sen-
suously postpone his pleasure, turning the volume over in his
hands, glancing through the jacket copy, while the author,
also watching, approves, *up to a point*: "Of course, this circling of the book . . . this reading around it before reading
inside it, is a part of the pleasure . . . but like all prelimi-
nary pleasures, it has its optimum duration if you want it to
serve as a thrust toward the more substantial pleasure of the
consummation of the act, namely the reading of the book."
This should be a hint of what is to follow: consummation
withheld—a series of beginnings, ten to be exact, ten novels
that break off just as they are getting interesting, ten cun-
ningly regulated instances of coitus interruptus in the art and
practice of fiction.

From the start, from the very first lines, like a barely heard
alarm-bell, "the new Calvino" induces slight anxiety in the
Reader preparing himself to recognize the "unmistakable tone"
of the author—one of the small initial sensations, highly
pleasurable, of opening a volume by an author one already
knows. But now the awaited sensation fails to materialize: this
new one does not read like a Calvino. There seems to be no
connection with any of his others. Nonetheless the Reader
persists, swallowing his first disappointment. In one who is
hooked on the potent old drug, the urge to read is greater than
the urge to read a Calvino.

In fact, as our marvelous story-teller fully demonstrates,
the addict can no longer be choosy; we behold him at the
mercy of his habit, suffering withdrawal symptoms when the
supply is abruptly cut off, unable to break himself of the solitary practice, so easily fallen into, of letting his eyes run from
left to right, then right to left on a swift diagonal, dropping
down a line, and again left to right, back and forth across any
bound sheets of printed white paper so long as order and serial pagination have been respected. And how little it takes,

for example, to compel reader-identification with the pronoun "I" in a first-person narrative, no matter where it is supposed to be happening and amid what company—more and more, these days, no introductions are necessary. In the course of this short book "You" will identify yourself with a series of complete strangers, some of whom, like the fellow with the suitcase in the first novel, never even let you know their name and occupation.

As my reader has surely heard if he is tuned in to literary events, *If on a winter's night a traveler* keeps turning into other novels, into, finally, nine successive polymorphs that break off at the point where the reader starts to feel real suspense as to what will happen next, the point where in an old movie serial the heroine is tied to the railroad tracks and the engine is coming steadily toward the viewer, who has to wait patiently for next week's installment not to be sure of the worst. Ten short cliff-hangers (though in some cases the drop is modest), ten contemporary authors (counting the false Calvino), ten titles, ten manners somehow familiar to the ear but by no means parodistic. The confusion begins with a rather common binder's error, always maddening to the innocent purchaser. By a duplication of "signatures"—as printer's folded sheets of multiples of four are called—after page 32 the bound copy of *If on a winter's night,* instead of going on to page 33, jumps back to page 17, repeating the sequence 17–32, and then, as really can happen, does it *again*, with the awful effect of eternity or of a stuck phonograph needle.

With the second chapter it is the next morning and we are back in the bookstore; the Reader cannot wait to return his defective copy and have it replaced so that he can get on with the story. There, between two rows of bookshelves, among the Penguin Modern Classics, he meets the Other Reader, by name Ludmilla, who has come on the same errand. The bookseller has been telling her, and now he tells the Reader, that unfortunately the signatures of the Calvino book got mixed up at the binder's with those of a Polish book, *Outside the town of Malbork*, by Tazio Bazakbal, so that the Calvino is being withdrawn temporarily from circulation with the publisher's apologies. By luck, though, the bookseller, having checked his stock, finds he has a few sound copies of *If on a winter's night*, which he can offer the two disappointed readers. But on the joint realization that it was the *Polish* book they had started on the previous night, they decline the Calvino. It is the Bazakbal they are now eager to finish.

The Reader goes home with the fresh volume, exhilarated by the thought that he will have a companion in his reading, with whom he can compare notes: he has taken her telephone number. The pages this time are uncut, and he arms himself with a paper knife to hack his way through the new obstacle to his impatience. But he has not advanced a page before it is evident that this is not the book he began yesterday. That one took place in a railroad station, and this one is on a farm, seemingly in central Europe. The style is quite different too: the other was foggy; this is clear-cut and precise, each character being promptly defined by an attribute, such as gnawed nails, or an implement, like a butter curler, that he is handling.

It is the wrong book but it is a book. The Reader reads on. Soon the story begins to absorb him, even though the names of places and people do not sound particularly Polish, which is odd. And then, as his knife goes ahead mechanically cutting, far more swiftly than he is able to read, his eyes suddenly come upon two blank sheets. Then two printed pages. That is how the book continues: an alternation of blank pages and printed pages. Those binders again. And that is not all. The more he considers the bit he has read of *Outside the town of Malbork*, the more he is persuaded that it has nothing to do with Poland. The names of a river and a town and the consultation of an atlas suggest that it is set in a locality called

190

Cimmeria, identified by Homer (*Odyssey* XI, 12–19) as a region of perpetual mist and darkness. And, as if this were not enough, when he telephones the Other Reader to hear whether her copy is the same, the voice that answers is different from hers. It is her sister speaking, a left-winger and feminist, named Lotaria.

There is no halting these metamorphoses; the book has taken on the extensible form of a telescope, with one part sliding into the next. Cimmerian, a modern language which has the distinction of being a dead language at the same time, is guarded by a mild dragon, Professor Uzzi-Tuzii, from infiltration by Cimbrian, spoken by a neighboring people who after the Second World War annexed Cimmeria and became the Cimbric People's Republic. *Outside the town of Malbork* proves to really be *Leaning from the steep slope*, the masterpiece of Ukko Ahti, a Cimmerian author of the first quarter of the century. The fragment Professor Uzzi-Tuzii is reading aloud to the two Readers, translating from the original as he goes, is unfortunately all we possess of Ahti's fictional work, so highly representative of Cimmerian literature. Upon finishing the first pages, the writer went into a deep depression and succeeded in taking his own life.

Now Professor Uzzi-Tuzii's little sanctum, already overcrowded with books, is invaded by Lotaria, insisting that the writing is not Cimmerian but Cimbrian. Moreover it is not unfinished. The title was later changed, and it was signed with a different pseudonym, that of Vorts Viljandi, a "complex personality" who wrote in both tongues. At this very moment the entire work is scheduled for analysis and debate by Lotaria's seminar on the feminist revolution, led by Uzzi-Tuzii's rival, Professor Galligani. As Ludmilla and the Reader take their places at a classroom table, Lotaria is holding a bundle of manuscript, *Without fear of wind or vertigo* (the true, postrevolutionary title), from which she will read aloud to the study group in a German translation.

Like each earlier attempt, the session with Lotaria's study group ends unsatisfactorily; as she cuts the reading short, to open the floor for discussion, she dismisses the Reader's plea to look at the rest. "The rest? . . . Oh, there's enough material here to discuss for a month. Aren't you satisfied?" Giving up on the University, the Reader decides to resort to the publisher of the initial defective volumes. There he is turned over to a Mr. Cavedagna, the house's pacifier and problem-solver, a little man shrunken and bent, familiar with the complaints of the trade, who leaps to the natural conclusion that the Reader is a writer, whose problem he knows: "You've come about your manuscript?"

In his relief at finding a Reader, so rare nowadays, where he had feared a writer, more and more a drug on the market, the small Dickensian being, himself an escapee from a library shelf, becomes genuinely expansive; for once he can be an open book. Behind the unhappy mix-up of the signatures, he explains, lay a villain of a translator, a certain Ermes Marana, doubling as a literary agent, who has been selling the firm a succession of specious foreign novels which he purports to have translated, covering his tracks when suspicion arises by a bewildering series of substitutions.

Thus the Cimbrian or possibly Cimmerian novel by Ukko Ahti was really the so-called Polish novel or can it be vice versa? This impudent sleight of hand, these brazen impostures might have gone on till infinity had it not finally appeared that the swindler did not know a word of those languages; he had merely inserted some appropriate proper names in a trashy text entitled *Looks down in the gathering shadow* that he had plagiarized from a little-known Belgian author, Bertrand Vandervelde. As a proof of confidence, Mr. Cavedagna offers the Reader photocopies of the opening pages of the real French text to look through in the office. It is a gangland story, a novel of the *milieu*; the "I" or reader-surrogate

192

is a retired mobster who has gone into the tropical-fish business in the Parisian *banlieue* and is at present having a hard time disposing of the dead body of "Jojo," a former associate.

We are now at the sixth chapter, almost halfway through. These numbered chapters, which at first seemed to be mere bridges leading to the narratives proper, are growing longer and more substantial, generating a suspense of their own, spinning their own plot. Around the Reader and the Other Reader, an independent cast of characters has been assembling: the two professors, Lotaria and her Amazons, Mr. Cavedagna, and now, just when he was needed, a villain, the *traduttore-traditore* of ancient ill repute, Ermes Marana, whose first name seems to link him with the god of thieves. And in the wake of the villain, coolly introduced by him in a series of letters to the publishing house, appears the mythic hero, a Celt of superhuman stature.

Meet Silas Flannery, author of innumerable best sellers that girdle the globe; a Zeus of the realm of book-production; legitimate successor to the old titan, creator of James Bond; at present residing on a mountain-top in Switzerland while in the grip of a majestic writing block, on a scale suitable to his fame and his royalties as well as the Alpine scenery. This sun-like figure's momentary (it is hoped) eclipse is spreading grief and terror among publishers, agents, banks, advertising firms, sponsors of the brands of liquor to be drunk by his characters, the fashions they are to wear, the tourist spots they are to visit, all stipulated by contract and now in jeopardy. Not solely the powerful corporate giants of the West but the infant economies of small developing countries expecting to be "put on the map" by a brief stopover of the old Irish author's imaginative progeny on their beaches or coral reefs. As in the case of Demeter grieving for Persephone, a whole world or, rather, industry is in mourning for the stricken creator who does nothing but write in a diary and observe through a spy-glass a young woman in a deck chair on a terrace at the bottom of the valley who is reading a book.

Our first acquaintance with Silas Flannery (other than the gossip relayed by Ermes) is made through a text, *In a network of lines that enlace*. The "I" of the narrative is an elderly jogger, a visiting professor at an unnamed university who, if I am not mistaken, has some of the lineaments of Nabokov's Kinbote. It is only a shadow, though, as one might say "Shades of Charles Kinbote," or, as the words "Belgian," "Bernadette," "Jojo," in conjunction with the previous narrative, make one wonder whether a cloud called Simenon has not passed overhead. There is no question, I repeat, of parodies here. There are faint resemblances, delicate reminders, some so evanescent that they cannot be pinned down to any one author or even school (Why do I sense that Ukko Ahti has something to do with Hungarian literature or just with the way Hungarians *talk* about Hungarian literature?), while others, for instance the Japanese novel, *On the carpet of leaves illuminated by the moon*, do seem to represent a whole distinct class of book. That "magic" effect, however, as Calvino (the real one) modestly lets us see, is produced by the manipulation of certain key words such as ginkgo tree, moon, waterlily, leaves, and certain stage properties such as suki-yaki and the kimono.

In general, though, what we are offered is ten volatile distillations of the novelistic essence bottled in ten diverse scent-containers. The little narratives are evocative in the same way as the white butterfly that flies across the valley from the book page the young woman is reading to alight on the page Silas Flannery is writing. What makes the white butterfly so poignant? What does it evoke? Literature, I suppose, because it is softly telling us that it is an author's device, a symbol; we are given an almost stolen glimpse of the author putting in a symbol. But, beyond symbolizing a symbol, it also evokes the errant, fluttery nature of communication, the perishability of message and messenger (it is an ephemerid), and conceivably the old lepidopterist, Nabokov, still haunting the Swiss peaks and valleys where he spent his last years. Yet if there *is* such an allusion it is less an *omaggio dell'autore* than a smiling acknowledgment of a presence.

A presence that in my opinion is wrongly evoked in connection with Italo Calvino, even though I have just been guilty of doing so, led on by the white butterfly. In the first place, I cannot escape the feeling that Calvino is no admirer of Nabokov, who likes to treat the reader as an adversary in a one-way hide-and-seek game. In the second place, I can see no influences at all at work on "the new Calvino," even of writers he has quoted admiringly in his critical prose, no literary genetic imprint, no trace of Borges, for example; if there is a hereditary line to be found, it winds back, surely, to the Orient, where all tales come from. There is an over-all congeniality with Queneau, but that is a matter of a shared playfulness, on the one hand, and a shared interest, on the other, in the possibility of literature as a semi-mathematical science, with laws to be detected.

In any case, we get to know Silas Flannery through the narrative of the old jogger, and, when we get to know him in person in Chapter 8, which is composed of extracts from his diary, we can distinguish autobiographical elements, quite recent ones, in *In a network of lines that enlace* having to do with "forgetting himself" in the presence of young women. And this in turn allows us to distinguish the real Silas Flannery from the false one; there are *two* sets of pages signed with his name, the second, *In a network of lines that intersect*, being the handiwork of his devilish counterfeiter, Ermes Marana.

When we examine the counterfeit, a curious literary phenomenon comes to light. If embarrassing autobiographical elements, creeping into the first fragment, seem to vouch for its authenticity, the counterfeit reveals itself as such in a not dissimilar fashion: the personality of its true author has "bled" into the work, which is volubly preoccupied with kaleidoscopes, with the "polydyptic theatre" (in which numerous small mirrors lining a large box turn a bough into a forest, a lead soldier into an army, and so on), and finally with a financial empire based on catoptrics, i.e., done with mirrors. In these involuntary revelations we are encountering the phenomenon known to medicine as ecchymosis (to use a Calvino-like word): an oozing of blood into the tissues as the result of a bruise. In other words, the wound and the bow. Ermes Marana's obsession with the dark arts of imitation, seeping into *In a network of lines that intersect*, betrays it as a forgery, just as in the old jogger's fragment a misfired pass made at a girl student proves (unless we have to do with a very clever and knowledgeable copyist) that it is a genuine Flannery. Thus a work can be "read" as an Identikit portrait of the author lurking inside it, unaware of giving himself away.

Of course there is nothing really new here. This kind of literary detection was initiated many years ago by Miss Caroline Spurgeon, who was the first to count the images in Shakespeare's plays, paving the way for a deconstruction of Shakespeare's own image ("Others abide our question, Thou smilest and art still") as a deep, fathomless person. And it was early in the century when Freud induced Leonardo to betray his secret. These are all modes of "reading" that many of our contemporaries vastly prefer to the older, "passive" kind. Lotaria, as a matter of fact, is still working the Spurgeon territory, drawing up lists of words used in a given novel or group of novels in the order of the frequency of their occurrence; her computer has proved invaluable to her in her labors, whose purpose is to catalogue novels in terms of atmosphere, mood, social background, and so on, thereby eliminating the wastefulness inherent in traditional reading habits. She is writing her thesis on Flannery, who finds himself unnerved by the prospect, unable to write a word in case it be "counted" against him by the electronic brain.

Meanwhile, in the seventh chapter, we have come upon a fresh kind of reading. The Reader, invited by Ludmilla to wait for her at her apartment, is seen "reading" the apartment in order to read Ludmilla. Nothing of course is more common. Who has not "read" a house, a set of bookshelves, a medicine cabinet, in the owner's absence? It is true that the objects in Ludmilla's house—or anyone else's—are "elements of a discourse." But with this reading of Ludmilla's house something different is starting to happen. This is at once felt by the pronouns, which suddenly shift places. Here at Ludmilla's, the "You" familiarly addressed is no longer the Reader; it is Ludmilla. "Calvino" is now speaking to her directly, over the head of the Reader, who has become a "he," that is, almost an intruder. And this reversal of the pronouns presages another, sweeter event. Before you can say Jack Robinson, they are in bed together, having metamorphosed into a "You," second-person plural, a single two-headed "*Voi*," two young heads on a pillow. And now half this plural is "reading" Ludmilla's body, her fleshly envelope, as, before she came home, for want of better, he was reading every crevice of the container that is her apartment. And Ludmilla is reviewing *his* body but more cursorily "as if skimming the index." The plot has thickened.

Separation, naturally, follows. He travels to Switzerland to find Silas Flannery. We learn of his visit from entries in Flannery's diary—another mold in which the traditional novel may be cast; we have already had the epistolary form in Marana's letters to the publisher. From the diary too, we learn of another of Marana's diabolical machinations—his arrangement with a Japanese combine to pirate Silas Flannery's complete works. Not exactly pirate, though—copy the model, using native workmanship. As Marana has explained to the old writer, "the great skill of the Japanese in manufacturing perfect facsimiles of Western products has spread to literature." Without revealing his own part in the fraud, he shows Flannery a book signed "Flannery" that Flannery has never written; a firm in Osaka has managed to get hold of the formula. Now the flood of imitations re-translated—or, rather, translated—into English will be indistinguishable from his personal output.

It is a nice touch that the Japanese novel that takes up the next pages should be, if not a perfect facsimile, at least a fair imitation of one, plausible enough to pass inspection in a drugstore paperback rack. Only two more samples remain to be exhibited. The Reader and the Other Reader after a number of vicissitudes are about to be reunited. We readers have seen pass in review, like a series of floats, to our cries of delight and recognition, a parade of the types and varieties of narrative experience, many of them in native costume with flags borne by persons having names like Ponko and Arkadian Porphyrich.

It is better than a parade. It is a *Summa fictionis* of scholastic rigor and, like all glorious codifications of divine mysteries, it has to do with love. The act of reading, when finally consummated, is seen to be parallel to the act of love. And at the same time, lest the foregoing seem too awesome for a book so sweet-natured and shyly merry, there is something here suggestive of an old-fashioned small-town garage (maybe an old Fiat place) with a car inside that has the hood up and a jack or so underneath. An inventor in a white coat, the top mechanic, is lovingly tinkering with it, tuning the engine and listening like a doctor. Just about every part of it is worn out and begging for replacement. It is a lovely piece of junk. And yet when the inventor shuts down the hood and takes his place

198

at the wheel of the contraption, removing his white coat (or maybe he is wearing a white short-sleeved jump suit), it actually moves, responding to the slightest touch of the accelerator pedal. And what does it run *on*? I think it must run on suspense, an organic natural product that nobody, not even (so far) our inventor, can tell us much about. If I can try to read his mind, I will say that, in the formula for suspense tentatively set out there, one should find at least three parts sex.

June 25, 1981

Politics and the Novel

SOMEONE SAID the other day that the American novel was, of course, not political: By comparison with the European novel— say Zola and the Russians—our home product was primarily domestic, unconcerned with public affairs. It was a surprise to me to learn that this strange notion was taken for granted— a truism—by common opinion; to me it was a new idea. At once a contrary list sprang into my mind, *The Bostonians* and *The Princess Casamassima* lining up with Henry Adams's *Democracy*; behind them marched *Uncle Tom's Cabin*, ("did much to hasten the American Civil War"—*Oxford Companion to English Literature*) and *The Blithedale Romance*, Hawthorne's satire on the Brook Farm experiment in communal living; ahead were Dos Passos' *U.S.A.*, *For Whom the Bell Tolls*, right up to Norman Mailer's *Why Are We in Vietnam?*

Indeed, Americans, I think, tend to get their political education through fiction—occasionally through poetry, though this is becoming rarer. Today a novel such as E. L. Doctorow's *The Book of Daniel*, currently a film, seems to have no other design than to excite a belief in the innocence of the Rosenberg couple or to reinforce a disbelief already held as to the charges against them. I do not know whether the Doctorow book changed anybody's mind on this subject—how could it, seriously, being fiction, deal with a concrete instance of fact?—but fictions do sway us to the right or left, and Americans, I suspect, more than most.

I can cite a case—my own—of a young person's being altered politically by a novel, but I cannot explicate the process, let alone explain it in terms of the author's intention or literary strategies. I believe there is often something accidental in these things, as with love, which gives them a feeling of fatality.

When it happened to me, at the age of twenty, it was the first time. I was probably not very susceptible politically; the year I was fifteen I had read an entire set of Tolstoy with no effect that I recall on my belief system. I was an atheist, a romantic, and an arch-conservative (except at elections, when I was a Democrat); none of this could have come to me from Tolstoy. The first real dent on my Cavalier-period armor was made in my senior year at Vassar in Miss Peebles's course in Contemporary Prose Fiction, where we studied "multiplicity" and "stream of consciousness" and were assigned *The 42nd Parallel* by Dos Passos as an example of those trends. I fell madly in love with that book—the first volume of the trilogy that was going to be *U.S.A.* No doubt the fervor of emotion—an incommunicable bookish delight—had been preparing in me for some time through other "social" books, just as two mild bee-stings may prepare you for a third that is fatal. I had been telling my friends, and believing, that in politics I was a royalist—an impractical position, I knew, for an American, since we did not even have a kingly line to restore. At the suggestion of one of those anxious friends, I had read Shaw's *The Intelligent Woman's Guide to Socialism and Capitalism*, but it rolled right off me, water off a duck's back. Then came *The 42nd Parallel*.

Though I did not yet realize it, it was the Book of Lancelot for me: "Quel giorno più non vi legemmo avante" (That day we read in it no farther) or, putting it in Manzonian terms,

"La sventurata rispose"—I responded. It was the title, I think, that captured me because I did not understand at first what the author meant by it. Then there was the unusual weaving of forms: the biographies, the newsreels, the Camera Eye (who was the author but treated in a wry, slightly embarrassed manner that I found very sympathetic), and finally the individual stories themselves: Mac, Eleanor Stoddard, J. Ward Moorhouse, Eveline Hutchins. . . . The one I most took to was Mac, who became a Wobbly or at any rate a socialist and was killed young. Best of all, I loved Debs, among the biographies, and disliked J. P. Morgan most.

I do not remember what I thought about a figure like Big Bill Haywood, the IWW leader who finished in Russia; I do remember what I did. I went to the library and looked up every line that Dos Passos had published that was in the card catalogue. I read them all. The last was a pamphlet on the Sacco-Vanzetti case, which I found and read in the library basement, feeling tremendously stirred by Vanzetti's famous words, brand-new, of course, to me, and by the whole story. But we were in 1933, I realized, and they had been executed in 1927. So there was nothing to be done. But I was moved to read up on the Tom Mooney case too (he at least was still alive) and to become aware of the *New Republic*. One thing leading to another, soon after graduation, I was writing little book reviews for the *New Republic*, then for the *Nation*, and I never looked back. Like a Japanese paper flower dropped into a glass of water, my political persona unfolded, magically, from Dos Passos, though he would have been saddened in later years to hear what his energy, enthusiasm, and sheer unwary talent had brought about.

So what do we mean generally when we speak of political novels? Some people—Marxists—will say that all novels are political, especially those, like Jane Austen's, that avoid the subject, thus lending tacit support to the status quo. This may

202

be true, insofar as no experience (even the solitary dialogue with the self) is without a political dimension, and to ignore this is to tell a falsehood. But awareness of that dimension varies greatly from person to person and no doubt from one civilization to another. I would guess that ours, democracy-haunted, equality-haunted, was especially sensitive to the political (i.e., the power games) in personal relationships: See *The War Between the Tates* or *Portnoy's Complaint* and compare Moravia's *Io e lui*. As a nation of lawyers (Tocqueville), we would be bound to have a talent for injustice-collection. But if one forgets the tense politics of personal relations and thinks of political novels in the common ordinary sense of the word—meaning political parties, voting, legislation, courts of justice, armies—one will nevertheless find that the term "political" can refer to several distinct types of story.

First, there are stories that engage in the highly political art of persuasion, aiming to convince a reader to take certain stands in a national or international debate—the simplest example is *Uncle Tom's Cabin*. But here *The Book of Daniel* may also be relevant insofar as, at one remove, it can affect a reader's attitude toward the Pershing missile. A second type of story deals with politicians, examples being *The Last Hurrah*, *All The King's Men*, Dos Passos' *District of Columbia* (whose weakness is to be biased), a good deal of Gore Vidal; I do not think this type is often found in combination with the first, since novels about politicians tend, like their heroes, to a worldly realism that would never change one's voting habits, except maybe to discourage one from voting at all. A third type ponders large political questions—essentially the nature and effects of power. The setting may be a village, a family house, a monastic community, a hospital, an air base, a hiring hall, an imaginary country such as those Gulliver visited or *Animal Farm*; the politics may be in the play between man and Nature, man and the universe, man and God. This third type too, being long-sighted, cannot coexist with the first, and not, I think, with the second either; a fascination with the corridors of power is always anecdotal, not reflective. Such anecdotes as appear in *War and Peace*, a supreme instance of Type Three, are there for illustrative purposes, to serve as *examples* in the ancient rhetoricians' sense of the term. This third and noblest type may be fully represented in our fiction only by *Moby-Dick*.

What we find most often, I believe, in American fiction is the first type, though we may not recognize it or, when we do, call it propaganda, which for us is a negative word, without any of the original wholesome connotations of missionary work (*de propaganda fide*, spreading the faith) implicit for the Roman Church. Actually the great majority of novels in this country—maybe everywhere—have been faith-spreaders. Those are the ones we name when we are asked what books have influenced or changed us.

Main Street was such a book, and *Babbitt* another. *Babbitt* was a generalized warning of what as an American one would not want to happen to oneself. (Type One, as I should have said, includes warnings—all sorts of wake-up calls, sirens, alerts.) When, with *Elmer Gantry, Arrowsmith*, and so on, Sinclair Lewis ceased to issue those wake-up calls to his fellow citizens and turned, instead, to cataloguing American social types by professions—preacher, scientist, businessman, social worker—he became a simple indexer, and nobody listened any more. Surprisingly, though, years after *Main Street*, he came out with an explicit warning to the nation under the ironic title *It Can't Happen Here*. It was Lewis doing his bit to alert his readers to the possibility of a native fascism, which of course would look different from Hitler's. The title was misunderstood even at the time, as a reassurance rather than the alarm-bell it was, which is perhaps a fate that lies in wait for such ironically titled, minatory books. Something of the kind happened with Eugene Burdick and William J. Lederer's *The Ugly American*—a clear lesson in the Do's and the Don'ts for the United States in southern Asia. The ugly American of the title was a homely simple fellow who knew the right way to win hearts and minds; in other words, he was *good*. But by those who did not read the actual story and doubtless through contamination from Graham Greene's *The Quiet American*, he was taken to embody the *bad* side of the USA, to the point where the term "ugly American" became proverbial, meaning someone suspected of being a CIA agent or, finally, just any American on neocolonial soil.

Is it an exaggeration to call *Main Street* and *Babbitt* propaganda? Certainly in 1921, when *Main Street* came out, it was understood to be a rejection of the values of Main Street, seen as narrow, rectilinear, conformist, deadly dull. And along with that was a notion that Main Street was a mistake, made with good intentions, which could be corrected, or repealed, like the Volstead Act—a product of just such prairie towns. Main Street could *not* be eternal, written in the natural order of things; thanks to Lewis and his readers, it could be just temporary. It is the underlying sense of something to be corrected in the American heartland that tells us that Lewis's novel is political, in comparison, say, with *Tess of the D'Urbervilles*. The wrongs done to Tess by the world surrounding her are infinitely greater than any injury done to Carol Kennicott in *Main Street*, who at worst could be said to be suffering from a slight personality impairment due to cultural deprivation. Tess is not a social fact, capable of multiplication to give a satirical picture, but the plaything of a cruel destiny. She is hanged at Winchester, like any common murderess, yet our knowledge that she is an uncommon, even a superior, person cannot let us fall on the book as a condemnation of capital punishment (see Mailer's *The Executioner's Song*),

though that could be a side-effect on certain readers of a passionate response to the book. That she is not changed—
coarsened—by her misfortunes (as in real life she almost surely
would be) is the clue to the supra-political dimension of Hardy's story. Politics, the art of the possible, hopes to change
the rules of society (or restore a former good order in the place
of a bad); at the same time, it induces change—for worse as
well as better—in individual subjects viewed as samples.

Naturally, the propaganda that works on us through fictions does not effect conversions (i.e., transformations) in ways
that can necessarily be charted. If our vote on ERA or a
nuclear-power amendment is changed by a novel we are
reading, that is only the tip of the iceberg. Probably in the
twenties there were more converts made to hedonism than to
any other faith, and that still may be the "message" of the
most influential fiction of today, from Mailer to Updike and
back, even when the evangel of self-expression is relayed
through fears of getting cancer (Mailer) by bottling oneself up.
But if we look at thirties fiction, it can be said, surely with
truth, that Cesar Chavez's grape and lettuce pickers unions
were helped, though with a delay of two generations, by *The
Grapes of Wrath*. And the Joad family, *Of Mice and Men*,
even the less accessible *In Dubious Battle*, had already had
consequences for the national psyche in a less evidently causal
way.

That American novels can be and often are political is
demonstrable. There was Mailer's second novel, for instance,
The Barbary Shore, laid in Brooklyn with an FBI man for the
villain. Not to mention the "proletarian novels" of the thirties, or Upton Sinclair, not to mention *Mr. Sammler's Planet*
and *The Dean's December*. Or Bellow's first book, *Dangling
Man*, the "alienated" cry of a character waiting to be drafted.
Or his second, *The Victim*: isn't *any* novel about anti-Semitism
political and almost any novel about race? Maybe novels about
the lot of women, such as *A Lost Lady*, were "domestic" at

206

the time of writing, but they have been drafted into the service of feminism, along with their modern sisters, *Fear of Flying* and *The Group*.

In a different vein, we have had the Boston pols of *The Last Hurrah* and their descendants in George V. Higgins. Good heavens, I was nearly forgetting *Gone With the Wind*. On the conservative side too, there was Cozzens's *By Love Possessed*—a goyish *Mr. Sammler*. Robert Penn Warren's *All the King's Men* was a political novel if there ever was one, being a highly recognizable picture of the career of Huey Long. If Updike's *Couples* was decidedly "domestic," what about *The Coup*, his study of an African leader? And *Bech: A Book*, where literary politics is never far from the other kind.

Most of our war novels have been pacifist in their general slant—enough to count as political. I am not sure of *The Red Badge of Courage* or *A Farewell to Arms*, but there is no doubt of *Three Soldiers, The Naked and the Dead, From Here to Eternity, Catch-22*(!). And the many works of Vietnam veterans such as *Dispatches* by Michael Herr.

Anyone who is in the mood can continue the list. To make the point there is no need to seek to prove (as some academic recently did) that *Moby-Dick* is an allegory of capitalism. What is interesting is that so many of the novels I have been naming have been high on the best-seller lists. The political novel in this country is certainly no fringe phenomenon. And it strikes me that we have almost more than our share of them, in comparison with England and Western Europe, just as we have had more war novels (in fact, a notable case of Type One) than our allies or adversaries, and this despite the fact that we entered both World Wars late and were never exposed to mainland attack or invasion.

In the First War, the English had war poetry, and the Germans had *All Quiet on the Western Front*; the French had part of Roger Martin du Gard's *Les Thibault*, Henri Barbusse's *Under Fire*, and a film, *La Grande Illusion*. Out of that war, the English, as far as I remember, produced only a single novel, though that was a masterpiece, first published, in expurgated form, as *Her Privates We* and written in fact by an Australian, Frederic Manning. It was reissued uncut a few years ago as *The Middle Parts of Fortune*. A curious aspect of this pure and beautiful work, dealing with trench warfare and behind-the-lines billet life on the Somme in 1916, is the absence of politics from it, as remarkable in its way as the same absence in *The Iliad*, and I mean politics of any kind—there is neither glorification nor condemnation of war, still less of "our" side in contrast to the enemy beyond the barbed wire, and, most unusual of all, no idealization of the class of privates as opposed to the officer class that made up the basic politics of American war fiction. We will not find that neutrality in our war literature, which has a strong accusatory ring; none of our soldier-authors could have written these two sentences (from the prefatory note to *Her Privates We*, 1929): "War is waged by men, not by beasts, or by gods. To call it a crime against mankind is to miss at least half of its significance; it is also a punishment for a crime."

Even Faulkner's *A Fable*, written toward the end of his life, after he received the Nobel Prize, but going back to the First War, is not dispassionate but, rather, hyperbolic about the redeeming mutiny it describes; with a silent admonitory black cross placed by Random House on the jacket, it is a pacifist parable, with funny echoes of *A Tale of Two Cities*, on the one hand, and of "Hinky-dinkey parlay-voo" (alias "Mademoiselle from Armenteers, She Hasn't Washed in Forty Years") on the other. Even though it is not fiction, one ought to mention E. E. Cummings's *The Enormous Room*, recounting his imprisonment, with Slater Brown, as a suspected spy in a French internment camp—a peak of imaginative prose writing by an American about the First War. *A Fable*, in fact, was Faulkner's third try at rendering some angle of that war; *Soldier's Pay* and *Mosquitoes* had to do with veterans, a political problem since Caesar's time.

January 1, 1984

In the Family Way

HERE, under the title *Marthe*, is a collection of family letters—found, we are told, in various château attics—which
constitutes a family portrait. It may be representative, though
one hesitates to think so, of an entire social class and period.
The exchange of letters covers ten years—1892 to 1902—and
considerable territory, from Normandy across to Burgundy and
down to the Alpes-Maritimes and the Hérault, but has a single, compelling center of interest, Marthe de Montbourg, the
pathological "case" who is causing so much ink to flow among
her relations.

   She is twenty, unmarried, and pregnant when the letters
start; it is not clear what obscure male is responsible, only that
he is "beneath" her—a pattern we will see repeated. The little *particule de noblesse*, the significant *"de"* in her name,
makes her delinquency especially painful to her sister, mother,
uncle, aunts, godfather, cousins; it means that certain solutions cannot be considered and that all solutions will be expensive. The family's position rules out marriage to the father,
and religion—the inevitable Catholicism transmitted in the
blood—rules out abortion.

   She can be married off to a station-master, a druggist, a
postal clerk (the money-order window), a tax collector (among
the prospects examined are two of these), providing he does
not drink, gamble, neglect his religious duties, or lean to the

210

left politically. But he cannot have parents in the retail wine business (wholesale might pass) or a baker for a brother-in-law. Given the handsome bribe of her dowry, she can even be married into her own class but with the great disadvantage that her in-laws will be certain to throw her past up to her. A grateful commoner (on Ben Franklin's principle of choosing an old and ugly wife) will be better, above all if the young couple sets up house far from any member of the family—Marthe's godfather's strong recommendation.

But whatever solution is elected, after consultation with the clergy, advertisements in the "Matrimonial" column of *Le Chasseur français*, advice sought from a *somnambule* (a paramedical practitioner who works with the subject's hair-combings and flannel undergarments), it is going to cost money. Not just the expenses of a discreet lying-in with the nuns at a St. Raphaël shelter, nor the price paid to a foster-mother for silence and anonymity, no, there is worse: even if the husband's agreement to recognize the illegitimate child as his own is stipulated in the marriage contract, there will be a strong likelihood of blackmail from him afterwards.

Marthe's widowed mother, the Baroness of Montbourg (born de Cerilley), has included that among her fearful fancies and she has been right. Even though the *parti* settled on is not the hard-featured tax collector but a debt-riddled aristocrat belonging to the same *petite noblesse* as the Montbourg and Cerilley clans, he is not above blackmail; nor are his mother ("Mamma d'Aillot" to Marthe now) and old-maid sisters. *"Sangsues,"* bloodsuckers, is the word Mamma de Montbourg usually finds for the lot of them. And to the American reader this is the surprise of *Marthe*. The *petite noblesse* behaves like our notion of the *petite bourgeoisie*—the class of shopkeepers. It is mercenary, grasping, petty, penny-pinching, mean. No code of honor restrains these ultras, with the qualified exception of Charles de Cerilley, Marthe's maternal uncle, who, though far from a chivalrous figure, does have *some* notion of fairness in dealing with people he disapproves of. This fairness of his, in fact, while never immoderate, leads his sister and niece, as the correspondence develops, to look upon him, each for her own reasons, as an enemy.

The English squires, the Anglo-Irish gentry, the American patriciate were never like this, or rarely. It may have something to do with the almost inbred eccentricity of the English squire class, passed on to the Americans and the Anglo-Irish. In comparison, the French provincial gentry as shown in these letters are all alike, seeing narrowly eye to eye except where some crass personal interest may impose a divergent view. There is not a trace of largeness, no capacity for surprising. Their main occupation seems to be the gathering of intelligence, i.e., spying, through a far-flung network of agents—above all, priests filing exhaustive reports: "Mr. Robert d'Aillot has two cows and three mares on his property at Mougins." Or, approvingly, "Mr. Robert d'Aillot is deeply conservative." Servants, too, are practiced in this type of police work: "Mme Clément [the housekeeper] assures me that he's after her night and day." All this no doubt accounts for the prevailing climate of suspicion, mounting readily to paranoia. From the very first letter, Mme de Montbourg talks wildly to her brother of emigrating to America, which is half a dream and half an ultimate threat.

In short, these people have no souls, despite the cloud of ecclesiastics surrounding them. This last points to another common trait among them that is not found in the English aristocracy: religious bigotry, here identical with political bigotry. The French Revolution, of a hundred years back, remains a fixed point of reference. For instance, when the baroness wants to describe the childish terrorism practiced on Marthe by her husband (he tries to persuade her that anything white she sees is a ghost), she is moved to compare it with the "homicidal" treatment a hundred years back of the little Dauphin, Louis XVII, in the Temple by the cobbler Simon, his keeper; the same methods, she prophesies, will be used on her poor little bastard grandson when "they" get their hands on him. Earlier, during the husband-hunt, Mme de Montbourg's devoted spy, investigating the tax collector from Condé-sur-Ifs, reports that his parents have a wineshop in Levallois-Perret (just outside Paris) with "Aux grandes caves de Danton" on the sign. "It's the name of the street," the baroness tells her brother, "but it can also be the name of their party hero." In other words, she has virtual ocular proof that there is socialism in that family.

Piety and avarice combine in these morose natures. Occasionally they are at cross-purposes, as when Mme de Montbourg confronts a dilemma in ordering Masses said for her beloved only son on the first anniversary of his death. In Normandy (where she is putting the château up for sale anyway in the hope of fleeing the scandal), she would have to send out engraved announcements, engage a whole raft of priests, distribute bread to the poor, etc. Moreover, Masses would call attention to the family. Instead, why can't she have a service said at the orphan asylum doubling as a home for unwed mothers where Marthe will be lying in? Rather than bread to the poor, she can distribute clothes to the orphans, killing two birds with one stone. Having decided that, for All Souls Day she orders a wreath which her brother can lay on her son's tomb in Burgundy and specifies that it be made entirely of beads rather than of natural materials, because beads last longer.

No seignorial largesse; economy is the watchword, as in the petty bourgeoisie. "Try to get it cheap," she enjoins a family connection who, she hopes, will be able to get "de Beauvoisin"—from the name of his village in Dauphiné—legally attached to the young station-master's surname. She and her brother keep sending each other all sorts of produce—bags of potatoes, butter, grapes, bulbs, flower-cuttings—and always by *petite vitesse* (slow freight), so that one wonders about the butter, at least. "Return the bags," each tirelessly reminds the other. Hampers also travel slow freight from mother to daughter, carrying blue flannelette from the Printemps department store, laxatives, dog biscuits.

Marthe asks her mother to send her her gray bedroom slippers, a bad-breath remedy (charcoal tablets), her father's steamer rug. On her own initiative, she sends her mother a new product, very economical, that will replace butter and lard in cooking—evidently a sort of margarine. And it is Marthe, the rebel of the family, who counsels her ailing mother to rub herself with oil that has been burned before the statue of St. Anne and to get another relative to send a flask of oil from the lamp that perpetually burns before the miraculous statue of Our Lord in Brussels. This ignorant credulity accords oddly with the pessary that her new Catholic family wants to equip her with and that her mother vehemently opposes. That Marthe, as we have guessed almost from the beginning, is sexually insatiable does not make her a free spirit, despite the tendency to bill her as an early women's lib heroine exhibited in some of the French reviews of the book. In fact it is not easy to place her on a map of the politics of sex. That she had a weakness for bus drivers, valets, peasants in the fields only means that she was predatory, like young *men* of her class then and now.

Currently she would doubtless be called a nymphomaniac; in her own day the term seems to have been "hysteria," from the Greek word for womb, used specfically here (sometimes chastely abbreviated to "*hist* . . .") for Marthe's complaint. Far from making her a liberated woman, this clinical oddity was the source of her enslavement. Robert Caron d'Aillot could do almost anything with her as long as he kept her supplied with sex (almost like a drug habit) of his own manufacture.

She let him pawn her wedding gifts, divert money her mother sent to his own use, wrote wills to suit him, sent abusive letters to her mother, threatened her, refused for long periods to enter her house, lied, lied, lied. . . . Depending on her mood or the effect she wanted to create, she lied when she said he beat her and when she said he didn't.

The most awful aspect of her slavery to him was not physical or financial but mental: the propitiatory habit of baby talk. She called him her "Cat," her "Tom Cat," her "Big Rat"; she refers to herself in the third person as his "'*tite femme*" (little wifey). "Poor you," she writes to her mother, "what would you do with me at the end of a week if you had me with you without my tom cat [*matou*]?" She could not have been more explicit. And she even applied this "little language," redolent of married sex, to her poultry; she calls her ducks "quack-quacks" and talks of "mummy hens." Her "Cat" has put the incubator in the dining-room, so she can feed her mummy hens in the kitchen. She and "Big Rat" have no children (can childlessness be an excuse?—her own by-blow has been farmed out to a foster-mother); but whether that is because of the pessary, or inherited syphilis, probably picked up by her father from a dancer in Caen, or a retroverted uterus, never becomes clear. The strange fact is that she retains this awful baby talk in different circumstances, when, at the end of her short life, divorced from her wife-beater, she lives in what quite clearly seems a lesbian ménage with a servant-companion, who is her "hedgehog," while her male cousin and contemporary is her "angora cat." It does not come as a surprise that when her will is opened, not her relations but her familiars pet-named for animals are found to be her heirs, the plebeian hedgehog getting the lion's share.

Yet, except for her sexual dependency on lowborn or brutal people, Marthe is a true member of her caste, just as hard and grasping as any of them, perhaps a little more. In

215

one of her last letters, she adjures her administrator-cousin not to be soft with a poor tenant of hers who is behind in his rent; she knows the type—the best thing to do will be to foreclose the mortgage before he can clear out, the way they do in Normandy. *Plus ça change, plus c'est la même chose*: if she runs true to form (already worrying in May about wreaths for the tombs on All Souls Day), so does the whole breed, to the point that, as some French critics remarked, it seems almost *too* perfect. This is exactly how these people are, clones of themselves. The economy of the race, the ingrained habit of saving, explains, indeed, the mystery of the survival of all this paper, when so many of the letters comprising it have ended *"Burn this!"* Thrift, it would appear, got the better of prudence; one can never be sure that a damaging document may not some day come in handy. As Mme de Montbourg wrote to her brother apropos his acquaintance with the brother of the bishop of Montpellier: "Be sure to keep his address, as we might well have need of him."

December 8, 1983

216

"Democracy"

Democracy, a novel, takes its title from Henry Adams's *Democracy*, subtitled *An American Novel*. On page 71 of Joan Didion's new book, the author speaks of a course she gave in the spring of 1975 at Berkeley, where she met with a dozen or so students in the English Department "to discuss the idea of democracy in the work of certain post-industrial writers." In that light, George Orwell and Ernest Hemingway, Henry Adams and Norman Mailer were considered as pairs of similars—to me an unlikely thought. In sentences of Orwell she heard an echo of Hemingway, and in sentences of Adams she heard a note of the Mailer to come. How the sentences she quotes from Orwell resemble any of Hemingway's or how Adams's forty-foot dynamo foretells Mailer is not elucidated, nor how they relate to their authors' notions of democracy.

In the same way, I have found it hard to make out what connection there can be between Joan Didion's *Democracy*, opening with a memory of the pink dawns of early atomic weapons tests in the Pacific, and Henry Adams's *Democracy*, which deals with the dirty politics of the second Grant Administration. And, leaving aside Henry Adams, I do not quite see how democracy comes into the Didion tale except for the fact that two Democratic politicians (both Vietnam-war opponents) and a CIA man play large roles in it. For Adams, "democracy" had become a coarse travesty of the ideal of popular rule, indissociable from the gravy train and the grease spots on the Congressman's vest. For Miss Didion too, the term is rich in irony, though corruption by now is so universal that it can no longer be identified with a party or tendency or grand ideal betrayed. There is nobody left like Mrs. Lightfoot Lee, Adams's high-minded Philadelphia mouthpiece, to feel shocked.

The Didion novel, which arrives at its climax in March 1975, while the character "Joan Didion" is teaching her course at Berkeley and the Vietnam War is winding down, can be described as a murder story set in Honolulu—a murder without a mystery in that the elderly "blueblood" killer of a nisei politician and of his own "socialite" daughter proudly announces culpability from his room in the downtown YMCA. I have put "blueblood" and "socialite" in quotation marks to indicate the colonial, road-show quality of the island's palmy social life, which always seems to have an airport (once dockside) lei around its neck. *Aloha oe.* In Hawaii, the fiftieth state of the Union, United States imperialism can claim a happy musical-comedy-style ending. And yet the islands, like Kenya, like the Bahamas, have been prone to quite classy murder, often, as in this case, though not always, involving a transgression of the color line. I remember the Massie (blond wife of a naval officer) case, *the* Pacific-coast newspaper sensation when I was a girl, and the intriguing name of the victim and rape suspect whose body was found in the white officer's car trunk—Joseph Kahahawawa.

As I say, in *Democracy* no mystery is made about the murder of Representative Wendell Omura, Democrat of Hawaii, and Janet Ziegler, daughter of the killer and Harry Victor's sister-in-law, on the Zieglers' lanai. For "lanai" read "porch," and for "Harry Victor" read "Democratic Presidential hopeful in the 1972 primaries" (conceded in California before the polls closed). What is left murky is what the Congressman was doing on the lanai early in the morning with Janet Ziegler. And that is the least of the arcana. "Cards on the table," the author declares, introducing herself to the reader on page 17. Yet despite an appearance of factuality achieved by the author's total recall of names, middle names, dates, by perfect chronometry of arrival and departure times and stereophonic dialogue of imaginary newsworthy figures, *Democracy* is deeply mysterious, cryptic, enigmatic, like a tarot pack or most of Joan Didion's work.

One way of looking at that work is to decide that it has been influenced by movies; hypnotized by movies would be more appropriate. Maybe that is what coming from California, even as far north as Sacramento, does to you. Like the camera, this mental apparatus does not think but projects images, very haunting and troubling ones for the most part, precisely because they are mute. Even when sonorized, as has happened here, they remain speechless and somewhat frightening in their stunned aversion from thought. This powerful relation to film, stronger that that of any other current author, must account for her affinity with Conrad, whose tales and novels—above all *Nostromo, The Secret Agent,* "Heart of Darkness"—seem to have anticipated film, like an uncanny prophecy.

What was new in Conrad was the potency of an image or images, often inexplicable in purely reasonable terms; why should "Mistah Kurtz—he dead" have been tumid with meaning for T. S. Eliot (who used it as an epigraph for "The Hollow Men") if he had not heard some pidgin sorcery in the summing up? Certainly one senses Conrad in Miss Didion's *Democracy;* he has passed through this territory, making trail blazes. The novel seems closer to "Heart of Darkness" than the literal-minded movie *Apocalypse Now* did, which was also trying to talk about the end of Vietnam and unspeakable "horrors," located upriver in the film. One odd development in *Democracy,* though, as compared with any Conrad text, is that the narrator—in Conrad usually the immensely talkative and indeed (dare I say it?) too garrulous Marlow—has been virtually silenced. What the character "Joan Didion" offers us is mainly brisk narration, impossible to construe as comment or rumination, unlike Marlow's chatter, but I shall come back to "Joan Didion" later.

For the moment, I want to forget about the cinematic influences and effects—the freezes and rapid fades and the humming sound track that make themselves felt in whatever she has done since *Run River* (1963)—and concentrate on examining the construction of this particular book as book. Yet here too I am reminded of what one might call an allied art. The construction of *Democracy* feels like the working out of a jigsaw puzzle that is slowly being put together with a continual shuffling and re-examination of pieces still on the edges or heaped in the middle of the design. We have started with a bit of sky (those pink dawns); now and then, without hurry, a new piece is carefully inserted, and the gentle click of cardboard locking into cardboard is felt—no forcing. Despite the fact that the pieces are known to us, face down and face up, almost from the start, there is an intense suspense, which seems to be causeless (no cliff-hanger this, no heroine tied to the railroad tracks), suspense arising from the assembly of the pieces, that is, from the procedures of narrative themselves. "This is a hard story to tell," the author says on page 15. It is a hard story to listen to, boring in the primal sense of the word—"making a hole in or through with a drill." Some parts of it are painful in their own right, shocking (or would have been to Henry Adams's Mrs. Lightfoot Lee), but what mainly hurts is the drilling, the repetition, in short, the suspense of waiting for the narrative line to be carefully played out, the odd-shaped piece inserted.

Here are three successive paragraphs and the start of a fourth from the first page.

"He said to her.

"Jack Lovett said to Inez Victor.

"Inez Victor who was born Inez Christian.

"He said . . ."

And here is a later paragraph, but still from the first pages, when we are getting into the story:

> "Oh shit, Inez," Jack Lovett said one night in the spring of 1975, one night outside Honolulu in the spring of 1975, one night in the spring of 1975 when the C-130s and the C-141s were already shuttling between Honolulu and Anderson and Clark and Saigon all night long, thirty-minute turnaround at Tan Son Nhut, touching down and loading and taxiing out on flight idle, bringing out the dependents, bringing out the dealers, bringing out the money, bringing out the pet dogs and the sponsored bar girls and the porcelain elephants. "Oh shit, Inez," Jack Lovett said to Inez Victor, "Harry Victor's wife."

Important information has just been passed: Harry Victor is "someone," a national celebrity. Before long it turns out that he has been a congressman, a senator, a war opponent, a Presidential candidate, that he has been photographed with Eleanor Roosevelt and Coretta King; the first tip-off that he is also a prize heel comes on page 55. So that phrase, "Oh shit, Inez, Harry Victor's wife," that keeps returning like a refrain is derisive for the one who speaks it—Jack Lovett, an "information specialist" and CIA man, a spook. The refrain comes back over and over, collecting incrementa, like a round. "Scotland's burning, Scotland's burning, Fire fire fire, Pour on water, Pour on water." Or: "Oh shit, Inez. Drop fuel. Jettison cargo. Eject crew. Down the tubes, the bartender said. Bye-bye Danang. Harry Victor's wife."

A round, but better, as I said, a puzzle. The enigma lies in the slow deliberation with which the picture is filled in.

The dialogue (or monologue) begins in the pink light of the Honolulu airport in late March 1975. The atomic tests of 1952, '53 ("Christ they were sweet") are a flashback. On page 29, a shooting is mentioned after some Honolulu social history, after the introduction of "Joan Didion" ("Call me the author"), after the introduction of a swiftly palmed photo of Paul Christian, Inez Victor's father, playing backgammon barefoot with John Huston in Cuernavaca in 1948, followed by a second photo of him—barefoot once more and in handcuffs—taken by a newspaper photographer on March 25, 1975, outside the Honolulu YMCA.

And so, finally, fourteen pages after the first mention, the name Harry Victor comes up again, with the strong indication that the individual referred to is a "name," as evidenced by the *New York Times*'s caption of the photo of the murderer: "Victor Family Touched by Island Tragedy." A few pages later, the group of interlocked pieces entitled Jack Lovett is fitted into the picture. Another flashback presents him as he first looked to the author (in 1960, in a photographer's studio on West 40th Street) when she and Inez Victor were both working on V*ogue*, the author in the features department and Inez Victor in fashion.

Jack Lovett is what was called then "an older man"; the author recalls "thinking that he could be [Inez's] father." Inez Victor is smiling at Jack Lovett in a certain way. "He can't stay," she tells Joan Didion in the V*ogue* photographer's studio. "Because he's running a little coup somewhere. I just bet." A few pages later, there follows a piece of WNBC film taken March 18, 1975, showing Inez Victor dancing at a party on the St. Regis Roof given by the Governor of New York— that would have been Hugh Carey, no? But the date of the network clip, "one week exactly before Paul Christian fired the shots" out in the mid-Pacific, refers to a quite different calendar of events.

Now, the fact is that from 1956 to 1963 Joan Didion did work at *Vogue* in the features department; it is in *Who's Who*. When you consider that Inez Victor, b. Inez Christian, d. Paul and Carol Christian, cannot be found in *Who's Who* or any other book of reference (not even *Who Was Who*), you may find that spooky, more so, actually, than Jack Lovett's occupation. It raises the question "What are we supposed to believe here?" in an uncanny way. Angels and ministers of grace defend us! What is a live fact—Joan Didion—doing in a work of fiction? She must be a decoy set there to lure us into believing that Inez Victor is real in some ghostly-goblin manner, as real anyway as the author herself is. For that purpose, the classic narrator, the fictive "I," could not serve, evidently. Or just seemed dated in a deconstructing universe. Before the end of the novel, in a flash-forward, the author is represented as actually flying to Kuala Lumpur to see Inez Victor, who by that time is working in a camp for refugees, having separated from Harry Victor and their children, Adlai and Jessie, and all their world. Does this mirror a real journey that Joan Didion has pressed into service to meet a fictional need (to end the novel), as other authors are apt to do with loose material that happens to be lying around?

In current theories of fiction, much attention is given to the role of the narrator, considered as sheer verbal device, without correspondence to any anterior reality. Yet if I understand Joan Didion right, here she is doing the exact opposite, inserting an attestable fact—herself—into the moving sands of fiction. I am not sure what the result of the undertaking is. It may well be to diminish the fictional likelihood of "Inez Victor" while leaving the reader to wonder about the reality of "Joan Didion."

In fact, the problem of "originals" haunts this peculiar fiction, intentionally, I should guess. It is an eerie lighting effect, making the strange appear familiar and the familiar

223

strange. At times Harry Victor seems meant to recall one of the Kennedys (most likely Bobby) or all of them. There is a hint of Jack's womanizing, and the suggestion that Inez Victor may have a "drinking problem" brings to mind Teddy and Joan. The new generation of the famous family makes its entry with Jessie Victor's teen-age drug habit. Yet when a flashback to the '72 primaries gives us a quick shot of Harry Victor conceding California (in other words, the ball game), it is a reverse image of 1968 and Eugene McCarthy conceding to Bobby, except that nobody could picture McCarthy as the original of a ruthless power-seeker capable of naming his son Adlai. Naturally, Adlai, who organizes a campus vigil for "the liberation of Saigon" virtually as soon as his voice changes, is a perfect Victor junior.

What is wrong with the Victors, father and son, what is wrong with their multiple originals, can be summed up in a word—celebrity. They are all media divinities, "names," a nominalist's nightmare, mere vocables. "Harry Victor's wife" can only escape the condign punishment that goes with the status by "burying herself" in Kuala Lumpur. Inez Victor's penance is the book's resolution—the final phrase in the canon of "Bye-bye Danang." It is odd how it reminds one of the last act of Eliot's *Cocktail Party*. Celia Coplestone, you remember, a smart-set Londoner, having found her vocation with a penitential order of nurses on an island in the "East," is crucified near an anthill by natives.

I have noted the cinematic quality of Joan Didion's work and the relation of the present construction to puzzles, specifically of the jigsaw kind. I might also have compared the narrative line to a French seam—one big stitch forward, one little stitch back, turn over and repeat on other side of cloth—valued in dressmaking for its strength and for hiding the raw edges of the cloth. Still another set of correspondences is discernible in literary reminiscences and allusions, beginning, obviously, with the title: Henry Adams, Hemingway, Mailer,

Orwell, Wallace Stevens, Delmore Schwartz, A. E. Housman, W. H. Auden, Kierkegaard. The ending must be a pointed reference to Eliot, and on page 16 one has met some lines in italics followed by the words "So Trollope might begin this novel."

This is part of the book's knowingness—not an altogether pleasant quality. The knowingness makes a curious accompaniment to the celebrity theme, for Joan Didion clearly does not care for the celebrity circuit and one of the attractions Jack Lovett has for her—and possibly for Inez too—is that he is not in *Who's Who*, does not have his name on his whiskey bottle in a Hong Kong restaurant (in fact has a false name taped to his quart of Black Label); Jack Lovett is a solitary who drowns in a hotel swimming-pool and is shipped out in a body bag. His profession requires him not to be known and to leave no fingerprints on what he touches.

Still, to be known and to be knowing are not so far apart. Everyone in *Democracy* is some kind of insider. It is not merely the Harry Victors and their entourages; the author herself has some complicity in the insider-outsider game—seven years at *Vogue* leave their mark. In the milieu of this *Democracy*, not just people but places and times can be poker chips: the St. Regis Roof, the Dalton School, Grant Park in Chicago at the '68 convention, where Harry Victor is not shy about getting himself tear-gassed for the camera of a *Life* photographer. But to appreciate that detail, you have to know about Grant Park, and not everybody does. To be knowing about the right names implies, moreover, being knowing about the wrong names—Dow Chemical, Air Asia, Air America. That is very important too.

The names of airports can be spent like coin: Anderson, Clark, Travis, Johnston, besides the old penny-ante ones like Tan Son Nhut. I am not sure where some of these airports are (I guess most of them are in the Pacific) or whether they are military or civilian. But I know that I ought to know. That is the special kind of insecurity—fear of not belonging to a club—that Hemingway had a genius for producing in his readers and in a colleague like Scott Fitzgerald, who even confessed to Ernest that he thought his own penis was too small. The spoor of Hemingway is all over *Democracy*, like the print of the Abominable Snowman. Not your table manners, not even your morals, but saying the wrong thing (as poor Scott Fitzgerald apparently did rather often) excludes one forever.

The greatest sinner in *Democracy* is Harry Victor, who infallibly pronounces sentences like "I've always tried to talk up to the American people. Not down. You talk down to the American people at your peril. . . . Either Jefferson was right or he wasn't. I happen to believe that he was." That "happen to believe" will cook him for all eternity—I agree with Joan Didion there. Yet to my mind, that is insufficient evidence for *artistic* damnation. A man who identifies a ghastly young woman he has brought along to a London dinner party as "a grandniece of the first Jew on the Supreme Court of the United States" condemns himself socially whenever he gives tongue; in real life, with any luck, one could avoid meeting him. But in a novel, once such people are met, I think one has the right to ask to know them better before sending them unpardoned to hell. Is the ear the ultimate moral judge?

For all its technical mastery and on-target social observation (Miss Didion is wonderful not only at hearing her characters but at naming them—take "Inez"), there is a depthlessness in *Democracy* as there was in *A Book of Common Prayer*. We would need to know a Harry Victor from the inside looking out to feel his real hollowness; it is tiring just to listen to his sound track playing over and over. This is true for most of the characters, though with the bit parts the effect is stunning: "'This is a stressful time,' the doctor said," following his previous one-liner, "It might be good to talk about therapy." The bigger role of Jessie, the Victors' teen-aged, heroin-shooting child, does not come off so well; perhaps the unexplained in her (like the manner of her arrival in Saigon without a passport) bulks somewhat too large. To my mind, the best character is Billy Dillon, Harry Victor's aide, who has the good fortune—which is also the reader's—of being a consciously funny man.

But, finally, what is one to make of Jack Lovett, inscrutable by profession from beginning to end? Whatever one decides, one must applaud the author's nerve in making a CIA agent in his sixties the love interest and *parfit gentil knight* of her book. Actually, this is a romantic, even a sentimental novel, with the CIA man and the congressman's wife as a pair of eternally faithful lovers, constantly separated and constantly reunited till his death and burial under a jacaranda tree—after which Inez Christian Victor has only one choice, in essence the choice of Guinevere: to take the veil. Kuala Lumpur is her Almesbury. "Mother Teresa," Billy Dillon dryly observes. That Inez Victor (and her creator) clearly prefer a CIA agent to a famous liberal senator may indicate a preference for action over talk or just a distaste for United States hypocrisy—the larger aims of Harry Victor and of "the store" being at bottom the same. Maybe those are the "cards on the table" that were promised when we first met "Joan Didion" in that early chapter.

Possibly. As I said to start with, the book is deeply enigmatic. For the reader willing to sweat over them, there are a number of half-buried puzzles. One riddling passage, I confess, has been tormenting me for weeks. It appears for the first time on page 18: "So I have no leper who comes to the door every morning at seven. No Tropical Belt Coal Company, no unequivocal lone figure on the crest of the immutable hill."

"Joan Didion" (she is the one talking) seems to mean that as a novelist she lacks some of the reliable old machinery that might have helped her tell her story. On page 78 the thought recurs. Inez is watching her unconscious sister Janet through a glass partition in the third-floor intensive care unit of Queen's Medical Center in Honolulu. Janet is on life support. Inez is still wearing a plumeria lei given her at the Oahu airport. "This scene is my leper at the door," the author tells us, "my Tropical Belt Coal Company, my lone figure on the crest of the immutable hill."

Does the reader recognize anything? For the leper, my friends and I have tried Conrad, Kipling, Graham Greene, Waugh's *Handful of Dust*—in vain. The Tropical Belt Coal Company looks more promising in that it is more specific. That leper could be anywhere. In *The Ten Commandments*, maybe, of Cecil B. De Mille, just as well as in Graham Greene. But no Tropical Belt Coal Company of fiction comes to mind, and indeed it sounds like a joke: Does anyone burn coal in the tropics? Yet coal is mined in Borneo; that is in the world atlas.* As for the figure on the hillcrest, it could be an Indian in any old Western. Perhaps all the elements in the puzzle are out of movies. Perhaps Joan Didion is just wishing that she were an old-time screenwriter rather than a novelist. If that is it, I am irritated. To be portentous, one ought to be deeper than that. I feel a bit like Alice when she heard the Duchess speak calmly of "a large mustard mine near here." Of course, the Duchess could speak calmly because that was Wonderland. And possibly that is the right way to take this latest Joan Didion—calmly, not setting out to solve sphinxine riddles, not looking for influences and analogues,

---

*Numerous readers wrote in to tell me that the Tropical Belt Coal Company is on the first page of Conrad's *Victory*. Yes. And one reader proposed that the leper came out of Flaubert's "St. Julian the Hospitaler." That does not ring a bell for me.

not hoping for the author's sake to exorcise the malign shadow of Hemingway, certainly not asking how Wendell Omura got on Janet's lanai or how, precisely, old Hem, than whom no more elitist writer ever took up pen, could illustrate in his sentence structure any idea of democracy. Just let it go.

April 22, 1984

PREFACES
AND POSTFACES

The American Revolution of Jean-François Revel*

LISTEN TO THE first sentence. "The revolution of the twentieth century will take place in the United States." *Pow!!!* The French reader was already seeing stars when the second sentence hit him. "It can take place nowhere else." Americans may feel bewildered, skeptical, glad, or sorry to hear the news, curious to know more. But you have to be French to get the full impact, the "visceral reaction." Ever since you could count up to ten or spell *c-h-a-t*, you have been secure in the thought that the United States is the citadel of imperialism, racism, vulgarity, conformism. And now a *Frenchman* returns from a voyage of discovery to say it is a hotbed of revolution.

Blandly, with a straight face, the enormity emerges, buttressed by figures and arguments, precedents, citations. Is it a joke? No and yes. It may have started out as a hardy quip or demolishing retort, and somewhere behind these pages Jean-François Revel is still suppressing an inadvertent smile. We, his readers, not required to school our features, laugh out loud in delight. At what exactly? At the French, of course, and their starchy preconceptions, which are being shaken, jostled, disarrayed, like a matron in some old slapstick comedy. But also at the author himself, that expressionless comedian,

*Written as a postface to the American edition of *Ni Marx ni Jésus* by Jean-François Revel.

233

swinging from a precipice, teetering on a tightrope. We laugh at his imperturbability in the presence of his imminent danger, at his reckless aplomb in courting ridicule—the reverse of sympathetic chuckles. He is serious, he protests: "Why are you laughing?"

All Jean-François Revel's books are cliff-hangers. He is a pamphleteer, and his first necessity therefore is to boldly secure attention. Characteristically, in his opening pages he risks being removed from the scene in a strait-jacket. His pamphlets are heresies and they generally result from prolonged exposure to piety. He is restive, like a schoolboy in church, surrounded by hushed worshipers and prompted to commit a sacrilege—stand up and *prove* to them that the Bible cannot be true. His anti-clerical nostrils are quick to detect the slightest smell of incense, and misfortune—or good luck—has placed him in a variety of churches, chapels, oratories, cenacles. He has passed most of his life among the devout.

Gaullist France itself is one huge basilica, consecrated to Glory. The Sorbonne is a monastery from which pilgrims set out for the wayside shrines of the national *lycée* system or go on foreign missions, spreading French culture. Revel started off in clerical disguise. He was an *agrégé* in philosophy and taught first abroad—at the University of Mexico and the University of Florence and at the local French Institutes—later in *lycées* at Lille and Paris: history of philosophy, history of art, French literature, geography.

His first published blasphemy or tale-told-out-of-school was *Pourquoi les philosophes*, an attack on the then reigning gods of French philosophy. Next came *Pour l'Italie*, a tract *against* Italy—for Revel a natural by-product of four years as a lecturer in Florentine classrooms. A simple corrective, he would have said, of Italophilia, a healthy explosion of the whole bag of myths about Italian art, Italian culture, Italian virility, Italian gaiety, good looks, liveliness, all of which he found non-existent, and backed up the verdict with real-life anecdotes and observations, many true, many funny, some brutal, such as the one, which gave much offense to feminine readers of *Epoca*, that Italian women have hair on their legs.

Not a word, I am sure, was invented, and yet the book was biased to a point that someone who loved Italy could have considered almost insane. Or the result of some personal grievance—an idea that was aired in the Italian press at the time and that I rather subscribed to myself simply from reading the book, which has many complaints about the unavailability of Italian girls. Knowing Revel, as I now do, I no longer think that explanation can have been right. There is something wonderfully disinterested about Revel's biases, a joy in bias itself as an artistic form, embracing hyperbole and conducing, finally, to laughter. He has a Falstaffian side and only cares that his "slant" should run counter to respectable culture and received opinion. If he has a personal grievance, it is a long-standing, deeply nurtured one against the immovable forces of entrenched beliefs that insult his sense of the self-evident.

There followed one of his most charming and persuasive works, *Sur Proust*. It is not so much controversial as, again, heretical. Revel loves Proust, which means that he is against orthodox Proustians, including Proust himself at certain moments. He makes the convincing argument that what is good in *A la recherche du temps perdu* is the worldly social side, the human comedy, whereas the "deeper" parts, the philosophy of time and memory, the *madeleine* and so on, are simply commonplaces of French philosophy already out of date at the time Proust wrote and often at variance with the book's real story. I.e., what is considered "superficial" in Proust is profound, and vice versa.

At this point in Revel's career, it might have been said that
the man was simply an attention-seeker, moving lightly from
field to field, in search of provocative positions to occupy and
abandon, a journalistic *enfant terrible* or disgruntled academic whose formula was to assert the opposite of what
"everybody" was saying. This would have been to ignore the
solidity and breadth of his learning but, more than that, to
mistake the impetus behind his contrariness, the irrepressible
spirit of contradiction that guides him, like a dowser, in the
hope of striking truth.

Self-dramatization, eagerness for the spotlight must count
very low among Revel's motivations. He has some traits in
common with Shaw (he was once meditating a book against
Shakespeare) but totally lacks Shaw's theatrical vanity and Irish
flair for personal publicity. Unlike Shaw, Revel does not play
the sage, ready for consultation by newsmen on all manner
of subjects; no Isadora Duncans, so far as I know, have been
asking to have babies by him. He is not a highly advertised
"brain," in fact makes no pretensions to having anything more
than common garden intelligence; if he is different from the
majority, he would say, it is only because he is not ashamed
to be caught using that very ordinary faculty—the natural light
of reason.

Far from being a star or aspiring to prominence, Revel
is very much the citizen, a bourgeois in the old Enlighten-
ment sense of the term—a townsman, fond of domestic tranquillity and the arts of peace and commerce. His nature appears placid, benevolent, easy-going, sentimental, that of a
private householder going about his business, reading his
newspaper without the expectation of finding his own name
in it, an urban Cincinnatus. He has a round, flat "Dutch"
face (though he is of pure French blood) that looks as if it
had seen service in the battles of William the Silent against
the Spanish oppressor. It is a moon face; indeed there seem

236

to be several moons perspicaciously turning in its dial, like in one of those grandfather clocks that keep track of astronomical time. He is a bettor and likes to go to the races, wears a gray suit and carries a briefcase.

Despite the stir of indignation excited by some of his broadsides, his person does not inspire fear or cause a swift turning of heads in a restaurant. His picture, in *L'Express* every week over his column, has something bullish about it, the broad-browed, head-lowered promise of some intransigent charge into the arena, and yet it is a *good* bull, scarcely more than a rambunctious steer. He is occasionally seen on television and once ran for office (Cincinnatus called from the plow) on the Federated Left ticket in the suburban district of Neuilly—not his natural territory. He came in a bad third, behind the Gaullist and the Communist. Notwithstanding the weekly photo in a mass-circulation magazine, his "image" somehow, as if from modesty, retires from circulation; if polled, fewer Parisians could identify J.-F. Revel in the rogue's gallery of current celebrities than could identify Robbe-Grillet, Marguerite Duras, Roland Barthes, Michel Rocard, Alain Krivine, or the man, *"La Reynière,"* who writes the restaurant column in *Le Monde*. Not to mention J.-P. Sartre, J.-J. Servan-Schreiber, Simone de Beauvoir, Jean-Luc Godard, etc.

Yet in terms of meritorious service in the combat against General de Gaulle and Gaullism, the outstanding antagonist was surely not any of the above-named opinion leaders, left or center, nor François Mitterand, nor Lecanuet, but Jean-François Revel. His spirit of contrariety found in the General its absurd predestined windmill to tilt at indefatigably. Three brilliant pamphlets sprang from his pen: *Le style du Général, En France: la fin de l'opposition, Lettre ouverte à la droite.* He slew de Gaulle again and again, and if the General had more lives than a cat and more heads than a hydra, that did not really daunt Jean-François, though he publicly confessed to battle weariness. In fact, like the deathless General himself, he came back refreshed, reinvigorated, having found a new point of attack, new weapons, generally captured from the enemy camp.

He is still fighting, this time on the left flank. *Ni Marx ni Jésus*, where the old Gaullist bugbear, the United States, is tenderly embraced as an ally, suddenly discovered, in the struggle, is another engagement with the adversary, resurgent in the form of Georges Pompidou, and that adversary's eternal cohorts, as Revel sees them, of the French Communist Party and the splinter grouplets of the left. If the emphasis here is more on the vacuities of the left, old and new, than it was in some of the preceding pamphlets, it is only a *shift* of emphasis.

From start to finish, Revel has seen the so-called left as the right's accomplice, and vice versa, two sides of the same worn coin—an agreement to perpetuate the status quo. What he holds against both right and left is their joint blocking the way to any real social advance. I am not sure whether Revel, like Shaw, believes in a theory of socialism, but at least during his short electoral career he was running on a Socialist ticket. Certainly he is a democrat and egalitarian. To him, plainly, right-left in France is a symbiosis mutually advantageous to both parties and deathly to human liberty. Or as de Gaulle is supposed to have said of Jean-Paul Sartre: "*Sartre, c'est aussi la France.*"

De Gaulle is France, Sartre is France, the CGT and the Communists are France. France, for Revel, is a suspended solution in which all these elements refuse either to precipitate or to dissolve. What Revel is fighting, single-handed, is "France," which has become to him the arch-symbol of all those forces of inertia that the original Adam in him felt bound to contradict when he still thought their locus might be Shakespeare or the obscurantist jargon of the Sorbonne chapel of philosophy. He is somewhat more indulgent toward the

238

young Maoists, Trotskyites, and Castroites because they are
young and the objects of a judicial campaign of terror, backed
up by riot squads. But for him they too are "France," in the
unreality of their perspectives, doctrinaire slogans, and practical failure to get anything done.

Sometimes one feels that Revel, as an infant, was nurtured
in a debating school where the training consisted of being
obliged to take the negative of such seemingly unassailable
propositions as: The earth is round; Proust was a snob; Fresh
air is good for you; Travel broadens the mind. And where daily
exercise in the gymnasium meant standing on their heads
maxims like "War is a continuation of politics by other means"
(*Without Marx or Jesus*, "Foreign policy is an initiation of
war by other means").

This would not be such a bad school for educating not
mere mental contortionists versed in paradox but free minds.
There is always the possibility that the exact opposite of what
you think (or think you think) may be true. At least it is worth
trying on for size, and experiment will show that the converse
of many dogmas, once stated, appear to be just as plausible
as the original. Moreover, anything repeated a sufficient
number of times has a natural tendency to upend itself, as
though obeying some physical law of balance, like a Carte-
sian devil or a Mexican jumping bean. E.g., if I hear often
enough "Poverty is no crime," I feel an urge to reply "Poverty *is* a crime," meaning that it is against the laws of humanity or that to be poor is to be already two-thirds of a
criminal in the eyes of the police.

In reality few propositions are entirely true and many are
lucky if they contain a grain of truth. Thus automatically to
take the opposite of any received idea, say, that Proust was a
snob or that the United States is the citadel of world reaction,
is almost bound to disclose unexpected evidence to the contrary. The danger in such operations is to mistake those grains

of truth newly brought to light for the whole truth and to fall into a reverse orthodoxy, which will not long have the merit of being your own private opinion or stubborn form of dissent but will soon be on "everybody's" lips. Far from being free to perceive what is there, outside, you are suddenly the captive of your own heresy and the adherents you have gained for it, many of whom have drawn near to listen from self-interested motives or simple love of novelty.

I do not think Revel has altogether escaped this danger in *Without Marx or Jesus*. Less than in his earlier polemics. The reason is that previously he stood virtually alone, his back to the wall, with not many more "voices" in his favor than he found to vote for him in Neuilly in 1967. But here the ally he has embraced in the shape of the United States is likely to smother him with warm moist grateful kisses. Even before U.S. publication, you can already hear those smacks resounding from the pages of *Time* and *Newsweek*. And in the French press, surprisingly, there have been quite a few huzzas. Only on the ultra-right and the ultra-left has the book been savaged. The Communist press, though naturally critical of his un-Marxist approach, has been remarkably unvituperative, no doubt because Revel's views, on some domestic issues, coincide with their own policy of parliamentary "opposition" and reprehension of extra-legal and guerrilla tactics. The fact that Revel is offering a happily distant, transatlantic alternative to the awful specter of helmeted local revolutionaries armed with Molotov cocktails and shrieking a Maoist or Castroite gospel must appeal to readers of *L'Humanité* as much as to readers of *Figaro* and *France-Soir*.

That is not Revel's fault, and if his thesis is true, it does not matter who takes comfort from it. Besides, if the French middle classes relax in the assurance that the revolution can only take place in America, they may get a surprise. More curious, and for Revel perhaps more disquieting, is that the

French reviews paid almost exclusive attention to the "positive" sections of the book, those dealing with the United States, and virtually ignored the "negative" sections, those dealing with France. Yet to my mind these contain some of his most splendid tirades, his highest comedy, and most acute observations: e.g., Pompidou rebounding from rough American reporters to deferential French journalists is as good as a play.

Up to now, the complaint about Revel's pamphleteering has been that it is "negative." "Why does he have to tear down?" and so on. He answered the judgment at length in the final section of *La Cabale des dévots*, where his defense rested on the common-sense argument, How can you expect me to be positive about a negative?—in that case the calamitous and self-satisfied state of French philosophy.

Of course his defense was right. The insistence on "constructive criticism" has no place in intellectual discussion. According to that notion, one could never "damn" a play, a picture, or a poem without putting in its place another play, picture, or poem, as though it were a question of an inventory and the withdrawal of one article from the common stock demanded immediate replenishment to maintain a constant level. A false equation is made with the necessities of practical life, where if I declare that the doctor treating a patient is a quack, I am under some slight obligation to try to find a more reliable man to speed to the bedside or the operating table. The idea that all doctors are quacks, true or not, is insupportable to a sick person but quite supportable in argument.

Without Marx or Jesus, however, breaks with Revel's critical habit by offering a positive model, the United States, to offset the otherwise gloomy picture he draws of mankind's revolutionary perspectives. If it were not for the United States, he is at pains to show, they would be nil. No hope. But why, one might ask, is a revolution called for? Why not gradual evolution? It is true that the world situation appears so grim, that to the emotions only a revolution seems capable of altering it for the better; we hope for a revolution as desperate peoples in the past hoped for a miracle to save them when all other resources had run out—battalions of angels flying in from the sky, manna flowering in the desert. A revolution *is* a sort of miracle, a widening crack in the social crust that is finally perceived to be an earthquake, and, like a miracle, it is outside the laws of prediction, except from the point of view of hindsight.

Given the common desperation, Revel can be excused for foreseeing a revolution in the United States, since he cannot see one in the offing anywhere else. But to *argue* it is something different. At the risk of being destructive myself, I would say that his "revolution" is only a metaphor, a play on words. If he means that the United States is different from the stereotype of it in French thought and that some changes are taking place there whose repercussions are already being felt elsewhere (the Berkeley Free Speech uprising anticipating "May" in Paris by nearly four years), then he is not saying anything very revolutionary, except perhaps to French ears.

I agree that draft refusal, dropping out, Woodstock, the drug culture, the Panthers, Women's Lib, the Yippies, concern about the environment, the back-to-Nature movement, open admissions to universities show that the United States is "ahead" of all its partners in the West, if that can be taken as a value-free term rather than a blanket endorsement, for we are also "ahead" in sophisticated weaponry. I agree too that all this diverse effervescence may add up to some kind of transformation already as alarming to most people over forty as a universal bomb threat.

Very likely, as Revel says, American traditions embodied in the Bill of Rights and an old history of civil disobedience going back to 1776 have favored these developments, although the very rootedness of those traditions or folkways could suggest the opposite of his conclusion, suggest, that is, that they are not very exportable. It seems to be easier to transplant Coca-Cola than hominy grits or habeas corpus. But in any case to propose that these changes are a revolution is to detonate images of the taking of the Bastille, the Carmagnole, Trees of Liberty, the storming of the Winter Palace, the shot-heard-round-the-world. The reader sometimes feels that he is poring over a rosy positive print of the negative that met the eyes of Attorney General Mitchell's wife, Martha, when she looked out her Washington window and saw a mob of "the very liberal Communists"—the Mobilization marchers against the war in Vietnam—and thought she was in St. Petersburg in October 1917.

Revel is of course careful to explain that he does not mean what everybody else means by a revolution, that most of what we call revolutions were really aborted revolts, e.g., the Paris Commune, the Russian Revolution, the Chinese Revolution, the Hungarian Revolution, which were either totally defeated or failed to achieve their ends and bogged down in tyranny. He believes that up to now there has been only one revolution—that which effectively took place in France, England, and the American colonies in the latter half of the eighteenth century (having originated in England in the seventeenth) and which, despite many setbacks, eventually replaced the old order by new democratic institutions.

One wonders, though, whether by his own strict criteria that protracted spasm was not also an aborted revolt, since many of its objectives have failed to this day to be realized, not only on a world-wide basis but in the countries where the whole thing started: The Rights of Man remain in large part on paper, like the Soviet Constitution, and equality is still a dream. So far as I can see, if one accepts Revel's definitions, the only successful revolution, up to now, has been the Industrial Revolution. . . .

243

If Revel does not mean what everybody else means by the word, why use it, unless to startle and amuse? Why not find another word, such as reform? Reform, in its root sense, is what Jean-François is actually talking about: a reshaping of society. He does not have in mind a violent overturn but a renovation brought about largely by legal means, such as strikes, marches, and boycotts, with little bloodshed and with a strong dose of voluntarism. Possibly this gradual evolution will take place in America. The trouble is, Revel does not say *how* in political terms, and that is what counts for us Americans.

Perhaps he expects politics to wither away. If in the future the young drop-outs of the counterculture do not vote, then voting will become a mainly ceremonial activity (which it is now, in a sense), engaged in by oldsters until they die off, and the Nixons of the future will be something like constitutional monarchs, useful for meeting their opposite numbers at airports, signing bills, redecorating the White House, throwing the first baseball of the year into the Washington stadium. . . . The Agnews would preside over the slumbrous Senate, another honorific body, like the House of Lords, and give employment to jokesters and makers of hate-dolls. Meanwhile the real majority life of revolutionized America would proceed undisturbed in communes and on campuses in a polyracial, polysexual ambience.

The drawback to this fantasy (my own variation on Revel's theme) is that the intervening steps are not clear. Who arranges the transfer of power? What do we do in '72? If there is nobody possible to vote for, which seems likely, what action do we take? While the occupant of the White House is gradually being defused, he still has his enfeebled hands on the levers of destruction. There still is such a thing as capitalism.

Revel bases much of his hope on the fact, indeed impressive, that the protest movement drove Johnson from office. Yes. But it did not end the war. The sad truth seems to be that whatever else the protest movement can accomplish—organizing marches and student strikes, draft-card burnings, moratoria, sending resisters to Canada and deserters to Sweden, blocking defense-research contracts in universities, promoting beards and long hair, the sale of love beads, pot consumption—what it cannot accomplish is the very purpose that brought it into being.

It looks as if *nothing* inside the country can do that, short of revolution (and not the gradual kind Jean-François means) or a massive economic depression. Or the second leading to the first. There, again, is the rub. One of the factors he considers essential for the renovation he postulates—a steady high growth rate—is the obstacle to even such a small step in a forward direction as withdrawal from Vietnam. On the one hand, the certainty of American technical superiority rules out for the Presidential mind the very thought of defeat or "surrender." On the other, American prosperity makes the country feel it can tolerate the war as it can put up with taxes, airport congestion, smog—the cost argument, repeatedly voiced by the war's critics, has never made the slightest impression, and as for morality, the scaling down of U.S. casualties, the changing of the color of the body count have allowed Nixon to do practically as he pleases. If, as Revel says, a large section of affluent youth is disgusted by the consumer society, the great majority of the country is not. Until something more than moral dissatisfaction with the ruling values is felt, the war will go on and expand.

Besides, Revel is too intelligent not to perceive and point out the flaw in his own argument, which in logic amounts to this: if turned-off youth drops out in increasing numbers, the growth rate will fall to zero, and one of his necessary preconditions for successful revolution will no longer be present. If its numbers fail to increase, then drop-out youth will remain a marginal phenomenon, which present society can afford or else move to repress. Revel does not follow up on this reasoning, but the consequence, it seems to me, is to be driven back to one of the old Marxist models and trust that an upheaval leading to renovation will come out of a capitalist crisis and not as an accompaniment of steady capitalist growth.

Perhaps it will never come, by that route or any other. Yet I do not wish to be forced by Revel's ineluctable logic into agreeing that if the revolution—whatever that is—does not take place in the United States, it will not take place anywhere. For an American, that is too discouraging a vista. And though Revel has proved to himself with dialectical relish that there can be no issue but that one, he is, again, too intelligent, too empirical, too in fact enamored of freedom not to be aware that any demonstration, no matter how rigorous, is only a demonstration.

If this little book is taken as a pamphlet, with all that connotes of provocation, surprise attack, deftness, rapidity, polemical sparkle, it will have done its work of disturbing—agitprop. But if American readers are led by it to believe that a Second Coming is materializing in the California desert, they will have misunderstood. They will be more right if they suspect that the "America" discovered by Columbus-Revel is an imagined and imaginary country, the antipodes of "France," though having many points of coincidence, naturally, with the homeland they know.

Revel is a satirist in the tradition of Montesquieu's *Lettres persanes*, Voltaire's *Lettres philsophiques sur les anglais*, *Gulliver's Travels*. Like these fabulists, he contrasts the institutions of his native country with institutions affirmed to exist among some ideal race of beings thought by the vulgar to be savages—the Persians, the English, noble horses. There is something of Molière in him too *(Les Précieuses ridicules)*; the French sections of the book constitute a delicious comedy

246

of manners. That was true also of *En France* and *Lettre ouverte à la droite*. For Americans, *Without Marx or Jesus* can be the occasion for a reciprocal discovery—of Jean-François Revel as a writer.

September 2, 1971

On F. W. Dupee[*]

"I HAVE *liked* being miscellaneous," Dupee roundly declares in the foreword to *The King of the Cats* (1965), sounding a note of defiance, of boyish stubbornness, where to the ear of a different author an apology might have been called for. "Fred" was taking his stand as a literary journalist, a *flâneur*, a stroller, an idle saunterer, in an age of academic criticism, of "field" specialists on the one hand and fanatic "close readers" on the other. The shorter pieces of *The King of the Cats*, originally written for magazines, seem at first to bear out the confession. He turns from the letters of Dickens to a life of Sir Richard Burton, to Behrman's reminiscences of Max Beerbohm, to "the secret life of Edward Windsor," to the letters of Yeats, to Kafka's letters to a Czech woman he was going to bed with, to Chaplin's autobiography. Quite a variety.

Yet Dupee was no butterfly, no moth singeing his wings at the flame of letters, no boulevardier. Or, rather, all that random sensuous delectation was both real and a masquerade. *The King of the Cats* was less miscellaneous than it appeared. It was not a series of peeps into literary shop windows where the mannequins were being undressed—stately Henry James, naughty Nabokov, Charlie the Tramp. In all its di-

---

[*]A preface to a new, University of Chicago Press edition of *The King of the Cats*.

versity that collection had a remarkable unity, which may or may not have been intentional—a unity of matter as well as of manner and style. Even the most fugitive of those essays (and there is always something fugitive, some touch of "light housekeeping" in Dupee's approach) is pinned down by slender ties to its fellows like Gulliver stoutly bound by the Lilliputians. The point in common, the *trait d'union*, is that Dupee's "remarks," as he called them, tended to be about letters of authors, biographies of authors (La Rochefoucauld, Sir Richard Burton), autobiographies of non-authors (Chaplin, the Duke of Windsor), late works of authors (Thomas Mann, James Agee), rather than about the primary work of authors. The big exceptions were Gertrude Stein, Proust, Nabokov, and Robert Lowell's *Life Studies*, which fitted, however, into the over-all Dupee pattern by being, itself, a prose-verse hybrid of autobiography and self-portraiture.

No doubt the unity I speak of was partly imposed by editors, who "typed" Dupee as they do any regular contributor. He was the right man to send a volume of Casanova to, a posthumous work of Jim Agee's (he *knew* him; they were friends through Dwight Macdonald), anything marginally to do with James, Proust, or Kafka, and, above all, any curio coming to light in the collector's corners of literature, e.g., a new, unexpurgated translation of Petronius's *Satyricon*. The only misfit (from that point of view) I find in *The King of the Cats* is a review of J. F. Powers's *Morte d'Urban*. Had I been an editor at *Partisan Review* then, I would not have thought of Powers as Dupee material. The Middle West, a golf-playing, Chevrolet-driving, go-getter of a Catholic priest?—I would have sent it to James T. Farrell or myself. But maybe Dupee *asked* for the book, seeing Powers as a *writer* rather than as a chronicler of Catholic rectories. Nevertheless the piece, even more so than its companion, a review of Bernard Malamud's *Idiots First*, seems a bit out of place in a collection so unconcerned with grading current fiction. Malamud too would hardly have been a "natural" for Dupee were it not for a curious resemblance noticed by him (and by no one else, surely) between *The Assistant* and *The Golden Bowl*. But there was something else: in the Chagall-like, Orthodox Malamud, Dupee had found an intriguing quality that he had already sensed in the Roman Catholic Powers—that of being *by choice* an outsider, a marginal figure, a minority, in the contemporary republic of letters, whose insiders at the moment of writing were Heller, Burroughs, Pynchon.

The essential art of Dupee is defined by himself in the foreword to *The King of the Cats* as literary portraiture. His models for that, he tells us, were Sainte-Beuve and Macaulay. More generally as influences he cites Gide, Mencken, the early T. S. Eliot, and Edmund Wilson. That is clear; it shines through his work with a wonderful perspicuity, and the visible line of descent going back to a vanishing-point is a beauty of his criticism: every debt is gladly acknowledged, and if he with his favorites occupies a slightly larger space than his masters lined up behind, that is only the law of perspective, which requires the present to come forward.

Modesty is one of his critical traits, and he is mannerly too: in the new, augmented collection of his work there is only *one* unfavorable review ("Leavis and Lawrence"); it advances the mild, sidelong suggestion that Leavis is a philistine. "What arrogant nonsense, one is tempted to say, while at the same time remarking on the amazing persistence and tortuous transformations of the philistine spirit in English letters."

The virtual absence of adverse comment is no sign of laxity. Luckily too his reviews are not free of mischief, even of delicate malice, as when he observes of Robert Lowell that Boston became "his Lake Country" and that the prose of *Life Studies* is "malign and dazzling." I am not sure whether it was mischief or malice that led him to say that there was something of the eternal bachelor in Yeats (and how true that was of Lady Gregory's star boarder!). Certainly a gleeful mischief dictated the following: "There are old photographs of Burton—dark, beetle-browed, his left cheek deeply scarred where a Somali warrior had put a spear through it, his gaze intensified by what is surely the Evil Eye, his moustaches six inches long and good for twirling. Such photographs suggest those sometimes reproduced on the jackets of books by our scarier contemporaries, Fiedler or Mailer." Blunter and less characteristic is: "*New Poets of England and America* [an anthology] assists us in penetrating the apparent anonymity, not to say nonentity, of the youthful band of men and women who make verse under these circumstances."

"He's French, you see," Edmund Wilson used to emphasize in his roaring voice, meaning, I suppose, that continental sophistication ran in the Dupee blood, making him suaver than his fellow *PR* editors—Rahv and Phillips and Dwight Macdonald. I don't know how much French blood Fred really had—perhaps a quarter or an eighth, certainly not as much as Wilson liked to imagine. In the distant past, Fred thought, the name had been "Dupuis." A true Middle Westerner, from Joliet, Illinois, he had no more command of spoken French than Wilson and probably less of the written language. I doubt that it was his major field at Yale. Yet he was almost fatally attracted to French literature, starting with Stendhal. (I never heard him speak of the old authors, not even the likely ones— Montaigne, Louise Labé, Maurice Scève. The exception was Rousseau, maybe not surprisingly in view of the *Confessions*. And there was also, I suddenly remember, Chateaubriand: *Mémoires d'outre-tombe*.) For *PR* in the early days, his undisputed "field" was French culture and politics.

Our interest in Gide was spurred mainly by him. At least it was at his urging that in *PR* we published Gide's second thoughts on his trip to the Soviet Union, which I translated.

And he was very much aware of Sartre—the Sartre of *Le Mur* and *La Nausée* in preference to the philosopher. When existentialism came in, after the war, our French specialist turned into William Barrett, who knew philosophy, the modern kind, and was able to read *L'Etre et le néant*. But Dupee remained the magazine's authority on Malraux and the aesthetics of action; I remember a very long article, in several parts, I think, that he was writing on Malraux and could not seem to finish. Composition was hard for him then. There was no question with him of a "writing block," like the one Dwight Macdonald got when the wind of radicalism went out of his sails, but the act of writing was painful, and Malraux was his most agonizing subject. He did finally finish that study, shortly after we had despaired. But he did not choose to reprint it in *The King of the Cats* or schedule it for inclusion in the present collection.

The truth was, he wrote extremely well. I do not think that we on *PR* were fully conscious of that. Knowing the pain he suffered over those pieces, we were conscious of the process rather than of the result. Only now, reading the essays over, I see how brilliant they are in what appears to be an effortless way. He is amusing, observant, nonchalant. The tone is that of conversation. The continuing flashes of insight appear almost casually, like heat lightning. There are many offhand lines, let drop as it were negligently, in an undertone. Kafka's letters are reminders of "the lost art of being unhappy." James Baldwin's sentences "suggest the ideal prose of an ideal literary community, some aristocratic France of one's dreams." Writing of *Pale Fire*, he lightly observes that Nabokov has made a "team" of the poet and the novelist in himself. Recalling James Agee, he mentions the Luce connection and lets fall the dreadful phrase "captive genius," without stress, without follow-up. In his essay on "difficulty" (a theme that recently took George Steiner a whole book to deal with), he calmly wonders whether "a high degree of dif-

ficulty is not an aspect of the modern poetic style just as a
peculiarly brilliant and aggressive clarity was a stylistic aspect
of the school of Pope." And, of Flaubert, very simply: "He
lived amid a clutter of dormant manuscripts."

He has a wonderful gift for quotation, bearing witness to a
memory stuffed with luscious plums, which he pulls out one
by one for our benefit. He gets his title for the 1965 collection from words Yeats is supposed to have spoken on hearing
from his sister that Swinburne was dead: "I know, and now I
am king of the cats." The quotations he pulls out often have
juicy traces of anecdote clinging to them, e.g., the following,
drawn from Burton's "Terminal Essay" to his translation of
The Arabian Nights: "How is it possible for a sodomite Mos-
lem prince to force a Christian missionary against his will and
the strong resistance instinctively put up by his sphincter
muscle? Burton could tell us: by the judicious use of a tent
peg."

Dupee's criticism, in fact, is strongly anecdotal throughout. That is what gives it worldliness—both kinds, the terres-
trial and the social. As he came to understand this of himself
as a literary artist, we can watch his work grow. In his unsur-
passed essay on *L'Education sentimentale*—one of the last
pieces he published—he asserts the sovereignty of the anecdote for a kind of new and modern epic, whose nature is
"mock" or comic. The enthronement of the anecdotal means
that the work affirming it will be flooded with irony. Flaubert's feat in *L'Education* was "to have made an epic novel
out of an accumulation of anecdotes." It follows that "each
episode extracts from the situation a maximum of irony and
then, having made its point with a precision consonant with
its brevity, is caught up in the furious current of the envel-
oping narrative." This accords with the mood of drift, so terribly modern, so twentieth-century, that pervades *L'Education*, which might have been subtitled "The Story of a Drifter,"

just as well as "The Story of a Young Man." No doubt it means something that our first glimpse of Frédéric Moreau is on a river boat that is bringing him home from Paris to Nogent-sur-Seine; he is susceptible to tidal currents, the ebb and flow of the age, the eddies of art and politics, and the net effect of the novel is of a general purposelessness. Dupee likens it to Joyce in its rigorous impersonality but distinguishes it from Joyce by the coldness Flaubert shows toward his characters, in comparison to which Joyce is "warm."

In this late and splendidly written essay, we seem to see Dupee at last finding himself. Always brilliant, succinct, intelligent, informative, "French," in Wilson's word, here he is decidedly more—emotionally moving, electric. I had often suspected, fancifully, that Fred identified himself with Frédéric Moreau, a bit because of the name and a bit because he too, in his younger years, had known "the melancholy of steamboats," if not in the most literal sense. But this penetrating essay is an act of total self-recognition (if Frédéric is Flaubert, he is also, transparently, Fred); it is the apotheosis of a wry, self-observing nature, and, as always happens at such moments of confrontation, the reader feels caught in the mirror too.

There is little left here of his faithful old models, Macaulay, Mencken, and the others. In some respect, even before this, he had left Wilson, his immediate mentor, behind: in the Gertrude Stein essay (cf. the *Axel's Castle* handling of her); in the several essays on Nabokov and *Lolita*; in the Samuel Butler foreword ("In Butler, the man and the writer were entangled as the drowning man is entangled with his rescuer"), which, after the Flaubert, is my favorite and shows a fineness of intuition of which Wilson with his wounds and bows was incapable; finally in his sympathetic short book on James (cf. Wilson on "The Turn of the Screw"). The difference, as I see it, is that Wilson took on himself the "heavy," huffing-and-puffing role of educator to his readers while Dupee made himself into a teacher in real life, first at Bard, then at Columbia, and in his writings did not seek to instruct but instead learned from his subject with a jaunty grace. The result was the sense of a mind and personality growing that buoys us up as we reach the end of this volume, knowing regretfully there will be no more. And it is perhaps not complete chance that the visible growth of Dupee coincides with the birth of the *New York Review* (1963), where he had not only a more amused, appreciative, in short, more sympathetic audience in Barbara Epstein and Robert Silvers but also more space. The earliest essay in the new collection that seems unmistakably and uniquely his is from the *New York Review:* the Burton portrait—"Sir Richard and Ruffian Dick." Moreover, it was in the *New York Review* that the final, Flaubert, essay appeared.

One aspect of Dupee I miss in what I have been saying is the side that—after Yale, after a short-lived little magazine called the *Miscellany* he and Dwight Macdonald edited with another friend, after a year of semi-slumming in Mexico—became an organizer for the Communist Party on the New York waterfront and concurrently literary editor of the *New Masses*. I do not see where a CP "streak" in him fits, unless he got it from the *Zeitgeist*, like a thirties Frédéric Moreau. He was always against authority, but that fails to explain it—the Party was authority incarnate. It was at some *good* urging, I now feel, that he joined and bravely passed out leaflets. He wanted to be helpful to our poor, foolish, grotesque old society. Could that have had something to do with coming from Joliet, which after all is a prison town? Prison towns are sinister and hateful, and in Marxism he may have seen a set of burglar's tools to smuggle past the guards to the inmates. You cannot grow up in the shadow of prison walls without a few generous daydreams of escape for those inside.

Maybe so, but I wonder where the boyish idealism *went*

when the Party let him down. Stalinism, now advertising it-self as twentieth-century Americanism, had shown its colors in the Moscow trials and the Spanish betrayal, and it was not too hard for Macdonald to convince him to leave the Party and the *New Masses*, taking the correspondence files with him. He appeared blithe about it; indeed, nobody breaking with Stalinism ever seemed to suffer regrets. And his sojourn there with Trachtenberg's "boys" had not been long: I first met him, just back from Mexico, at a party to raise money for the sharecroppers, given by Macdonald in 1935; by 1937, at the second congress of the League of American Writers, he was on our side. And I don't think he lost his idealism in the course of that adventure. It must have turned into an underground stream, making his teaching (he was very popular) fertile. Was it out of pure non-conformity that he never got his Ph.D.? I cannot find the idealism, as such, in his later writing. But it may be its long-term effects I notice in the growth indicators exuberantly branching and swelling in his later work. In 1968, anyway, at Columbia during the student strike, he risked some brand-new dentistry to join a line of faculty drawn up to pro-tect another group of "boyish idealists" from the forces of or-der and got a black eye for doing so.

October 27, 1983

256

The Paradox of History*

WHEN THIS BRILLIANT, searching book was brought out in England in 1970, it got generally respectful, even laudatory reviews, which differed from each other only in their degree of deafness to what the author was saying. To his misfortune, "Signor Chiaromonte" had run up against British practicality, empiricism, dread of abstraction—all aspects of Blimpishness. In *The Paradox of History* a man was visibly *thinking* about his topic, musing, almost meditating, not English practice in expository prose: if you want to muse and ponder, verse is your medium.

The reviewers felt fairly sure—if not quite positive—of what Chiaromonte was getting at. Anthony Powell (*A Dance to the Music of Time*) put it in his own plain English. "What have we got to do about it all?" he summed up on behalf of the reader. In other words, what does this Italian recommend doing in a thoroughly bad situation when "things have got finally and totally out of hand through a combination of action, blind interpretation of history and doctrinaire theory"? Some people might call for "something positive" to combat "the . . . political abstractions of Communism/Fascism, and their aggressive tactics," but not Chiaromonte, if Powell has

*To serve as postface to a University of Pennsylvania Press publication (Fall 1985) of a book by Nicola Chiaromonte.

understood him. In reality Chiaromonte has been proposing that we accept the fact that the world and our perception of it are "only fragments of an eternally impenetrable whole," and Powell, God bless him, "take[s] that to mean" that "Mr. Chiaromonte thinks we are much better rubbing along as best we can, dealing with problems as and when they arise, rather than committing ourselves to more oppressive theory."

Another reviewer concluded, more cautiously, that Chiaromonte "has set himself a problem which is central to the contemporary human predicament and will continue to be so, as long as men are unable to resolve it. Nicola Chiaromonte does not claim to have done so; what he has done brilliantly and convincingly," etc., etc. Still a third, writing in the *Times Literary Supplement*, saw disturbing evidence of "fatalism" in Chiaromonte and/or the writers discussed, fatalism being the conviction that events "do not cause each other: all of them are independently caused by some single, external, superhuman agency of which human beings are merely blind instruments." Absorbed in his private nursery game of dividing fatalists between optimists and pessimists (Dr. Pangloss, I guess, would be an optimistic fatalist), the reviewer failed to notice that the "blind instrument" notion was expressly and vigorously rejected by Chiaromonte. A few sentences later the *Times Literary Supplement* was cheerily reassuring the reader: "There is no need to feel disappointment that Mr. Chiaromonte veers sharply to a pessimistic conclusion." An "interim judgment," surely; given time, there was every reason to hope that Chiaromonte would change his outlook. Finally, a writer in *Tribune*, i.e., a Labourite, voiced a sorrowful suspicion: "Chiaromonte's prescription for twentieth-century nihilism . . . would appear to be some kind of religious commitment."

All these reviews, wherever they sprang from, right, left, or center, had one thing in common: a "problem-solving" approach. That in itself may explain the above absurdities, since if there is any predictable result that the reading of this small volume might lead to, it would be loss of faith in arriving at results through an act of thought, however prolonged. Yet results, prescriptions, solutions, remedies, optimists vs. pessimists, "What are we to do"?—the whole vocabulary of those reviews speaks of a cultural gulf, not to say chasm, between audience and writer. One feels that the reviewer ought to have been told to remove his pack of preconceptions on the threshold of this experience, as shoes are removed on entering a mosque or Japanese restaurant.

It is too bad, I think, looking back, that this deeply thoughtful and original six-part essay should have been exposed at its launching to the well-meaning philistinism of the English educated class. Fortunately this reissue, in our different climate, offers the book—and its readers—another chance. We Americans have our share of British-style insularity, but not to the same point of saturation. Other strains— ethnic, racial, religious—have made our reviewers, when literate, less resistant by instinct to abstract ideas, indeed in some cases not resistant enough. Nor are we as deadly empirical as the English, even though pragmatism is supposed to be our national faith. It will be interesting to see how Chiaromonte's thought (so very well translated, by himself with his wife's help) will "take" in this country.

Yet, before going on, I want to say a final word about the English press reception of *The Paradox of History*. The odd fact is that the book is anti-abstract, empirical, non-theoretic. In all his writing and throughout his life (he died in 1972), Chiaromonte was always a stubborn rebel against the dictates of theory. Of course what was abstraction to him could be demonstrable reality for another mind—and vice versa. For example, the notion of material progress, so palpable and on the whole desirable to everyone else, to Chiaromonte was not only odious but also an immaterial illusion or, at best, a theoretical conception requiring careful testing to determine its actual existence. Similarly, the "arcane but ubiquitous realm beyond the world of events," which for him was the realm of Fate for the very practical reason that, by definition, it was the enormous realm of the unknown, might be dismissed by others as pure mystic claptrap, for an almost identical reason, *because it could not be known.*

The relativeness of all this, too, can be frightening, like a seesaw, as a true-life anecdote will demonstrate. Many years ago my great friend Hannah Arendt and Chiaromonte had agreed to meet in Florence during a trip of hers to Europe, for they had much to talk about (he had greatly admired *The Human Condition* and written her a long letter about it, which she answered, also at length, I believe). In Florence, they spent a couple of days together looking at the city, but when afterward I asked one of them (I forget which) how it had gone, he or she shrugged: "All right, I suppose. She/he is intelligent. But so abstract!" The other reported the same.

In any case, Chiaromonte's mind, even more than Arendt's, was questioning, skeptical to the point of doubting the solidity of any proposition outside geometry. All abstractions but two—justice and freedom—were anathema to it. And if I ask myself now why he made an exception of justice and freedom, I can only think that it was because—unlike Progress, unlike History—they make no claim to be incarnate in the material world, but exist in it, so to speak, negatively, in bits and pieces, never "adding up." In short, they really are Ideas, of the true Platonic stamp. Thus I can conceive a just act without ever having beheld one; I construct it in my mind as the *reverse* of the whole sum of unjust acts I am familiar with. Hegel's famous utterance "I have seen an Idea on horseback"—Napoleon at Jena—would have made Chiaromonte laugh.

But to sum up: though he loved reason and reasoning, theory was repellent to Chiaromonte except in the realm of pure speculation, which is its natural home. And I suspect that the awful misunderstandings in the minds of those English reviewers, the yearning, evinced by all, to attribute a theory or a prescription to him, were caused, at least in part, by the absence of any such thing in the work they were trying to evaluate.

The message contained in *The Paradox of History* is mysteriously simple: the faith in History, which was shattered by an historical event—the impact of the First World War— cannot in good faith be restored, since the confidence in Progress underpinning it, tacitly or explicitly, is no longer there. The collapse of that man-made structure can be dated—summer 1914—when a credo in a forward-directed History fell instant victim to history with a small *h*, history in a raw state, a "senseless" accumulation of happenings. That is the paradox, the irony, the joke if you wish; it suddenly emerged with a painful shock that history unprocessed, history in the raw, is what the ancients knew as Fate.

Yet this discovery, like all discoveries (which are only *un*coverings), had been anticipated some time ago. Stendhal had glimpsed it in *The Charterhouse of Parma*; Tolstoy saw it full face in *War and Peace*. And between the two World Wars, Roger Martin du Gard in *Summer 1914*, the concluding volume of *The Thibaults* (today forgotten except possibly as an example of the *roman-fleuve*), showed the trusting faith in History, which for the educated had replaced religion, in the act of collapsing as French and German Socialists voted war credits in their respective parliaments. The assassination of Franz Ferdinand at Sarajevo and of Jaurès in a Parisian café triggered—for once the awful word seems suitable—a kind of rapid, out-of-control automation in world events. Yet these assassinations could hardly be viewed as "causing" a chain reaction of trench warfare lasting four years, nor as historically inevitable—the result of deeper causes themselves: Prinzip could be said to have acted for "historic" reasons, but Jaurès was the victim of a crazed fanatic, i.e., of a psychiatric accident.

In *Dr. Zhivago*, Pasternak saw the Bolshevik revolution in somewhat similar terms: as an upheaval, an uprooting, a shaking and tossing that nobody was prepared for (though it could be viewed as predictable through hindsight) any more than a violent windstorm or a raging flood. But the analogy with nature could not have been applied to World War I and, in any case, for Chiaromonte it is misleading. To equate revolution with a natural event is to declare it to be somehow affirmative, belonging by its very might to the sempiternal order of things and hence not to be resisted by a mere individual in its path. In Pasternak's vision you "bend to" a revolution as to a hurricane. Yet, as Chiaromonte points out with his invariable acuteness, we do *not* bow to an historical occurrence as we do to a natural force (though of course there are always those who try to swim with the current). There is a difference; even in daily affairs, ". . . it is not possible to resign oneself to the evils of society in the same way as one submits to the adversity of nature."

The underlying theme of *The Paradox of History* is, simply, fate. What happened, like a roll of thunder on August 2, 1914, was the rediscovery of fate. It was not the intellectuals that the War forced to open their eyes. They had been discovering necessity in the awful freedom of nihilism for the past thirty years. "Clinging to the 'notion of Man' would mean . . . fearing to draw the logical consequences of atheism, which demands that *nothing* be an obstacle to the realization of a human project. What is possible must be." For them, there was no failure of belief in Progress on that "fatal" date, because they believed in nothing anyway. It was ordinary people who bore the brunt of looking into the face of fate suddenly exposed like the featureless egg in the Chinese tale of the traveler.

Fate is the unknown, the uncalculated and incalculable, what the Greeks called the sacred, meaning merely (to start with) that which is hidden. For Tolstoy, as Chiaromonte understood him, the perception of power as a relation of maximum dependence meant that "destiny has, for man, the face of his own neighbor." Or, as he stated it on his own behalf, speaking of *The Thibaults*: "What is violently revealed in the transition [from peace and freedom to war and coercion] is the extreme dependence . . . in which each individual finds himself with respect to others." And, again, referring to the characters in *The Thibaults* at the outbreak of the war: "Individuals are no longer alone. History invades their lives and, with history, the nation, the State, and all mankind."

Chiaromonte's book is descriptive, not prescriptive. The encounter with fate is shown almost novelistically, in episodes, which amount to a single prolonged encounter. As in a work of fiction, one of the figures tries to escape: Malraux, who in the person of his hero seeks to make himself the invincible lord of his destiny by invoking the demon of action. Or, as Chiaromonte puts it: "What matters to Malraux's 'conquerors' is not history but force, and the problem of force in history. . . . They represent, pushed to the extreme, the great heresy of our time: the attempt to control force by becoming its servants."

Chiaromonte is not really a difficult writer, but a dense writer, a compact writer; insights, *aperçus*, brief analyses, pungent observations are packed together in a continuous flow or stream of narrative, carrying the entire baggage, miscellaneous yet related, along with it as in the *roman-fleuve*. I will mention a few examples: the "arias" of Fabrizio's soul (is Chiaromonte the first to notice the operatic element in *The Charterhouse?*); Anna Karenina's passion is condemned not by the sixth commandment but by "universal entropy"; "Was it God who brought about Napoleon? It is hardly conceivable"; the "Stoic morality" of Martin du Gard, a phrase evoking not only a distinctive quality of the novelist but the decline and fall of Rome; in Malraux, action is analyzed with "such vehemence" that it becomes "immaterial and transparent"; Malraux's heroes as inheritors of Pascal's wager; Malraux as the poet of defeat. Finally, and in my view most wonderfully characteristic, apropros of war and politics: "Why is war an extreme situation? Is it because of death? This is what a certain kind of pacifism (that of Barbusse, of Céline and Giono, for example) has maintained. Yet the most terrible thing about war is not death."

The pithiness of such a remark (which hits a reader with the double force of surprise and recognition) points to an essential trait of Chiaromonte's that is summed up like an ideogram in his very name: "clear mountain," "bright mountain." I mean his absolute realism and clear-sightedness, which were illustrated in nicely abridged form in an incident related to me by an American who had been sent in 1940 by the Quakers or Unitarians (maybe both) to help anti-Nazi and anti-Fascist refugees in unoccupied France. One of the American's first concerns was to supply all these people around Toulouse with false papers. Shortly afterwards, one of them—Chiaromonte—was halted on the street by a Vichy policeman who, naturally, demanded his papers. The reply came smilingly. "Which do you want? The real ones or the others?" Chiaromonte denied that it had happened that way, adding mildly, almost by way of confirmation, that those ridiculous forgeries would have deceived nobody.

That realism, which shines through this book, is Italian, I think, and by no means, if Joseph Frank will forgive my disagreement with an observation he makes in his preface, uniquely a peasant's trait, even though it seems to be con-

nected with some basic simplicity. It has in it a strong element of naming things by their names, as though returning
to our forefather, Adam, who gave a name, clearly the right
one, to everything on the earth. There is also wit—an effect
of compression, that compactness I spoke of. Chiaromonte had
a humorous mind; that it was dark-complected prevented many
people from observing the fact. There was a saturnine cast on
occasion, I admit, and sometimes a rasp of sarcasm. But anyone who takes the pains to look will find a striking kind of
humor in *The Paradox of History*, not only at intervals (as in
some of the remarks quoted above), but in the fundamental
conception, which is a wry joke, after all, an irony at the expense not only of "evolutionists," progressives, and historical
salvationists but also of our poor race as a whole, which had
become over-hopeful and so was bound to meet Nemesis,
another joker, on the high road to Utopia.

Yet if there were not a utopian, a thirster for justice and
freedom, in Chiaromonte, this book of his, summing up in
brief form a lifetime of meditation, could have been cruelly
reductive rather than inspiring in something like Tolstoy's way.
To firmly conceive a notion of limit, of a boundary beyond
which there stretch expanses of the unknown and unknow-
able, is no more gloomy or "confining" than the sight of the
huge sky to Prince Andrei lying wounded on his back at Aus-
terlitz. Moreover, as Chiaromonte puts it, paraphrasing Tolstoy on freedom, "If we could get to know the consequences
of our actions, history would be nothing but an idyllic and
constant harmony of free wills, or the infallible unfolding of
a rational design. . . . But then we would not be free. We
are free, however, and this means literally that we do not know
what we are doing."

So, if man had the choice between knowledge and freedom, which should he choose? Knowledge, of course, we
chorus, which to the "man" we have come to be means mas-

tery, supreme control. Today's genetic engineering—surely more significant for the future if there is one than the manufacture of nukes—leaves no doubt how the vote has been cast.

January 1985

INTERLUDE

La Traviata Retold

The Metropolitan Opera, working with the publisher Little, Brown, had the idea of inviting writers to tell in their own words the stories of some "beloved" operas. The rules laid down were simply that the narratives should be about seventy typed pages long and should contain no allusion to the music.

The result was an expanded program in hard covers, to be sold in the opera-house lobby as well as in bookstores and containing the libretto, analyses of the score, photos and drawings of former performances, in addition to the writer's narratives.

The first to appear was Anthony Burgess's Der Rosenkavalier; *then came V. S. Pritchett's* La Bohème; *then me. I was always glad not to have picked one with a plot like* La Forza del Destino.

PART ONE

The "woman gone astray" of our story is a classic product of her century and of a single country, France—you would not find her in Madrid or London. She is as much a Parisian distillate as perfume is of Grasse. But she is also a universal, an archetype of the misunderstood woman of easy virtue—the Magdalen, Moll Flanders, Dostoyevsky's Sonia, Tolstoy's Maslova, Sartre's "Respectful Prostitute." The type perhaps goes back to the temple prostitutes of ancient religions—opposites and counterparts of vestal virgins tending the sacred flame. Is it in the temple of love that Violetta Valéry, a highly successful cocotte and our special fallen woman, is serving as a votary or somewhere else? The story will show.

In our own century, this Violetta, so alluring to aristocrats, might have been a Coco Chanel, kept by the Duke of Westminster, or the Mlle. Modiste of an opera by Victor Herbert (whence the song "Kiss Me Again"). Or a famous model—there is a continuing relation to fashion. But actually she belongs, historically and in spirit, to the reign (1830–1848) of Louis Philippe, the so-called citizen king. The kept woman, of course, was not invented during those years; the mistresses of French kings over several centuries had been acting as "role models" for young women of luxurious tastes and accommodating habits, and they did not even have to be beautiful to catch the royal eye—look at the portraits. Nor was it necessary to be vicious—think of Madame de Maintenon.

The kept woman, or high-class courtesan (the same as "court lady," originally), was well known to readers of romances long before Violetta's time. Indeed a key book that may well have guided her footsteps was *Manon Lescaut* (1731) by the Abbé Prévost, about a well-born youth, the Chevalier des Grieux, ruined by the bewitching girl of fatally acquisitive propensities he undertakes to keep. Much later, this story became an opera, in fact, two, but Violetta can have known only the novel. She identified herself, very likely, with Manon (higher up than she, to start with, on the social scale), though this would have been a guilty identification; her sympathies, since she is a young woman of heart, must have gone to the Chevalier des Grieux.

The difference in birth between her and Manon is significant. It contributes to making her a girl of her time. She never says where she comes from or how she got where she is. All we know is that she is completely alone in the world, without parents or relations; she must have envied the fictional Manon her army-officer brother, even though he is a bad lot. She might have been a flower-seller, a theatre-usher, or a seamstress with a smart dressmaker when she attracted the notice of her first "protector." Her good heart seems to testify to simple origins (though the equation is not always correct); most women of her kind at the time—like Chanel, later—came from poor farms and villages. Violetta reads; she is literate. This is a tribute to the conquests of the French Revolution, thanks to which primary and even secondary education became more than middle-class privileges. Despite her education, Violetta has retained a certain innocence, the mark perhaps of her origins, and even in her dissipations there is something high-minded, abstract, almost principled.

She is not, strictly speaking, a demi-mondaine; that implied somebody half in good society and half out of it. Violetta is not a well-nurtured girl who has made a misstep (had an illegitimate child, say) and thus *fallen* into vice; she is not déclassée (a term designating once upon a time a married woman no longer received socially and the title of a movie of my girlhood starring Corinne Griffith); nor is she exactly a demi-rep (an eighteenth-century term for a person of dubious reputation), though she may come closer to that. She differs from a Greek hetaera in that she is part of a social revolution in which those from below have been rising to the top. She is a ripple on the surface first unsettled by the French Revolution fifty or so years before; when we come to know her, it is around 1845, the apogee of her delicate ethereal type.

By the eighteen-forties, France has undergone the Terror, the rise and fall of Napoleon, the Bourbon restoration, the insurrectionary "July days" ending with the installation of the Orléanist branch of the Bourbon family in the form of the moderate, pear-shaped Louis Philippe. It can be said that under that relatively easygoing monarch the French Revolution finally "took," like a vaccination: as with a vaccination, the body politic experienced a mild form of the dread disease of social leveling or equality—slight, feverish symptoms which, it was hoped, would insure against a recurrence of the real, virulent thing. By and large, that hope was not mistaken. Although Louis Philippe was overthrown in 1848, by the uprising that inspired the *Communist Manifesto* ("A specter is haunting Europe"), his reign nevertheless had been the heyday of mild, reformist progress. Once the '48 revolution was bloodily put down, Napoleon's nephew, Louis Bonaparte, calling himself the Emperor Napoleon III, inaugurated a permissive, coarsely acquisitive society well characterized by Emile Zola in novels picturing real-estate speculation, meat-packing, art, prostitution, alcoholism, coal mines, and the new department-store business.

If Zola was the inspired chronicler of the corrupt Second Empire with its vulgar, driving businessmen and their debased clothes-horses, the *poules de luxe*, it was Balzac and Victor Hugo who described the ebullient and still sometimes generous ruling class of newcomers and former aristocrats of Louis Philippe's time. This is evident in the treatment of the kept-woman figures of Balzac, so often tender-hearted, but also in Victor Hugo's touching picture of Fantine *(Les Misérables)*, the orphaned grisette from "M. sur M." who goes wrong with the leader of a gay band of Sorbonne students, themselves provincials, and thus becomes the mother of Cosette. Sweet unworldly Fantine, tubercular, eventually reduced to streetwalking, is wholly altruistic, sacrificing her beautiful hair and her very teeth for her child, and even Balzac's courtesans, who know their way around, far from demanding a luxurious scale of living for *themselves*, are bent on maintaining their poor young lovers in style. Their ideal is to be kept by an old, indulgent (or preoccupied) man who visits once or twice a week and has the further privilege of escorting his cocotte to the theatre, where he will be seen by the *beau monde* with her charms on his arm: when her Pantalon returns her to the love-nest he pays for, she is able to serve a delectable after-theatre supper to the young genius she adores.

Some such ideal arrangement appears to be in the mind of Violetta Valéry in the early stages of the relation with *her* young man from the country, Alfredo Germont. She is a long way from the destitute Fantine, and yet there is an uncanny resemblance, even to the tuberculosis: "There but for the grace of God," Violetta might well have murmured to herself, had she read Fantine's history in one of the books she is fond of.

It is to a smallish intimate supper in her flat near the Opéra that Alfredo has been brought by a friend somewhat better born than himself—Gaston, the Viscount of Leto-rières. Alfredo has been yearning to meet the famous cocotte, at present kept by a Baron Douphol. He is shy and feels the honor of being taken to one of her occasions. The young blades are dressed in evening clothes, and the women, when they begin to appear in the arms of the gentlemen escorting them, have the air of society ladies in low-cut silks and velvets, flounces and ribbons—it is the age of the crinoline—carrying fans and with jewels in their hair. Only a certain freedom of manners will reveal them to be high-class tarts.

Violetta has been ill. When we first see her, that evening in her drawing-room, she is sitting on a sofa with her doctor—Grenvil—and some friends, as a party of other friends arrives late, having lingered playing cards at the house of a woman named Flora. Another fashionable demi-rep, we can surmise, watching her come in, preening, with the Marquis d'Obigny, a young man who is now keeping her. "We've all been at Flora's," they chorus, to excuse themselves. "Flora!" cries Violetta, rising to greet her and her train. The flower names of these women—before Violetta's launching there had been a Camille, so called for her white and red camellias, and a Marguérite (Daisy)—give a whiff of the fashions of the period.

An immense table is laid for the supper to come, with cold fowl and game, pâtés of little birds, galantines, chaud-froids, lobsters, Russian salads, hams from York and Prague. Champagne is being served by liveried footmen; later there will be sherbets, pineapples, and Italian ices. It is an August night (hence no oysters). Other servants are bringing platters, richly decorated, and wine bottles in iced coolers of highly polished silver. Everyone drinks, even the doctor. To us, the gaiety—clinking of glasses, raised voices, familiarity of manners—may be slightly reminiscent of some "wild party" of the twenties or a Hollywood soirée of silent-film days, when the Mary Pickfords and Gloria Swansons were the style leaders (and often kept women) of an extravagant new class.

In Violetta's suite of reception rooms, one opening into another, the atmosphere is unusually fevered and hectic, even for this milieu. This is a sign, surely, of her disease, like the doctor's presence at her side, an omen, as in the big mirror over the dainty marble fireplace on the left of the principal room, furnished with sofas, *faces-à-faces*, love seats, footstools, small tables and tabourets, rosewood and buhl cabinets full of Sèvres and Meissen. This is a room designed for moments of intimacy and suggestive of a boudoir. The mirror is Violetta's eternal, warning companion, like the mirror in the fairy-tale ("Mirror, mirror, on the wall"), a necessity of her profession—the kept woman must constantly know the truth about the fluctuating bank account constituted by her beauty. As the saying goes, her face is her fortune, or has been up to now, but it is also her misfortune.

Now, as her guests pour in from Flora's (significant that they should be late, indicating that to them one kept woman's house is the same as another's), Violetta promises an evening of riotous pleasure, to the point where Flora and her new "protector" wonder aloud whether the hostess is allowed to stay up late drinking champagne with so much abandon.

"I want it," Violetta says with a little air of obstinacy, glancing at the doctor, who says nothing. "I have the habit. The life of pleasure agrees with me. It's the best medicine I know."

At that very moment, at the entry to the drawing-room someone appears who will be her fatal drug: Alfredo. He has hardly been presented to her, as a great admirer, when Flora's marquis speaks to him, tapping him on the shoulder, and the two shake hands. He is a young fellow from the provinces, of middle-class background, and most of the others are titled playboys, but in this house equality reigns; he is greeted by his first name—"Alfredo!" "Marquis!" he replies. Meanwhile Violetta's baron has showed his face among the latecomers who had stayed gambling at Flora's. This seems to be Violetta's signal to summon a servant: "Is everything ready?" At the servant's nod, she calls the company to table as champagne still makes the rounds.

Violetta has put herself between Alfredo and his sponsor, the viscount, who tells her in an undertone about the new young man. Opposite are Flora, with her marquis on one side and Violetta's baron—Douphol—on the other. This is the key group; the rest find places where they can. "He's always thinking of you," Gaston says softly to the hostess. "You're not serious?" she answers, laughing. "When you were ill," Gaston persists, "he came running to ask after you every day." "Oh, stop it!" she decrees, but with a touch of archness. "I'm nothing to him." When she tries to ward off flattery, she is half-serious, half a trained coquette. "I'm not fooling," Gaston retorts, looking toward Alfredo, as if to draw him into the exchange. "Is it true, then?" No longer laughing, she turns to Alfredo. "But why? I don't understand." With her look fixed on him, he speaks to her, shyly, for the first time, to confirm what his friend is reporting. "Yes, it's true." He sighs. Sweetly and seriously, she thanks him for his concern. Then, across the table, to the baron: "But you, Baron, how is it you didn't do likewise?" "I've known you only a year," says the baron, harshly. "But this one has known me only a few minutes," she points out.

Alfredo, with his seriousness and shyness, is getting on the baron's nerves. He does not like the change the young provincial is effecting in Violetta. Flora notices this, and, sotto voce, out of the corner of her mouth, chides the baron for his manners. *She* finds Alfredo charming, she adds.

Meanwhile, across the table, Gaston is chiding Alfredo, who is *his* responsibility. "Aren't you going to open your mouth?" he inquires. Flora's protector, the marquis, knows Alfredo well enough to put the burden on the hostess. "It's up to you, my lady," he tells Violetta, "to wake the young fellow up." "I'll be Hebe, your cupbearer, and pour you a glass," she announces to the still dumbstruck Alfredo. "And may you be immortal, like her," he answers, gallantly; he is schoolboy enough for a classical allusion to have loosened his tongue. Then the others join their voices to the wish, raising their glasses. This inspires the viscount to try to jolly up the moody baron. Can't he find some verses—a song—to suit the festive occasion? Without a word, the baron refuses. "All right, it's up to you, then," Gaston tells Alfredo. The others loudly second the suggestion. "A drinking song! Let's have a drinking song!" He, too, declines. "I'm not in the proper mood." "But aren't you a master of the art?" teases his friend Gaston. "Would it please *you* if I sang?" Alfredo turns to Violetta, abruptly altering the tone. "Yes," she tells him, simply. That is all he needs. "Yes? In that case I'll sing. I have the song here in my heart." He rises. "Everybody listen!" cries the marquis. "Attention for the singer," they chorus, the baron excepted.

Alfredo, on his feet, sings in praise of wine—a fairly standard paean. As he goes on, however, more and more carried away, he is singing directly to her, and words and music take on, as it were, an undertone of deeper meaning. Through wine, it is love he is hymning—the hotter kisses that lie at the bottom of the cup. "Love . . . love . . . love"—the word repeats itself like an incantation, as though he were compelled. At one moment, intoxicated by the song, he has pointed straight to Violetta, and now, as his young voice ceases, she too rises to her feet as if compelled also, and sings her own paean. Not to wine nor to love but simply to pleasure. Anything but pleasure is folly. The flower of love is born and dies in a day. Take it, joy in it. Seize the alluring occasion, revel in every pleasure, laugh and make merry till dawn.

It is her creed she is pronouncing, of feverish enjoyment, without distinction between sensuous delight and sensual pleasure, a creed, at bottom, of forgetfulness. She has addressed herself to the whole like-minded company and, when she has finished, all but Alfredo join in. Then, in quite another voice, she speaks to Alfredo: "Life is jubilation." Is it an apology for herself or an instruction to him? "Do you hear me, life is having fun," she seems to be telling him, ignoring everyone else. And he replies in the same tone, as though they were alone in a room: "For those who haven't yet loved." This is a mild reprimand or gentle correction. Each of these young people—for all her amorous history, she is not yet twenty-three—is playing teacher. Surrounded by her guests, by a veritable chorus of inane worldlings, they are all by themselves in a schoolroom, as it were, each reciting a lesson, solo. "Don't tell it to somebody who isn't in the know." (To somebody, she is admitting, who has never loved.) "It's my destiny," he says grandly, as if embracing the fate of loving. It is a kind of quarrel—their first falling-out, based on assertions and counter-assertions of principle. Then the mindless chorus breaks in, supporting her side of the argument ("Wine, jesting, and song, All the night long"), but without her desperate dependence on pleasure as oblivion.

At this appropriate moment a band strikes up in the next room. The guests show surprise. "Wouldn't a dance be nice now?" inquires Violetta, who of course has planned it. There is a cry of general delight ("What a lovely thought!"), and Violetta, once more the hostess, leads the way to the center door. "Let's go in, then." She urges them ahead, to the ballroom. "Oh, my!" She has turned deathly white. "What's the matter?" the choir of guests tunes up. "Nothing, nothing," she replies. "What in the world *is* it?" other voices exclaim, some almost irritable. "Let's go," she repeats. "Oh, God!" She takes a step or two and is obliged to sit down. "Again!" they all cry out. "You're in pain," says Alfredo. "Heavens, what is it?" the others chime. "Just a trembling that comes over me." She makes a gesture toward the inner room, where the band is still playing a waltz. "Please! Do go in! I'll be with you soon." "As you wish," they tell her. And amazingly all of them, except the mute, motionless Alfredo, pass into the next room, drawn by the music like children by a Pied Piper of Hamelin. They leave the drawing-room (as Violetta thinks) empty. She goes up to the great mirror over the fireplace—her truth-teller. "Oh, how pale I am." She looks at herself a long time; then a warning instinct makes her turn, and she becomes aware of Alfredo, behind her. "You here?"

He timidly approaches her. "Has your indisposition passed off?" "I'm better," she says curtly. The reserve of her tone tells him that she is trying to put him off, and almost angrily he bursts out. "This way of life will kill you." He moves a little closer so that he can study her still pallid face. "You must take care of your health." "And how am I to do that?" she teases, opposing her experienced lightness to his youthful solemnity. He ignores the levity, and his answer is like a vow. "If you were mine, I'd take *such* care of you. I'd be the faithful guardian of every one of your precious days."

Violetta is startled. "What are you saying? Am I in someone's charge, perhaps?" "No," he replies promptly, flaring up as though a fire in him had suddenly been fanned. "That is because no one in all this world loves you." "No one?" she rallies him. "No one but me." "Is that so?" she gives a trill of laughter, deciding to be amused by him. "Oh, yes, I'd forgotten that grand passion of yours." He is hurt. "You laugh. Is there a heart in your bosom?" "A heart? Well, yes, maybe. And what do you want with it?" He shakes his head sorrowfully. "Ah, if you had one, you couldn't jest."

Up to this point, the dialogue between them in the deserted room has been earnest preaching on his side and on hers a light, practiced fencing, a quasi-professional scoring of points. In other words, she has been firmly treating the interlude as a flirtation, disturbed only by the gravity of his insistent reference to her health, more appropriate to a doctor than to a suitor. But gradually something somber in his tone or the burning expression of his eyes catches her deeper attention, and for the first time she responds with a seriousness matching his.

"Do you mean it?" "I'm not deceiving you," he answers, with the same knightly earnestness. "Is it a long time that you've loved me?" she wonders, curiously, having never felt the sentiment herself. That question is all Alfredo needs. He knows the answer by heart. It is why he is here this evening, having persuaded his friend Gaston to bring him. In the next room the band music stops as if to listen to his declaration. And he begins by taking her question literally; his is a literal nature. "Oh, yes, for a year," he tells her; the true son of a burgher, he counts. But then a simple poetry that is also in his character starts to tug at the earthbound prose in him; he goes up as if in a bright balloon, recalling the first day he saw her—ethereal, a bolt from the blue. Since that day he has loved her, in secret, with a tremulous love throbbing in him like the heartbeat of the entire universe—a mysterious sovereign love, so very mysterious, a torment and a delight.

The rapture of this extravagant declaration takes Violetta aback; she recoils from the fiery furnace of the young man's ardor. If what he says is true, she tells him, he had better leave her alone. Friendship is all she can offer him. He must understand her position. "I don't know how to love. I can't sustain such heroic emotions. I am telling you frankly, in all candor, you must look for another kind of woman. It won't be hard for you to find her, and then you'll forget me." He is paying no attention, continuing to talk raptly of a mysterious, sovereign power, when the band in the next room strikes up more loudly and at the same moment his friend the viscount appears in the doorway as though blown in by a gust of sound. "What's going on here?" "Nothing," Violetta tells him quickly. "We're talking nonsense." "Ah ha!" the viscount exclaims, seeing how the land lies and starting to beat a retreat. "Fine! Stay there!" And he hurriedly withdraws.

But the mood has been dispelled by the intrusion of the world. Violetta once more has the ascendancy over her intemperate suitor. He must make a pact with her, she enjoins him: no more talk of love. He agrees and promptly turns to go. But she detains him. Somewhat surprised or even hurt, she draws a flower from the bosom of her dress. "Take it." "Why?" "Why, to bring it back to me," she says with a little laugh. This catches him midway in his departure and makes him whirl about. "When?" "When it has faded," she replies, on a note of self-evidence. She is amused with him again: evidently there is a language of flowers unfamiliar to the inexperienced youth. We are reminded of the story of Camille, another kept woman, and her red and white camellias. But Alfredo, though ignorant of that history, has finally understood. "Good heavens! You mean tomorrow?" "Well, then, tomorrow," she tells him, indulgently, though that is sooner, apparently, than she meant.

"I am happy," he declares, taking the flower in a transport of bliss. She smiles on him tenderly. "Do you still say you love me?" If she asks, she must want him to repeat it, contrary to the "pact" she has just imposed. "Oh, how much!"

he declares, bringing his hand to his heart. Once again, he starts to go. "You're leaving?" she exclaims, wistful all at once. "I'm leaving." During this lingering exchange, it is as if Violetta has grown childish, and he has become a man. "Good-bye," "Good-bye," they tell each other softly. For a last time he returns and kisses her hand.

No sooner have they separated than the band of others bursts in, ready to take their leave and totally forgetful, it emerges, of their hostess's indisposition only an hour or so before. Not a single inquiry from her seeming "best friends," the very ones who were wondering at the outset whether champagne and a late night might not do her harm. Inside, the musicians have stopped, but the parting guests, volleying out their thanks and their dreadful *joie de vivre*, are making enough noise for a whole military band. "Time to go home," "The dawn is breaking," "Thank you, thank you, dear lady, for a marvelous time," "It's the height of the season, everyone's giving parties, so we must get rested up."

This burst of cheerful, unfeeling chatter makes a peculiar contrast with the pitch of intense feeling that Violetta and Alfredo have mounted to when left to themselves. In this very contrast there are premonitions of tragedy. Two beings of extreme sensitivity seem unprotected, like a pair of orphans in an unfeeling world—despite Violetta's sumptuous style of entertainment, they are both babes in the woods. "Life is a tragedy for those who feel"—Violetta, long ago, has learned that lesson and taken measures to ensure herself against love, the most powerful feeling of all. Alfredo, on his side, is less prescient; he finds nothing but joy and ecstasy in his capacity to feel.

What we have just witnessed is a scene of temptation with the sexes reversed: Alfredo, our innocent Adam, is urging a reluctant and fearful Eve to taste with him the delights of something more than mere carnal knowledge—a love-apple that for a girl in her position is poison. It is already evident

281

that she has consumption, that is, something inside her, within her frail chest, that is burning her up. This consumption is allied to the passion that will inevitably devour her, a wasting disease beside which mere dissipation—wine and late hours— is harmless child's play.

Now the beautiful kept woman is alone in her salon. Alfredo has gone off in high spirits and great expectations, not much more sensible than the departing revelers to the struggle she is left to carry on, for self-protection, with herself. The baron has departed and apparently will not return tonight. She thinks aloud. It is strange, strange, she meditates, that those words of his have carved a design in her heart. Would a serious love be a misfortune for her? She cannot answer, never having known one, and there is no one to give her counsel, not even Flora, certainly not the doctor. She can only ask her own confused, ignorant soul. The sensation of being loved while loving (mutual love) is foreign to her experience. But ought she to disdain it for the arid follies of her present life? She paces the room, thinking more and more deeply on the matter.

She asks herself whether Alfredo is not, finally, "the man of her dreams." Didn't he appear to her, as a lonely girl, to paint her soul's prison in vivid, arcane colors? And didn't he in fact, just recently, stand modest guard outside her sickroom and kindle a new fever in her bosom, awakening her to love? She is seeking a supranatural explanation for the novel feeling in her, pretending that she had known him, dreamed him, in an anterior life or that his presence, at the door of her sick chamber, when he came to inquire every day, had been felt by her in the midst of her fever as an "aura" or emanation of love. Sunk in these mystical thoughts, as if in a trance, she is soon like a creature possessed, by this young man or by a kindred spirit speaking his language of mysterious sovereign powers, balms and crosses, torments and delights.

Then she shakes herself out of her reverie. "Follies," she scolds, getting herself in hand. "Madness, vain delirium." Having cast out the love demon, she sighs. "Poor woman, alone, abandoned, in this populous desert they call Paris, what more have I got to hope for? What must I do? Enjoy, enjoy, enjoy . . . Die on the summits of pleasure." She seems to hear a voice—Alfredo's—in a serenade below the balcony of her open window. Still those heartbeats, crosses, and delights. Her own private music has quite another theme. "Free, forever free, flitting from joy to joy. Let me live for pleasure only. Down the primrose path I fly." This mundane hymn to liberty is raised to a higher plane by the frenzy in it; a fever of commitment redeems the triteness of the pledge this poor young woman, gesturing with a champagne glass, is taking to the principle of enjoyment.

PART TWO

Five months have passed. It is January. Nothing has turned out as a realist might have expected. Violetta has not persisted in her giddy life of pleasure. Instead, she is living in the country near Paris, and with Alfredo. Where is it? Perhaps Auteuil. These kept women, even when they reform, cannot leave Paris far behind. It was the same with Manon Lescaut, before the Revolution. When she and her Chevalier des Grieux decided to play house in the country, living the simple life and saving taxi fares, they removed to Chaillot. (Today both Auteuil with its racetrack and Chaillot have become indistinguishable parts of Paris, but Chaillot got swallowed up earlier.) Violetta has taken a pleasant country house. French doors give on a garden from the ground-floor living-room. There is an abundance of chairs and little tables, as well as a writing-desk and a few books—"serious" items that had not been visible in her Parisian dwelling. Another symptom of change is the absence of flunkeys; here one little girl,

Annina (Annie), in cap and apron, seems to be doing most of the work. At the back of the room, once again there is a fireplace, rustic this time (built of stone), with a mirror hanging over it and under the mirror a clock of the Empire period.

Alfredo comes into the empty room; when he was last seen, he was in evening clothes, and now he is in hunting dress with a gun on his shoulder, which he lays down. The hunting season must be nearing an end. It is three months since Violetta left Paris—lovers, parties, cards, furniture—to devote herself to creating an idyl for him. And it has worked. His boiling youthful spirits, under her serene management, have been tempered to a quiet happiness. He has changed. Ever since the day she told him "I want to live for you alone," he has been living in a kind of heaven.

Now Annina comes in, dressed in traveling gear. She has been to Paris. Alfredo is surprised. "Who sent you?" Clearly, such trips are unusual. "My mistress," the girl replies. "Why?" he persists, and Annina tells him: it was to sell the horses and carriages and whatever else Violetta still had. He is thunderstruck, unable to believe his ears. "It costs a lot to live alone out here," Annina informs him. "And you said nothing?" "I was forbidden to." "Forbidden?" he repeats, still staggered by what she is revealing. "So how much do we need?" "A thousand," she replies. He has no visible reaction to the sum of money named—is it a still worse shock? But he at once tells the little servant to make herself scarce. *He* will go to Paris himself. "And you're not to tell your lady about this conversation. With what I have, I can still repair the damage. Go, what are you waiting for?"

When the little servant goes out, he apostrophizes himself in horror. How can he have been so unnoticing? Infamous! Shameful! To live in such delusion! At last the truth has shattered that rotten dream. There's still time, though, if offended honor will only be patient, to wash away the shame.

With that thought, he rushes out, bound for Paris. A

moment later, Violetta returns, her own transaction accomplished. She comes in slowly, in traveling dress, talking to Annie, her little maid, at the door. In her gloved hand she holds papers—bills of sale, receipts, and so on. Seeing no one in the room, she calls his name. "Alfredo!" There is no answer. Then Annina steps forward, to say that he has left for Paris only a few minutes before. A presentiment seems to grip Violetta. "Is he coming back?" The maid fails to hear the trouble in her mistress's voice. "Before sundown," she says. "He asked me to give you the message." But Violetta is not wholly reassured. "Strange!" she muses aloud. While she stands wondering, Joseph, the old manservant, appears. He has a letter in his hand. "It's for you." As a servant, he is no more stylish than Annina. "Good," says Violetta, opening the letter with a paper knife from the writing-desk. "A man of business will be here to see me soon. Have him come in at once." The servants withdraw.

Now Violetta opens the letter, which proves to be in fact from Flora, who has found out her hiding-place and wants her to come to a dancing-party in Paris that evening. Violetta tosses the letter onto a table and sinks into a chair. She is tired from her journey and all the business she has done. "Well, well! She'll have a long wait for me." Of course she won't go. She yawns. Joseph again appears in the doorway. "There's a gentleman here." "It must be the one I'm expecting," Violetta decides and she motions to the servant to show the caller in.

A handsome old man, stiff as a ruler, enters the room. "Mademoiselle Valéry?" "I am she," Violetta replies curtly, as though sensing a need to assert every bit of her dignity. He makes no move to come near her. "You see before you Alfredo's father," he announces in a deep, austere voice. In her surprise, Violetta utters a cry. "You?" She gestures to him to sit down in a chair opposite her; she had not risen at his entry. "Precisely," replies the elder Germont, taking the seat.

"Of the reckless young man you've bewitched and sent rush-ing to his ruin." Having formally stated this, he leans forward and looks her keenly in the eyes. Violetta, incensed at this language, rises to her feet. "I am a woman, sir, and in her own house. Please allow me to leave you, as much for your sake as for mine." She starts to go out. "What style!" the of-fended father mutters. He decides to curb his tongue. "How-ever . . ." he continues, in a milder tone. "You have been misled," she tells him but returns to her chair in time to hear him say: "He wants to make you a present of every sou he owns." "Up to now he hasn't dared," retorts Violetta. "I'd re-fuse." Germont glances around the sitting-room. "But all this luxury," he comments.

Violetta has followed his glance. "This is a secret from everyone. Let it not be one from you." Without a further word she hands the unbending old man the papers she has brought back from Paris—papers that speak for themselves. He runs a hurried eye through them. "Good God! What a revelation! You think of stripping yourself of all your possessions—every-thing you have?" Then an explanation occurs to him. "Ah, because of your past. Why let it accuse you?" He is moved to pity. "That past no longer exists," she announces proudly. "Now I love Alfredo. And God has annulled the past because of my repentance." Germont is more and more struck. "These are noble feelings," he observes. Here is not the kind of wan-ton he had expected to deal with.

With her acute sensibility, Violetta is immediately aware of the change in his feeling toward her. She leans forward impulsively. "How sweet your words sound to me." Germont ignores this winning speech, intent on his main purpose. "Such feelings demand sacrifices. I am asking one of you." He has stood up. She leaps up herself, affrighted, trembling like a hunted deer. "Ah, no. Be quiet. You'd ask for terrible things. Yes, I foresaw it. I expected you. I was too happy." The old man squares his shoulders and stiffens his bony spine, making himself look even taller. "Alfredo's father demands it in the name of two destinies—the future of his two children." "*Two* children?" She is startled. Seeing her surprise, Germont takes a deep, preparatory breath. Now he can speak to her of the little sister, the daughter God gave him, pure as an angel.

Pure as an angel. But if her truant brother refuses to return to the bosom of the family, then her fiancé—the youth she loves and who loves her in return—will have to back off from his commitment, which had been the joy of both. On the theme of that pure maiden, Germont waxes eloquent. He soars to a pitch of feeling. As he pleads his suit (or the suit of his daughter), the old burgher in his virtuous plain attire curiously recalls the figure of his son in evening dress in the salon of Violetta's apartment holding forth on ethereal rapture, mysterious, sovereign love, and so on. Like father, like son. Violetta listens, transfixed. We are witnessing a seduction scene—nothing less than that.

And, like so many women mesmerized by a seducer, Violetta does not understand at first what Alfredo's father wants of her. "You're not going to turn the roses of love into thorns," he has been pleading, carried away on a fresh rhetorical flight. "You won't withstand my prayers. Your heart will not refuse." "Oh, I understand," she cries, brightening, her next words a clear indication that she does not. "For a little while I shall have to live apart from Alfredo. That will be hard. However . . ." "That's not what I'm asking," he says bluntly.

"Good heavens, what more can you want? I'm offering a great deal." "Not enough, though." "You want me to give him up for good?" "It's necessary." His terse, staccato replies reveal a different, wholly determined man. They come like short pitiless stabs at her tender, quivering heart. At last she understands what this Nemesis wants of her. As comprehension pierces her, she screams. "Never! No, never!" she shrills, like somebody on the rack. Then she gets hold of herself, her voice drops to a soft pleading tone that begs him pitifully for mercy.

Germont cannot know the love she has burning in her heart. That among the living she has neither friends nor relations. That Alfredo has sworn to her that he will be all of them for her—parents, brother, friends. Nor does her torturer know that she has been stricken by a dread disease, that the end of her days is already in plain sight. And yet he is asking her to give Alfredo up. To such heartless torture, she decidedly prefers death.

Again his attitude changes, to one of respectful sympathy. The resolution of her last few words has showed another side to her, which he must treat with a new deference. The sacrifice will be heavy, he acknowledges. "But still—listen to me calmly—you're beautiful and young. With time—" "Don't go on," she interrupts, as though to spare him useless effort. "I understand you. But for me it's impossible. I can love only him." "Granted," he tells her. "And yet men are inconstant, you know." To this terrible hint, Violetta reacts with a start, as though the idea that Alfredo could be faithless were coming to her for the first time. "Good God!" she cries out. The paterfamilias, confident that he has touched a vulnerable spot, presses on with his insinuations. A day may come, he prophesies, when the pleasures of Venus pall and boredom is quick to follow. . . . What will happen then? "Think!" he bids her. "For you the sweeter affections can never serve as balm, since unions like yours cannot be blessed by heaven." Violetta drops her eyes, again touched to the quick. The fact that Alfredo cannot marry her, which she has accepted with an easy heart, takes on its full, bleak significance in the father's relentless optic: they can never have children, a real home, family life, an assured place in society; when love-making loses its first charm, they will find nothing to occupy them, no binding agent to hold them together. "It's true!" she whispers, excruciated; again the torment he skillfully produces in her is like a physical pain.

"Well, then, abandon that seductive dream." Germont is close to attaining his object; he has only to drive home his points. Vigor and manly confidence now visibly exude from him, like an athlete's sweat. He has shown her enough of the bad and threatening aspects of the future; it is time to point to the rewards in store if she behaves. "Be my family's consoling angel. Violetta"—for the first time he pronounces her name—"think, do think. There's time still, don't you see? Young woman, believe me, God is speaking through a father's voice." It is a privilege he is offering her if she will only understand. Through the sacred character of the family tie (which she has never known, apparently), she will be drawn into the embrace of the *Padre Eterno*, stern but forgiving, like his human simulacrum. Germont, as if bathed himself in holy light, is showing the fallen woman the path to salvation.

But the prevailing erotic undertone, the caressing voice, deeper and more virile than the son's mere tenor, start to make one wonder. Isn't this grave old party the devil? To one more versed in the Gospels than Violetta, this is the familiar temptation in the wilderness, with a perverse Victorian twist. The family is the god to which she and all her sisterhood are required to sacrifice. Indeed, without Violetta and her sisters to "take care of" the coarse lusts of the male, the family as temple of purity could not be enshrined.

Meanwhile, Violetta, writhing on the cross prepared for her, is sadly aware, at last, of her fate. She has been deluded—now she knows it—to suppose that she can rise from ashes and create a new life. There's no hope for a fallen woman. Even if God in His indulgence can forgive her, man will be implacable.

Bitterly weeping, she turns to the parent-extortioner to tell him to tell his daughter, that fair, pure daughter, how a poor wretch, victim of misfortune, had a single ray of happiness and sacrificed it to her. Having done so, the wretch will die. The extraordinary thing is that Violetta, as though to bear out the father's well-worn arguments, is transfigured while speaking by her good (as she thinks) action. Although she weeps bitter tears, her feeling for the fortunate, sheltered maiden has no trace of animus or sarcasm; if there is envy, it is a kind of holy envy, suffused with tender piety. And now Germont, perhaps sincerely, is able to offer consolation to his suffering victim. "Weep, weep," he tells her, "weep, poor woman." Her tears are good for her—a therapy; she must let them flow. And, now that it is over and she has given way, he is able to see—and admit—that it is a supreme sacrifice he is asking of her. In his own breast already he feels the pain of it. "Courage!" he concludes, on a brisker note. "Your noble heart will conquer."

A silence intervenes, as at the conclusion of a rite: *ite, missa est*. Then, like a soldier or a hired assassin, she asks him to give her his orders. "Tell him you don't love him." "He won't believe me." "Leave." "He'll follow." "Then . . ." Germont is at a loss; he has no experience in these matters. In his stead, Violetta decides what she must do. But first, like a young knight, she needs his blessing. "Embrace me like a daughter," she instructs the old man. "That will make me strong." He puts his arms around her, and for a moment they stand clasped. Then the newly armored woman, the "daughter," speaks. "He'll be delivered to you shortly, but he'll be in a pitiable state." She points to the garden. "Please wait for him there and comfort him." She goes to the writing-desk. "What's in your mind?" he asks, uneasily. She shakes her head. "If you knew, you'd try to stop me."

Germont is more and more impressed and surprised by her. "Generous woman! And what can *I* do for *you*?" Violetta has the answer ready for him—another surprise. Advancing from beside the desk, she takes a few steps in his direction. She has been thinking ahead. "I'll die! When it happens, don't let him curse my memory. If you do feel something for me, at least tell him what I've suffered." "No, generous spirit, live. You must be happy. Heaven will reward you one day for these tears." In a new way they are still at cross-purposes. Her realism and urgency are met by uplifting speeches of a deeply conventional sort. Alfredo's father prefers not to know the truth, which Violetta, for her part, has accepted—almost, in a strange fashion, embraced.

She replies calmly. When she is dead, Alfredo should know of the sacrifice she has made for love of him. He should know that her heart has been his up to her last breath. Germont's answer to this is, of course, the predictable set of clichés. "Your heart's sacrifice will find its reward. You will be proud then of such a noble deed." Violetta is no longer listening. She has heard a sound perhaps from the garden. "Someone's coming! Go!" "Oh, my heart is so grateful," he says, turning to leave. "Go!" she repeats and adds, on reflection: "This may be the last time we'll see each other." Very simply, she turns to him, and they embrace. Each then enjoins the other to be happy—impossible in both cases—and they bid each other farewell. He goes out by a garden window, and she is alone.

"God, give me strength." She sits down at the desk, writes something, then rings the bell. Annina appears. "You wanted me?" "Yes. Deliver this yourself." Annina glances at the folded sheet of paper and is surprised by the name of the addressee. She gives a little shriek. "Quiet," her mistress tells her. "Be off." The girl goes out. Violetta ponders. Now she must write to Alfredo. But what will she tell him? And where will she get the courage? She writes and seals the letter.

Alfredo enters, in city clothes. "What are you doing?" he immediately wants to know. "Nothing," she tells him, hiding the letter. "You were writing!" he exclaims. "Yes, no, no," she answers in confusion. "Why so perturbed? Whom were you writing to?" She faces him. "To you." "Give me that sheet of paper." "No, not now." He is embarrassed by his own brusqueness. "Forgive me. I'm a little upset." She rises. "What has happened?" "My father has arrived." "You've seen him?" "No. He left me a stiff letter. But I'm waiting for him. He'll fall in love with you as soon as he sees you."

She becomes extremely agitated. "He mustn't find me here. Let me leave. . . . You calm him, and then I'll throw myself at his feet." She can barely hold back her tears. "He won't want to separate us any more. We'll be happy. Because you love me. You do, don't you, Alfredo?" "Oh, so much! But you're crying?" "I just felt the need of tears. But now I'm over it. See? I'm smiling at you." She makes an effort. "I'll be there, among those flowers, always near you, always, always near you. Alfredo, love me as much as I love you. Love me, Alfredo. . . . Good-bye." She runs out into the garden.

Strangely enough, Alfredo seems quite undisturbed by this precipitate departure. "That dear heart lives only for my love," he observes, somewhat fatuously. As we have already seen, he is not a noticing young man. He sits down and opens a book (can it be *Manon Lescaut?*) and glances at the clock on the chimney-piece. "It's late. Maybe I shan't see my father today." The old servant, Joseph, comes in. "Madame has left. A carriage was waiting for her and by now it's speeding along the road to Paris. And Annina left even sooner than she did." "I know it," Alfredo tells him. "Calm down." Joseph mutters to himself. "What does it all mean?" After the servant has left the room, Alfredo puts down his book and ponders. Violetta, he decides, has gone off to speed up the disposal of her property. But Annina will prevent it. Through the French windows the father's tall black-clad figure can be seen crossing the garden. "Somebody's in the garden!" Alfredo exclaims. "Hello, who's there?"

A gold-braided messenger appears in a side doorway. "Monsieur Germont?" "I am he," answers Alfredo. The messenger is out of breath. "A lady in a carriage, not far from here, gave me this for you." He hands a letter to Alfredo, pockets a tip, and leaves. Alfredo studies the letter. "From Violetta! Why am I disturbed? Maybe she's asking me to join her. Why, I'm trembling. Oh, Lord, courage!" He unfolds the letter and begins to read. " 'Alfredo, when you get this letter—' Ah!" Turning, with a wild cry, he finds himself face to face with his father, who stands silently waiting as Alfredo falls into his arms. "Oh, Father!" "Oh, my son! Oh, how you're suffering!" He is shocked by the young man's racking sobs, evidently an unfamiliar spectacle for him. To the original surge of pity, parental impatience is a natural sequel. "Oh, dry those tears. Come back to us. Be once more the pride and boast of your father."

The invitation to dry his tears and come home does appear somewhat ill-timed. It's as if Germont were blind to the awful grief he is witnessing, with the wilful blindness of old age. While the young man sits unhearing, the old man decides to rally him by singing the praises of their native Provence. The father, like so many Southerners, is a patriot— not to say a booster—of the local air and light. Provence, he seems to be saying, can cure whatever ails anyone.

He invokes the blue sea, the soil, the glittering sun of Alfredo's forefathers. Who could expunge them from the heart of a true-born Provençal? If only Alfredo in his sorrow would remember the joy he once knew under those sparkling skies, the peace that once again can shed its effulgence on a native son! In the course of this reverie laced with exhortation, he has convinced himself that all Alfredo's troubles came from leaving home. And he has treated himself to a bath of sentiment on his own account, the pitiful old sire of a distant son, his white head bowed with shame. He has suffered more than Alfredo can ever know. But if he has found his boy again, if his own power of hope does not falter, if the voice of honor has not been entirely silenced in the errant youth, then God has heard him!

Alfredo, seemingly, has not. Old Germont gives him a shake. "Don't you have any response to a father's affection?" Alfredo shakes himself out of his absorption. "I'm devoured by a thousand furies. Leave me alone." He pushes the old man away. "Leave you here alone?" Alfredo ignores him, speaking to himself with determination. "Revenge!" Germont has no perception of his son's mood or the direction of his thoughts. Characteristically for this story, they are talking at cross-purposes (like Germont with Violetta), each intent on his privately nurtured design. The father supposes that the son is ready to leave with him for the curative blue skies of Provence. "Enough delay. We're leaving. Hurry up." Alfredo remains fixed to his chair, brooding to himself. "It was Douphol," he decides, his fevered brain fixing on his former rival, Violetta's protector of five months before. Germont grows peremptory. "Do you hear me?" he demands. "No!" shouts Alfredo, who at length understands what is being asked of him.

"So it's useless to have found you again, is it, Alfredo?" But from his son's taut face, Germont realizes that he is wrong to antagonize him. "No, Alfredo, you'll hear no reproaches from me. We'll bury the past together. Love has brought me here to find you and love knows how to forgive. Come! Let's surprise your dear ones with the sight of us together. You can't refuse that joy to those you've pained so much. A father and a sister, even now, are hastening to console you." Alfredo is taking no interest. Again he shakes himself, as if to focus his attention. His eye lights on Flora's letter on the table beside him. He reads it. "Ah!" he cries, enlightened. "So she's at the party. I'll fly to avenge the insult." He rushes out, headlong, with his father on his heels. "What are you saying? Stop!" The doors to the garden bang. The love-nest is empty; all the birds have flown.

It is quite another décor that meets our eyes, still that same night. We are at Flora's. A long, richly decorated room is brilliantly lit by crystal chandeliers and bronze candelabra. There is a small refreshment table laid with snowy linen and flowers in silver epergnes. In the middle of the room is a gambling table, holding cards, a roulette wheel, dice. Flora is escorting her first guests into the salon. We recognize the habitués of Violetta's former circle: the doctor, the marquis, and so on. There will be a masquerade this evening, Flora promises; the viscount has got it up. And she has asked Violetta and Alfredo too. Her lover, the marquis, smiles. Hasn't she heard the news? Violetta and Alfredo have separated. Flora and the doctor can hardly believe it. But the marquis is very sure. She will come tonight with the baron; the company will see. The doctor shakes his head, still incredulous. He saw them only the day before, and they seemed so happy.

Just then a distraction occurs: the masquerade. Flora calls for silence, and a band of ladies enters disguised as gypsies. Some are picked out by the guests as members of the familiar select circle. Thus when the "gypsies" begin the game of pretending to tell fortunes, they are able to make use of their intimate knowledge of the private lives of the company—e.g., that Flora's marquis is a rake who gives her countless rivals—without causing too much surprise. Following on the artificial storm raised by this intelligence—common knowledge to all, Flora included—new maskers come in: the viscount and his friends disguised as matadors. They put on a frankly amateurish show, reciting parts and singing a Spanish-style chorus of love and bullfighting. But this somewhat perfunctory "theatre" soon gives way to business, as masks are removed and everybody either makes for the gambling table or prepares to stroll about, idly flirting.

At this moment Alfredo, having waited perhaps for a lull, chooses to present himself. "You?" they all exclaim, not concealing their astonishment. "Why, yes. It's me, friends." He is alone, manifestly, yet Flora feels that she must ask about Violetta—where is she? Alfredo shrugs. He has no idea. And this casual disclaimer wins him a flurry of applause. They admire his parade of detachment, which leaves them free to pursue their own concerns—the gambling they have promised themselves. He joins the group around the table. His friend Gaston—the viscount—cuts the cards; Alfredo and the other young blades put down stakes. As they do so, Violetta appears, in a low-necked dress, on the arm of the baron—the prediction was right. Flora, as the hostess, hurries up to welcome her. "How delightful that you were able to come." "I could only yield to your very kind invitation." Flora turns to the baron. "So pleased that you, too, were able to accept."

The baron's look lingers on the group at the gaming table. "Germont's here," he murmurs to Violetta. "See him?" "Oh, God, it's true," she whispers to herself. Then, to the baron: "Yes, I see him." "Not a word from you tonight to this Alfredo," the baron warns her in a fierce, sibilant undertone. He is older than the other men and has a deep, disagreeable voice. "Reckless girl, what made you come here?" a frightened Violetta demands of herself. "Oh, Lord, have pity on me!" Then Flora sweeps her off. "Come, sit next to me. Tell me everything. What's this sudden change I see?" Violetta has no choice but to sit down by her on a sofa; the doctor, as always, hovers near the two women. The marquis, tactful, draws the baron to one side and holds him in conversation.

At the table, the viscount cuts the cards; Alfredo and the other players put down stakes. Some guests are strolling up and down the long room, as though it were their private boulevard, holding the promise of some exciting diversion—a new coupling, a quarrel. Alfredo's light voice can be heard announcing that he has a four. He has won again, marvels his friend Gaston. "Lucky at cards, unlucky in love," Alfredo says dryly. He bets and wins. The onlookers are pressing around the table, making a dense hedge so that Alfredo's play cannot be seen. "He's always the winner," they report. "Oh, I'll win this evening all right," Alfredo declares headily. "I'll take my winnings to the country and be a happy man." "Alone?" The sharp, pertinent question comes from Flora, on the sofa. "No, no," the young man answers, turning to stare at the two women. "With the one who was with me there once and then fled my company."

Eyebrows go up around the room; fans are agitated. "My God," whispers Violetta, stricken to the quick. The viscount nudges Alfredo, pointing to poor Violetta. "Have pity on her," he says. Meanwhile, the baron, detaching himself abruptly from the marquis, pushes up to Alfredo with barely contained fury. "Monsieur!" he says in an insulting tone. But Violetta, rising with determination, interposes in a low voice. "Restrain yourself or I'll leave you." "Were you addressing me, baron?" Alfredo coolly inquires. The baron answers on a note of irony. "You're so very, very lucky that you tempt me to play with you." "Really?" replies Alfredo. "I accept the challenge."

Violetta drops her eyes, unable to bear what she fears is coming. "Oh, dear God, have pity on me. I feel I'm about to die." "A hundred louis!" The baron puts down his stake. "I'll match you!" says Alfredo. They play. Gaston deals cards to Alfredo. "An ace . . . a jack . . . You've won!" "Double it?" says the baron. "Very well, two hundred." Gaston cuts the cards. He deals. "A four . . . a seven." "He's done it again!" the crowd exclaims. "I've won," says Alfredo. "Bravo!" they chime. "Really and truly bravo! Luck's on Alfredo's side." "The baron will foot the bill for that 'month in the country.' That's clear," observes Flora, provocatively. Alfredo lets this pass. He turns to the baron. "Your play."

But now supper is served. A lackey comes in to announce it. "Come along, then!" commands Flora. Obediently, her guests start filing out into the next room. Alfredo is close to the baron as they leave the gaming table. "If you wish to continue . . ." he suggests, in a low tone. "For the moment we can't," replies the baron, his voice low too. "Later I'll have my revenge." "At any game you like," answers Alfredo. "Let's follow our friends," says the baron. "Later." "At your service, then," Alfredo agrees. The two follow the other guests out through a big set of doors at the back of the apartment. The room stands empty, strewn with discarded masks that the servants have not yet picked up. After a longish interval, Violetta bursts in, breathless.

She has asked Alfredo to follow her and is not sure that he will obey. And even if he comes, will he listen to her? She is afraid that hatred may prove to be stronger than her pleading voice. Alfredo enters. He has obeyed her summons. "You wanted me?" He bows stiffly. "What is it you wish?" Knowing better but unnerved by his manner, she plunges straight to the point. "Leave this place!" She is still breathless. "A danger is hanging over you." Alfredo gives a cynical smile. He has understood, he believes. So she thinks him as vile a creature as that. He is no coward—this much he can show her. That was never in her mind, Violetta protests. "Then what is it you fear?" "I'm in deadly fear of the baron," she confides. Alfredo's answer is chilly. "True," he agrees, "there's bad blood between us that's bound to be fatal to one or the other." If the baron falls by his hand, obviously she'll lose both her lover and her protector at a single blow. Can that be the disaster that terrifies her?

Violetta ignores his sarcasm and replies from the heart. "But if he should be the slayer? That's the sole misfortune that I fear like death." "My death!" he says contemptuously. "Why should that trouble you?" At that she flares up, impatient with his foolishness. He must depart this place at once. To her surprise and relief, he agrees. But then he turns equivocal; he bargains. He will leave but on one condition: that she will swear to follow him wherever he goes. "Ah, no!"

she cries out. "Never!" The force of that stuns him. "No, never?" he shouts back. She is angry now herself, an effect of desperation. "Go, unhappy wretch! Forget a name that's infamous to you. Go, leave me at once. I've given my sacred oath to put you out of my life."

In her anger and fear for him (she truly does quake before the baron), she is giving the show away. Hearing herself, she catches her breath: another word of that and she will have gone too far to retract. And of course there is something soft and tender in her that is aching to tell him the truth. "Whom did you swear such an oath to? Tell me. Who could ask it of you?" She first tries an evasive answer, which will be true enough and yet misleading. "Someone who had every right." But the hint does not make him curious. "It was Douphol," he states. In other words, the baron. He has put the lie into her mouth for her. "Yes," she faintly assents, with a supreme effort of her will. But the weakness in her voice only suggests to the young man that she is ashamed of the admission. "You love him, then?" he demands. This lie comes easier. "Well, yes . . . I love him." For her, the crisis is over. She falls limply back on the sofa.

But for Alfredo it is far from over. He runs furiously to the big central doors and yells into the dining-room: "Everybody come here!" In confusion the guests enter from the supper tables; some of the men still have napkins tucked into their evening waistcoats. Behind the guests stand the servants, full of curiosity. "You called us? What do you want?" guests demand. In their bosoms there is evidently a conflict between anticipation of a scandal and desire to finish an exquisite meal in peace. Alfredo draws himself up. He points to Violetta. "You know this woman?" There is something almost biblical in the tableau; he must sense himself as an accusing prophet. She flinches and supports herself by leaning on a table. "Who? Violetta?" They all know her, of course. "But you don't know what she did?" She can half-guess what is coming and tries to stop him. "Be still," she begs, closing her eyes. But the others want to hear. He goes on to recount to the company how this woman they see before them squandered her whole property on him while he, blind, vile, abject, was able to let her do it right down to her last possession. The company listens in silence to this public confession.

"But there's still time!" he begins again, his convulsed voice rising to a shout. "Time to clear my honor of the infamous stain. I call everyone in this room to witness that I have paid her off—here!" With furious contempt he throws a purse at Violetta's feet. Coins tumble out onto the carpet as she falls fainting into the arms of Flora and the doctor.

In his frenzy Alfredo has not noticed the entry of his father, who has been in time to witness the gesture and hear the last scornful words. The severe, soberly dressed Germont cuts a path between the worldlings as they give voice to their shock and horror. They do not doubt that he has committed an infamous act. He has put himself beyond the pale. Not only has he struck a death blow at a sensitive heart but he has dishonored womanhood. This is the sacrilege for which he will be banished from society. No door will open to him again.

His father is in absolute accord. "No man insults a woman without dishonoring himself," he decrees in deep, measured tones, constituting himself the spokesman of the social establishment and the natural judge of his son. The fact that this is not a "respectable" gathering and that the insulted and injured party is a professional woman of pleasure is not felt by anyone as ironical but on the contrary seems to deepen the crime. "Where is my Alfredo?" Germont continues inflexibly, running his eyes over the criminal. "In you I don't find him any more." In other words, through his action, the beloved son has vanished as a member of the human race.

In a curiously parallel reaction, as he comes to his senses, Alfredo before our eyes is driven to *ostracize himself*. He, too, feels horror at his abominable deed and no longer knows the person who was capable of it; "mania" is the only word he can find to characterize the force that propelled him. And, naturally, he believes that he has put himself beyond forgiveness, at least Violetta's, which is suddenly all he cares about.

Simultaneously with his torments of repentance, Violetta is recovering consciousness. As she comes out of her swoon, she is conscious only of Alfredo, addressing herself to him or, rather, to the memory of him in feeble, passionate accents. The real young man, sunk in hopeless remorse, she apparently does not take notice of. Or else he is hidden from her by the throng of sympathizers that press forward to surround her the moment she sits up.

As she is conscious only of an ideal Alfredo existing as a central fixture in her unhappy mind, so her only concern is that he should comprehend how much she has loved him and loves him now. He does not know the lengths she has gone to to prove it, earning his contempt. But one day he will; he will learn of her sacrifice, and she prays God to save him then from bitter remorse.

"Even in death I shall continue to love you." It is another Violetta who weakly sits up in her chair—a pale prophecy of her dying self but already seeing visions and talking, as it were, to a ghost. He does not hear her, and she does not see him, or only indistinctly, like a reflection in the mirror of her thoughts. This is the ultimate case of cross-purposes in this ill-fated story, of a dialogue of the deaf.

Meanwhile Violetta's well-wishers crowding around her chair give the baron the chance he has been waiting for—to address Alfredo unheard by anyone and promise him the duel he asked for by his atrocious insult to a woman. From his point of view, Alfredo, besides being a rival, is an upstart—a little bourgeois from the Midi thrusting his way in—and he intends, with his weapon, to humble his "pride." Pride, though Douphol is too insensitive to guess it, is the last attribute that the wretched Alfredo, banished from his own society by his conscience, is in a position to sport.

At the same time old Germont is fighting a temptation, which is to tell what he knows. He is aware of being the only one in this whole milieu to be able to gauge the full measure of this kept woman's virtue, fidelity, nobility of spirit. But he must be cruel and keep silent. That, he tells himself, is where his duty lies.

In fact, were he to speak out now, the story would be over. Leading a quiet life in the country with her lover by her side, Violetta might even recover her health. Who knows, they might finally brave the conventions and marry. That could lead to children—Violetta is still under twenty-three—and children could serve to reconcile the family to an accomplished fact. But such a solution is not dreamed of, just as it has entered nobody's mind that the fiancé of that pure and spotless sister might marry the girl anyway, whatever her brother's truancy, if only he loved her as devotedly as the father claimed. No one among these people concerns himself with what one might call practical morality, involving concession and compromise. The ruling principle is sacrifice. For Germont, a skilled missionary of renunciation, it is a lofty program to be carried out by the kept woman mainly and to a lesser degree by Alfredo, who, however, can be expected to suffer less because of serene family influences and the "cure" of Provence. It may actually be that old Germont now sees himself as sacrificing pleasure to duty: it would be pleasant to speak up on Violetta's behalf since she has stirred grateful emotions in him and he is not insensitive to her beauty and charm. But, as head of the family, acting in its best interest, he must reject temptation and bow to duty's command.

Without a word to the deeply injured Violetta, he takes stern leave of the pleasure-den, pulling Alfredo along with him and followed at a discreet distance by the baron, stalking his prey. The remaining guests do their best to comfort Violetta, assuring her that they share her sufferings, that she is among friends, that she must dry her tears now. From this noisy, though well-meaning, consolation, she is rescued by the doctor and by Flora, who lead her into another room, where she can at least be quiet.

PART THREE

Hardly a month has passed. It is February now, carnival-time, and Violetta's disease has made its classic "galloping" progress. It is another, poorer, part of Paris. Her circumstances seem to be reduced; there are no signs of luxury. She is in bed with the bed-curtains half drawn; at the single window, closed inside shutters prevent the entry of light. In the fireplace a fire is burning. On the table by the bed are a decanter of water, a glass, bottles of medicine, a thermometer—all the accoutrements of the serious invalid. Across the room there are a dressing-table and a sofa, indicating that she is still able to get up occasionally. A night-light burns on another table. The closed shutters and dim illumination produce a disorienting effect, as though the sickroom were adrift in space. There is no way of knowing where we are or what time it is. In this room there is no clock. Behind the half-drawn curtains Violetta is asleep on the big bed, and in front of the fireplace, in a chair, there is another sleeping figure, apparently a maid—the same one, Annie.

It *is* the same girl. Violetta, waking up, calls her name to ask for some water. The sleepy girl pours her a glass from the carafe. Then Violetta wants to know whether it is morning yet. Nearly seven o'clock, Annina thinks. Violetta orders her to let in some light. Annina opens the shutters and looks out into the street. "Dr. Grenvil!" she exclaims. "What a true friend," Violetta murmurs, touched by his calling so early to see after her. She wants to get up to receive him and tells Annina to help her. As soon as she has put her feet down and tries to stand, she falls back on the bed. But then, supported by the maid, she manages to walk slowly toward the sofa. The doctor is in time to give her an arm to lean on.

Again, she is touched by his goodness and tells him so, revealing how alone in life she must be. He takes her pulse. "How are you feeling?" Her body is in pain, she replies honestly, but her soul is at peace. Last night she had a visit from a priest, who brought her some comfort. Religion is a solace for those who suffer—she confides that discovery with an innocent soft smile. Clearly she has never heard before of the consolations of religion. "And how did the night go?" She thinks back. "I slept well." "Take heart, then. Convalescence can't be far off." She gives a half-teasing shake of her head, then lets it fall back wearily on a cushion. "You doctors have the right, don't you, to tell us kindly lies." He presses her thin hand. "Good-bye, till later." "Don't forget me," she begs, sitting up as if in a flurry of alarm.

As Annina is showing him out, she asks him softly how Violetta is. Only a few hours left, he whispers. "That's the way it is with consumptives." Hiding her own disquiet, the girl makes an effort to cheer the patient. "So then, take heart!" Violetta, not deceived, changes the subject. "Isn't today a holiday?" Carnival, Annina tells her (i.e., Mardi Gras); Paris is going wild. This moves Violetta to reflection: amid the general merrymaking, God alone knows how many unfortunates are suffering. It is lonely to be sick or poor on a holiday. She points to a little money chest. "How much have we got left?" Annina unlocks it and counts out some gold coins. "Twenty louis." "Go give ten to the poor." "But that won't leave you much," protests Annina. "Enough to last me," Violetta answers calmly. It is hard to guess whether this sudden profligate gesture springs from the generosity we already know in her character or whether she is using a reliable magic formula to conciliate fortune—women of her profession are superstitious.

"Afterwards, fetch my letters." She dispatches the girl, who seems hesitant to execute the charitable commission. "But what about you?" wonders Annina, turning back at the door. "I won't need anything. But hurry, if you can." As soon as the door has closed, Violetta takes a letter from the bosom of her nightgown, carefully unfolds it, and reads it softly aloud. It is almost a recitation, so well does she know the contents. " 'You kept your promise. The duel took place. The baron was wounded. He's recovering, however. Alfredo is in foreign lands. I myself have revealed your sacrifice to him. He's coming back to you to beg your forgiveness. I shall come, too—take care of yourself—you deserve a happier future. Giorgio Germont.' "

"Too late!" she moans in a dead lusterless voice, letting the letter fall. She gets up. "I wait and wait and they never come." She struggles to the mirror on the dressing-table. "Oh, how changed I am. Yet the doctor tells me to hope. Ah, with this sickness every hope is dead!" She hovers before the mirror, peering at images of the past she seems to see reflected— roses in her cheeks, now cruelly faded, Alfredo's love. . . . She misses it even now, on the edge of the grave. What a comfort, what a support it would have been for her weary soul. . . . She cannot tear herself away from the mirror. Memories mingle with tears; laments finally yield to prayers for redemption. But the sudden vision of her earthly tomb, coldly intervening, is too much for her: no flowers, no mourners, no cross with her name on it to cover her bones. . . . Will God not consent to smile on the last desire of "the woman gone astray" and welcome her to Himself?

She sinks down hopeless on the sofa while outside the window a wild pagan song is heard. The populace is acclaiming the Fatted Ox, king and lord of the Carnival, who is being drawn in procession down below in the street with garlands of flowers and vine-leaves around his neck to the shrilling of pipes and drums. The piercing sound coming in the window is a hymn of worship to the ribboned victim. At a thousand altars across the city of Paris, the guild of aproned butchers awaits his coming with sharpened sacrificial knives. Violetta is not attending. The analogy with herself as sacrificial victim would not be present to her.

The procession moves off, and Annina hurries into the room. There is something hesitant in her manner. "Madam . . ." "What's happened?" "Is it true, madam, that you're feeling better today?" "Yes, but why?" "You promise to be calm?" Violetta can hardly fail to guess that some important news is about to be broken to her. "Yes, yes. What is it you want to tell me?" "I wanted to prepare you for an unexpected joy—a surprise." "A joy, did you say?" "Yes, dear madam." Violetta lets out a cry. "Alfredo! You've seen him!" The girl nods. "He's coming! Oh, make him hurry!" And, despite her weakness, she is able to rise and post herself in the doorway. "Alfredo?" In a minute, he is there, still in traveling clothes, and they fall into each other's arms, exclaiming and marveling, both talking at the same time in a veritable Babel of happiness.

His first distinguishable words are a confession of guilt. He has learned the truth and blames himself for everything. But she will not have that. No explanations or accounting. All she knows or wants to know is that he has come back to her. He takes her hand and presses it to his heart. Its beating will teach her whether or not he loves her. He knows that he will not be able to exist without her any more. She smiles slightly at this, touched by the characteristic hyperbole. She has made a discovery, she tells him: grief cannot kill. If it could, he would never have found her still alive this morning.

But he has missed the seriousness behind her frail little jest, not observing in his excitement how fearfully changed she is. She must forget grief now, he tells her, and pardon him and his father. "But no, I ask *your* pardon," she answers with great sweetness. "I am the guilty one. But only love could

306

have made me do what I did." She is referring to her re-sumption of the relation with the baron—a risky subject, one would think. But Alfredo receives it very calmly, which looks like a sign that he has matured.

Together they bury the Douphol interlude. Neither man nor devil, they agree, will ever come between them again. The emphasis they bring to this joint declaration sends a light shiver down the spine. By naming the devil, will they make him appear in their path? And when they speak of him, the Prince of Darkness, what or whom do they mean? It cannot be a mere roué like the Baron Douphol whose advances they must pledge themselves to resist. Douphol is no real danger. Rather, it must be Alfredo's own father—the formidable mis-sionary of middle-class morality, Giorgio Germont. Are these young people alert enough, now that it is too late, to recog-nize the Father of Lies, smell the whiff of brimstone?

In any case, Alfredo has the remedy for their troubles, which is to leave Paris. Violetta is of the same mind. And this time it will not be to Auteuil they will go, virtually at the city's gates, but to the genuine country. Far from the great world's lures, he will be able to look after her in peace and she to regain her health. Our pity goes out to their igno-rance, for we have heard what the doctor said. And in the midst of the plans they are sketching for a smiling future in the classical *rus* (reminiscent of Germont's apostrophe to the purifying sun and sea of Provence), Violetta herself has a *fris-son* of foreboding. She halts her joyful lover in the middle of his farewell to Paris. Her voice is unsteady. "No more, please . . . Alfredo . . . Let's go to church and give thanks for your return." Moving toward the clothes-cupboard with the inten-tion of dressing for church, she hesitates, sways on her feet. He stares at her, taken aback, observing her, really, for the first time since they left each other a month ago. "You're get-ting pale!"

She tries to reassure him. "It's nothing. *You* know. I can

never stand a sudden access of joy." But even as she offers this half-plausible explanation, she lets herself fall, exhausted, onto a seat. He is terrified. He holds her up and looks into her face with horror. "Good God, Violetta!" "It's my illness. A sinking spell. Now I'm better. See? I'm smiling." That smile, a product of her will, appalls him more than her feebleness. Under his breath, devastated, he laments this last cruel turn of destiny. "It's nothing," she repeats tenderly, still forcing her mechanical smile. "Annina, give me something to put on." "Now?" He is incredulous. "Oh, please, wait." She is determined. "No, I want to go out."

Annina, who understands her mistress, is standing by with a flounced dress. Violetta starts to put it on and then, hindered by her feebleness from getting her arm through a long tight sleeve, throws it on the floor. "Oh, God! I can't do it!" Once more, she falls back onto the seat. Alfredo, still hardly able to believe his eyes, orders Annina to go for the doctor. The mention of that faithful friend somewhat revives Violetta. She sits up straighter. "Tell him," she directs, "that Alfredo has come back to my arms. Tell him that I want to live."

The maid hastens out and, alone with Alfredo, Violetta seems to have regained a little more of her strength. Raising her head, she looks straight at him and utters the truth. "But if you, coming back, can't save me, nobody on earth can." She reflects. "Oh, God, to die so young when I've suffered such a lot already. To die when I'm so close to drying my tears at last." This is said not in a tone of self-commiseration but soberly, with a clear-sighted awareness of the irony of her "narrow escape" from happiness. "But it was a delusion," she goes on, "that credulous hope of mine. It was a waste of effort to fortify my heart to be true. Alfredo, what a rough ending they've reserved for our love."

He does not want to hear this. His torn soul is in no mood for stock-taking. She's his breath and his very heart-

beat, he cries out, his dear delight. Her tears call forth his—
he cannot tell which are which. But more than ever—she must
believe it—he needs her steadfast spirit. For his sake, she must
not close her mind to hope. He begs it of her. "Oh, calm
yourself, my own, my dear Violetta. Your grief is killing me."
What he cannot admit, of course, is that she *is* calm, facing
her own extinction. It is he who is agitated. And what he is
really begging her is to spare him her death, in other words,
not to die.

At that moment, without preparation, when his son's
demoralized state has reached a point close to total abjection,
Germont enters the sickroom. He is a breath not of fresh air
but of authority, and his concern is not with love but with
dignity. Standing in the doorway, he speaks Violetta's name,
loudly, like a summons. "Ah, Violetta!" Behind him appear
Annina and the doctor. "You, sir!" she cries happily, struggling to sit up and arrange her laces and ribbons. "Father!"
puts in Alfredo, surprised. He has not been aware of the special relation that has grown up between these two. Wholly
intent on each other, Violetta and Germont seem for the
moment to forget him. She is oblivious, too, of the doctor,
who is taking her pulse. "So you didn't forget me?" she marvels. The father draws himself up. "I am here to keep the
promise I gave you. To take you to my heart as a daughter."
His stiff form bends down toward her; his deep voice darkens
with emotion. "Oh, generous girl." In deference to his father's
feeling, Alfredo steps aside. "Alas, you've come too late." The
flat words escape her before she can stop herself. "Still, I'm
grateful. . . ." She would not wish to take away from his pride
in the keeping of the promise. With his assistance, she pulls
herself upright and embraces him. As they stand clasped in
each other's arms, she catches sight of the doctor. "Do you
see this, Grenvil? In the arms of all my dear ones, I'm drawing my last breath."

Startled, Germont releases her, so that he can study her

better. Her tone just now with her medical attendant has been gay, almost teasing, but the father does not like what he sees in her over-bright eyes. "What are you saying?" he exclaims. Then he examines her wasted form. "Great Heaven, it's true!" he mutters to himself.

He bows his head, shaken, remembering how he had doubted her when she had spoken during their last meeting of her failing health. He had taken it for a lie she had invented to put him off. Obviously he had not known this woman at all, despite the god-like part he had played in her unhappy destiny. Or was the part he played diabolical? The thought occurs to him for the first time. Unfortunately she has to die to prove what she really is—a dying woman—and absolve herself of the last of his suspicions. "Do you *see* her, Father?" the son says vehemently. Germont bows to the stinging reproach. He will have a great deal to forgive himself, if he is able.

"Don't torture me, I beg you. No more, please! I'm devoured with remorse already. Every word of hers goes through me like a bolt of lightning. Imprudent old man!" Repentance, as always—is that not its nature?—is too late, just like his arrival in this dingy room in a "popular" neighborhood. He shakes his head. "Only now I see the wrong I did her."

With father and son brooding on either side of her, Violetta is called on to exercise her force of character. The moment is ripe for a universal reconciliation, and she must reconcile these unhappy men, her dear ones, with themselves—their past errors and cruelties—and, more important, with the future. And, wonderfully, she has a plan. From a hiding-place at her elbow, she takes a jewel-case that contains a miniature of herself. Unlocking the little casket—unique relic of her worldly past—she turns to Alfredo, her real love, from whom in her simplicity she has let the hideous specter of duty tear her away.

"Come closer, dear Alfredo. Listen, won't you take this?

It's the picture of me as I was then, in the good days. It can serve to remind you of her who loved you so." Alfredo still refuses to hear the note of finality, maybe because it speaks to him in that dreamy, dulcet voice, which affects him like a caress. "No, you won't die! Don't tell me that. God cannot have put me here to bear such a torment." But the dulcet voice overrides his protest and grows dreamier still.

It is telling of the life to come, where Violetta sees a vision, of a pure young girl. Is it the little sister for whom she has made the heroic sacrifice? No, it is another maiden, a girl he does not know yet, the girl who will offer him her heart and whom he must marry, because Violetta wishes it. Sister and bride blur as Violetta gazes raptly into the future. This is the ultimate sacrifice, the cruelest and sweetest of all. She has died on the altar of the family and looks down on it from Heaven.

"Give her this little image. Tell her that it's a present from one who is praying for her, one who's up above with the angels and prays for her and for you." The fusion is complete. She has made a gift of her life to a young girl "pure as an angel" and now, in reward, she is an angel herself, offering the gift of her image to another chaste spirit. The unchaste one, chastened, is leaning down from Heaven dangling a holy eidolon, like the girdle that the Virgin on the day of her Assumption tossed to the Apostle Thomas doubtingly watching her mount.

In an ideal sense, it is all true. Violetta, who was never bad except in the eyes of middle-class morality, has become wholly and visibly "good." This can be a moral fact even if a deception has been practiced on the aspiring soul, even if the new-made angel does not receive a genuine, twenty-four-carat harp, even if it is a shocking case of victimization. In any event, the struggle is over, or nearly so. *Consummatum est.* They gather round her deathbed, Alfredo still begging to be told it is not true, his father repenting, and the doctor and

Annie bidding her suffering soul farewell as they see it fly off to join the blessed spirits they believe are "up there." And, for a pseudo-miraculous moment, Violetta herself is brought back to life, rising to her feet with no sign of weakness. All her pains have left her; her former strength, as if by magic, has come back. But only Alfredo is deceived, crying "Violetta!" in an access of joy. It is a phenomenon familiar to medicine—a last flare-up of life. She falls back on the bed. The doctor feels her pulse. She is dead.

Fall 1983

NATURE PIECES

The Rake's Progress*

ELEANOR PERÉNYI'S TITLE is from Marvell: "Annihilating all that's made / To a green Thought in a green Shade" ("The Garden"). Her genius here, though, is Johnsonian, and I mean it as a high compliment. These witty and useful sallies on the art and practice of gardening are arranged in dictionary form; the entries proceed alphabetically from "Annuals" through "Woman's Place," with an appendix on catalogues.

The loose-leaf arrangement is ideally suited to the material, each entry fitting into its well-dug bed of history and legends and yet retaining a certain branching liberty of form. Other non-technical books on the subject have been based, with logic, on the calendar, like the ancient *Works and Days*. The first twelve chapters of Gertrude Jekyll's *Wood & Garden* (1899 and a bible to the present author) run from January through December. The longer English growing season recommends that approach: "There is always in February some one day, at least, when one smells the yet distant, but surely coming, summer," Miss Jekyll's second chapter—*February*—begins. A four-part division by seasons, harking back to Thomson and Haydn, is possible too. But Mrs. Perényi's

*A review of *Green Thoughts: A Writer in the Garden*, by Eleanor Perényi.

315

method, not needing to stick to Nature's fairly iron-clad schedule, can be pithy or expansive ad libitum, which allows her pleasing changes of tempo. The entry "MAZES," for example, two sentences long, offers the following counsel: "Should you ever find yourself lost in one, choose either the right or the left wall and follow its every turning. You can't fail to emerge."

I wonder whether Eleanor Perényi was conscious of Dr. Johnson's accompanying shade as inspiration in these pages. It may be just an affinity of temperament. If the great lexicographer had been reborn after undergoing a sex change and been interested in the outdoors in the first place he would not be averse, I think, to putting his name to many of these "green thoughts." The point in common is an unshakable firmness of opinion, often looking frankly like prejudice, as in the famous definition of "RENEGADE," or Mrs. Perényi's decided views on "EVERGREENS," "SEED TAPES," wood-chip mulches, almost any gardening fashion. Like Johnson, she has a vigor of expression to match her ideas and a range of erudition that surprises by its freedom from pedantry. I knew about fuchsia and funkia, but never guessed (though one could have) that dahlias were named for a botanist Dahl and zinnias for a Herr Zinn. Johnson, though not musical, might have been diverted to learn that Handel assigned his Xerxes an ode to the plane tree: "amor vegetabile, cara ed amabile." But the basic, the profound, resemblance between the two lies in an empirical cast of mind combining with strict principles to give a dappled effect of waywardness—the signature of a majestic and authoritative yet noticeably human nature. One could not reasonably expect Sam Johnson to be a humbly devout Christian, and yet he was close to that, nor would one expect Mrs. Perényi to be a humbly devout apostle of *Organic Gardening*, and yet she is close to that.

One of the many charms of this delightful book is its lack of claim to professionalism. It is manifestly directed to amateurs by a more advanced member of their tribe. Mrs. Perényi has been an amateur longer and more inveterately than most gardeners and is unashamed of it. In fact it is this in the end that constitutes her authority, even gives her the papal right to an occasional ex-cathedra pronouncement. Confessions of failure, uttered in a forthright, no-nonsense tone, give the author an ascendancy over professional gardening experts, who are in no position to make such avowals without supplying an explanation of the *cause* of the failure.

That is the difference between literature (Mrs. P.) and "science" (Your Garden Columnist). To get to the bottom of her repeated annoying failures—giant blue delphiniums, gentians, sweet peas—Mrs. Perényi, were she an expert, would send samples of her soil to her county extension agent for the usual series of tests. Just like checking yourself into the hospital for the annual exploration. But she has *never sent her soil for analysis, nor her compost, nor the salt hay and seaweed she uses as mulch.* In gardening circles this is as peculiar as it would be to meet someone in New York intellectual circles who has never been to a psychoanalyst or smoked pot. And I will bet that she doesn't even own a home soil-testing kit. Or a rain gauge. Like any normal gardener, she has failures and sometimes she suspects what has caused them (a dog peeing, for example; a street light shining on the chrysanthemums). But sometimes she can find no culprit. It is a mystery. Like why the hollyhock and foxglove seeds I plant in *my* garden never come up—no, the seed is not old.

Not just the failures. The successes (or luck) she has in her garden are frequently a mystery to her too. She does not know why her tomatoes fail to get the blight, why in fact the whole village of Stonington is blight-free. It is (to repeat) luck. Yet luck by itself cannot account for or excuse success or the lack of it in gardening. Obviously study and hard work are factors. Mrs. Perényi says she does not believe in a "green thumb." But I imagine that she is simply tired of hearing about it; she is irritated by clichés.

It is clear that experience and common sense, plus luck, count for a great deal with her. Yet isn't a "green thumb" the proverbial name assigned by common sense to cover a mysterious run of luck in making things grow? Common sense, thus—an ally of folk wisdom—has noted an x factor in the whole gardening business. Mrs. Perényi herself subsumes it under "MAGIC." "The lesson for the gardener," she counsels, "is not to swallow everything he reads in books. . . . If you have a question, don't write your newspaper either. Better to consult the old lady down the road, the one whose porch is covered with moon vines and who grows the blessed thistle (*Cnicus benedictus*) in her garden."

This old lady, of course, is a witch. Mrs. Perényi has been writing in anger against what she calls establishment thinking in the gardening world—thinking with an automatic, unquestioning bias in favor of the arsenal of herbicides and pesticides employed by the majority. It is understandable that in the context she would prefer "white" witchcraft to black "science," lunacy (the moon vine, night sister of the morning glory) to sanity. Mrs. Perényi, for all her rationality, is a romantic. If she were not, she would give up the struggle.

Worse, she does not really believe in her anti-scientific magic. When there is no longer any old lady down the road, where does the reader turn? The whole passage is a groan of future-shocked despair. More than a hundred pages later, toward the end of the book, she is writing prophetically: "Already I am something of a freak in this community on account of my vegetables, herbs and fruits. I foresee the day when I graduate from freak to witch."

———

318

Gardening, in this country, is an eccentricity. It is wasteful, time-consuming, expensive, impractical. That home-grown fruits and vegetables *taste* better cannot justify the mad investment of labor. The growing of flowers is still more indefensible as long as there are florists in practice (or, for people who cannot afford florists, goldenrod or Queen Anne's lace growing free by the roadside). Both pursuits rest on indemonstrable premises. Taste better to whom? Or taste *how much* better? Enough to repay the cost-computed labor? The answer "immeasurably better" will not do. As for home-grown flowers, by what standards, pray, are they superior to florists' flowers, to say nothing of the eco-approved wild flowers and grasses? Are flowers in fact necessary at all in the ordinary home? Ceremonial occasions seeming to require them, traditionally connected with the rites of marriage and death, are no longer held at home but in the reception rooms and "parlors" of hotels and funeral directors. There is no evident answer to these questions. Only in terms of what are admittedly prejudices can you put up an argument for a dish of garden peas on the table and some home-cultivated flowers (wild don't last as well) in the middle.

In any case it is obvious to the naked eye, at least in my part of the country, that flower gardens are disappearing, along with family fruit trees and vegetable gardens. Even roadside stands, which were a cross between home growing and market growing, are getting scarce, so that you are lucky this year to see a couple of cucumbers with a hand-printed sign "CUKES" beside a rural mailbox. And to find a passionate, straw-hatted lady gardener at work in her rows is as arresting a sight as a scarecrow dressed in the straw-hatted lady's old clothes. Mrs. Perényi is aware of all this. She knows full well that it is not "worth it" to attempt to grow the quinces, pears, apricots, gentians, Himalayan poppies that she does keep trying and is conscious, too, that even the more co-operative subjects such as peonies and phlox ("Pansies are a *thankful* flower,"

319

a young countrywoman said to me once) are a folly she indulges herself in for no better reason than that a garden without them "would be sad."

There are pages where she treats her garden ruefully as a sort of addiction, and this view of it may help solve a puzzle: the thriving state of the seed, bulb, and gardening-tools industry in the teeth of what looks to me like the general disappearance of gardens. As Mrs. Perényi points out, most of the old firms like Burpee's—selling by catalogue to home growers as well as to nurserymen—have been taken over by conglomerates, which strongly suggests that there is still pay dirt there. Even granting that the breeders today, like publishers, concentrate on the mass market—the best-selling petunias, zinnias, marigolds—to the neglect of old favorites like sweet peas, bachelor's buttons, love-in-a-mist, this is a bit peculiar. I can only think that people buy more seeds, tubers, corms, bulbs, rhizomes, than they ever plant, more tools and gadgets than they ever use, that there is a gardening itch, like an addiction, that comes on strongest in the fall and winter, when the catalogues hit the mailboxes, and that the craving, in the end, proves to be purely mental (platonic, you might say), getting no farther than the filling out of an order slip and writing of a check. Still, though I can verify the suspicion to some extent from my own practices, from the packages of ancient seeds (wild strawberry, for instance, angelica!) gathering dust in the toolshed, it cannot be the whole story. Perhaps there are secret gardens, like the Mary gardens, or *giardini segreti*, mentioned by Mrs. Perényi, that right this minute lie hidden from a prying eye down loggers' trails in the woods, in mobile-home parks, town dumps, and cemetery plots.

Making things grow, at least in Connecticut, where the author lives, and in Maine, where I spend half the year, is a continuing struggle in which it often appears that Nature, far from being on your side, is actively against you, attacking with bugs, molds, rot, cankers, neighboring dogs, raccoons, skunks, porcupines, drought, torrential rains, "black" frosts, snow heaves, winter-kill. And I cannot think that the satisfaction derived is in the results, however beautiful or tasty. Even my exquisite Mme Hardy rose with its green center like a curled-up worm and faint blush of pink on the first creamy petals (unobtainable at any florist) or the messes of tender lima pole beans harvested and cooked by Mrs. Perényi (try and find them at the Shop 'n' Save) will never quite compensate the grower for the anxious pain and fret of cultivation. If they *are* the reward, then greed (of eye or tongue) would be the chief motive for gardening: you dig and scratch so as to be able to sit back and savor the end product. I do not believe that that is how it works. That is not why the Risen Christ appeared to the Magdalen in the likeness of a gardener. Certainly there is a joy in fruition, and some pride, too, but it is more in the strange process of growth brought to completion than in the testimonials to the *value* of the process represented by the yield.

That value, as I have been suggesting, can always be called into question by somebody who doesn't "know about" old roses or care for lima beans and thinks the time consumed would be better spent in a boat or on a tennis court. Only a fellow gardener can judge your rose or lima bean in the light of an ideal product, which both you and he see in the mind's eye. And only another gardener can appreciate the components of luck and accident in the mysterious process of growth, that is, sense the history of inscrutably simple and complex causes leading up to the eventual fruit or flower nodding on the stalk, as though to nudge you into recognition of a numinous presence—related to L., *nuere*, to nod.

The fact is that gardening, more than most of our other activities except sometimes love-making, confronts us with the inexplicable. Like a rock struck by the spading fork in ground long worked over and hence presumably free of boulders, mystery rears up to meet us from a restless subsoil constantly turning in its bed. Mrs. Perényi seems to find this particularly true of the behavior of vines; she does not know *why* a clematis refuses to follow the course laid down for it and instead crawls along a telephone cable or why a *Hydrangea petiolaris*, disobeying all Nature's rules, heads sidewise into the thick shade of a hemlock hedge rather than upward to the sun. But vines, admittedly, are serpentine.

The mystery suddenly met, "surprised," almost, in the garden (as in "Coming Through the Rye" or the Apparition to the Magdalen) is omnipresent, though lurking. It is tied to the life process, an idea we can accept, but, more disturbingly, to what is commonly called the "supernatural." Appropriately, the subject is tackled in the entry called "SEEDS," when the author is talking of "Adonis gardens"—spring baskets or pots planted with quick-sprouting wheat, fennel, and lettuce by women of antiquity to welcome the risen god. Then, all at once, she gruffly interjects: "I am an agnostic. I don't believe a word of any organized religion and go to church only to look at the architecture, listen to music I could hear nowhere else. . . . And yet, that isn't quite right either. When it comes down to it, I am as superstitious as any savage about the origins of life and as disposed to propitiate the powers that govern nature. True gardeners will know what I mean. You can't work among plants for long and remain altogether an unbeliever: it is too obvious that *something is going on.*" The italics (hers) come down like the full stops of an organ.

This must be the core and pith of the book. As so often when one is dealing with Nature, explanation would seem out of place. We do not wish to hear *what* is going on, in the author's opinion, any more than we want her to send a sample of her soil to her county agent for analysis. *Better leave it alone*, in both cases. Maybe what she is saying is only common sense, and common sense, for all we know, may be natural wisdom transmitted genetically. Tolstoy seems to have believed something of the kind and so did Socrates.

I confess that I do not follow all Mrs. Perényi's principles in my garden practice. I lack the strength of character *not* to spray fruit trees that are manifestly being eaten by enemies and if I find it easy to resist chemical fertilizers, it is because supplies of wood ash, manure, and seaweed are locally available. We have a thing called the Rotocrop (which I found in an ad in the *Observer* and which she would surely scoff at) that makes compost out of kitchen garbage—best to leave out large animal bones—as well as leaves and grass cuttings. But if we could not get manure, I doubt whether I would be heroic enough to go it on compost alone; anyway there would not be enough.

We have also used Weed-and-Feed on the lawn, and when we gave it up, it was not because our lawn was wrecked by it as hers was by some similar product—in fact ours was greatly improved—but because the wind blew the stuff all over the lilacs. So she was right about that, even if for her own, to me not quite tenable reasons. I am a much softer gardener than the author, which means I am a bad gardener. I would not have the heart to emulate Miss Jekyll in a "vigorous thinning" of the nut-trees in January or hack out some of the Scotch fir "that are beginning to crowd each other." To be a good gardener, you must be ruthless and decisive, and I am neither. I am a temporizer.

But you do not have to be a good gardener to fall in love with *Green Thoughts*. Its willingness to talk of failures is an encouragement to lesser lights. Probably the author's frankness promotes a spirit of confession in the reader, which permits him to face up to his defects. As an inveterate realist, Mrs. Perényi is full of good counsel; the soundest remedy is often simply to throw the erring plant away. She is reassuring about garden "subjects," such as leeks, commonly regarded as difficult. Of modern hybrid lilies, said to be "fussy": "All they require is a hole dug for them in sun, or semi-shade. . . . I plant them a little deeper than is usually suggested, putting into the hole a tablespoon of bone meal or dried cow manure topped with a pad of sand for good drainage. Then I forget them—which is why a label with their names must be attached to a stick placed in their vicinity."

The book reads as though it had been immense fun to write. It also reads with the intrepid assurance of a classic, which it will be, I think, for a very long time, possibly in years to come as "escape literature" when there are no gardens left to relate to it. In anticipation of a string of future editions, I have two small hesitant questions to raise. The first has to do with the "Mary garden" of medieval and Renaissance painting; Mrs. Perényi calls it the *"hortus inclusus."* My own recollection is of a *"hortus conclusus."*

The second concerns the dessert called Apple Charlotte, from which other desserts including Charlotte Russe derived. Mrs. Perényi tells us that four varieties of apple were named for Queen Charlotte, consort of George III of England "—hence, it is said, Apple Charlotte." For my part, I have always understood that the dish—like the Charlotte mold it is made in—was named for Goethe's Lotte. To quote the first stanza of Thackeray's parody, "The Sorrows of the Young Werther":

> *Werther had a love for Charlotte*
> *Such as words could never utter.*
> *Would you know how first he met her?*
> *She was cutting bread and butter.*

And here is the last stanza, following on Werther's suicide:

Charlotte, having seen his body
Borne before her on a shutter,
Like a well-conducted person,
Went on cutting bread and butter.

Sliced bread and butter are the "basics" of the dish, which originally contained apples but today may use other fruit. The Charlotte Russe uses sliced cake rather than bread, but the principle is the same. Yet even if Mrs. Perényi is wrong (as the persistence of the bread-and-butter theme suggests) in her notion of the provenance of the dessert, I am grateful for a nice bit of information contained in the same sentence: not just apples, the *Strelitzia* (bird-of-paradise flower) was named for Queen Charlotte, an ardent botanist who was born Mecklenburg-Strelitz.

November 5, 1981

The Very Unforgettable Miss Brayton

I<small>N THE LAST QUARTER</small> of her life, Alice Brayton's garden in Portsmouth, on the island of Rhode Island, became a social magnet for visitors to Newport, "society's summer capital," a fifteen-minute drive away. I was first brought to see it in 1949, when I had moved to a farmhouse on Union Street, Portsmouth, and already, on that first afternoon, I had the sense of being taken to a delightful little circus with its own P. T. Barnum in the form of a small white-haired spinster ("I'm not an old maid, I'm a spinster"), the owner, the impresario, and a principal exhibit of the show.

Officially the property was famous for its topiary work, the "Green Animals" she had decided to name it for at about the time I met her. Before that, it had no name, not pretending to be an estate; the address was simply "Cory's Lane, Portsmouth"—an address it shared with the Priory, a boys' school run by "black" Benedictines across the country road. The land sloped down to Narragansett Bay, which made for very mild winters allowing her to grow figs, virtually unheard of elsewhere in that part of the world, and bamboo for staking. The topiary collection stood on an elevation like a grassy platform behind the large white frame house, and several of the privet animals—the giraffe, the camel, the ostrich, the elephant, the horse and the rider—besides being raised on clipped green pedestals, were unusually tall in their own right, so that the impression on one coming from Cory's Lane was of a sheared family of Mesozoic creatures—dinosaurs, ptero-dactyls.

That impression remained even though the greater number of the animals belonged to the classic repertory—a swan, a pair of peacocks, a unicorn, a bear, a boar, a cock, a she-wolf (copied from the Roman bronze of Romulus and Remus's foster-parent); there were also baskets with handles, tall tubular forms resembling tops, and (the greatest hit) a po-liceman at the entry with a night stick and a metal star on his bristly green chest.

The general assumption was that the animals were a col-laboration between Alice Brayton's fancy and the clippers of a family of Portuguese gardeners who worked and lived on the place. But sometimes she would disown her own part in the creation. "Folk art," she said dryly when in that humor. "It all came out of Joe's head." At other times she insisted that the topiary was as old as herself; in that version she was just the curator, maintaining it "as it was"—this despite the fact that there were accessions to the collection, including, if I'm not mistaken, the policeman, who could hardly have been "in restoration" when I first saw the garden.

It was the same with the inside of the house: she could never decide whether she preferred to have us think that wall-papers, draperies, and so on were "original," i.e., more than 150 years old (the age of the house varied too, according to her mood), or testimony to her prowess as a decorator. Was it better to have had "ancestors" or to be a genius in one's own right—self-made? I don't think Miss Brayton was ever able to settle her mind on that point, which nevertheless was the pivot of her existence. The truth was she had created something indisputably her own—her gingery self, her evolv-ing animals, her continually revised mythology of wallpapers, draperies, carpets, bell-pulls—and never knew whether to be proud of that or ashamed.

Alice Brayton did not come from Portsmouth. She was a Fall River woman, from one of the ruling mill families; Lizzie Borden she claimed as a cousin or cousin once removed. The Fall River gentry—Hazards and Durfees, Bordens and Braytons (there was also a "Satan" Drayton)—were plain people, largely undisturbed by their wealth. In Fall River, I was told, husbands and wives were seated side by side at dinners, on the ground that at least they would have something to talk about. Practical, hard-headed people; the main business block was called "Granite Block" and looked it. Another Brayton I knew, a granitic young lawyer with an office in the block, gave me his matter-of-fact prescription for surviving the "wild" late-starting (6:30 P.M.) cocktail parties of a Westport Harbor hostess: "I have my supper first."

In fact, as I now know, the Portsmouth house was not a family property but a purchase Alice Brayton's father made. It was normal for well-off Fall River people to have summer houses near the seashore, which was how, I suppose, "Green Animals" started out. But the vicinity of Newport, for Miss Brayton later a strategic height to be scaled with rope ladders, was a little "different." Usually Fall River men did not take their wives and children so far; they went (and still did in my time) to Westport Harbor, Sakonnet, *à la rigueur* to Little Compton. I would love to have seen the inside of Alice Brayton's "real house" in Fall River; if I remember the outside right, it was gray, stone, square, without frills—no gazebo on the lawn, not so much as an arbor. But she had not lived there for many years when it was pointed out to me, on Cliff Street, naturally—she herself never spoke of it, as though it were a divorced relation.*

Now, ten years after her death, I learn from a book on

---

*In fact, her nephew tells me, I was shown the wrong house, the property of some other Braytons. Her own had been torn down.

Eastern public gardens that her father, Thomas Brayton of the Union Cotton Manufacturing Co., Fall River, bought the Portsmouth house in 1872 and that the topiary dates from 1893. According to this authority, he had seen topiary work in a botanical garden in the Azores and hired a gardener, Joseph Carreiro, a native of the Azores, to make something like it for him on Narragansett Bay. But *is* there a botanical garden in the steep volcanic Azores, mainly noted for the growing of pineapples? And what was a Massachusetts mill owner doing in the Azores anyway—hiring Portuguese labor to sweat? I feel very skeptical about that part of the tale. It sounds like a typical Alice Brayton invention, very much in her narrative vein, and has the virtue of providing her animals with ancestors.

Miss Brayton was a fabulist. I do not think she lied about other people (she was mischievous but not malicious), nor to obtain advantage or get herself out of a scrape. She was a pure spinner of tales and myths centering on herself and her life story. She lied constantly, inveterately; it was almost one of her charms. You discovered to your amazement that you could not trust anything she told you pertaining to herself or to anything she owned.

And did she sometimes catch herself lying? If so, what an awful experience. She professed to hate liars, and I believed her. As she grew older, she grew more class-obsessed, and it distressed me to hear her talk more and more wildly after her second martini on themes of class and race—I felt ashamed for her. One of her phobic convictions on the subject of "them"—Portuguese, Catholics, Irish, the whole race of millhands—was that they lied. When the fit was on her, she liked to explain that the difference between "us" and "them" boiled down to the fact that "we" never told a lie. As an observant little party, she knew better. It is a puzzle to me where she got her obstinate delusion of being a truth-teller either as an individual *or* as a representative of her class. I wonder whether for her it may not have figured as a synonym for outspokenness, the habit of speaking her mind. Maybe she honestly did more of that than the lesser breeds—she could afford it.

But to leave general speculation and get down to brass tacks: *did* she plant the pair of Turkish oaks that stood at the head of the garden, by the water-lily pool? She maintained that she grew them from two acorns that she had buried at the spot when she was a little girl. Oaks are slow growers, yet here the two were, nodding as she told their story, ninety or a hundred feet tall. Years ago, alas, when I looked them up in a tree book with the thought of planting a pair of my own, I found reference only to a "turkey oak" (*Quercus laevis*), a small Southern variety whose popular name is said to derive from the wild turkeys attracted to the sweet acorn—no resemblance to the ones on Cory's Lane.

But wait. Hers, I now discover, trying an older book, must have been *Quercus cerris*, also known as "turkey oak," a fast grower that was brought to England from the Turkish peninsula and became fashionable with nurserymen in late Victorian times. So Miss Brayton stands vindicated; even the dates tally. If the trees had reached their full height when she was seventy years old, she could well have been eight when she planted them. There is just one bothersome note: in today's descriptive flyer, issued by the Newport Preservation Society, no Turkish oaks are listed, and in the spot where they ought to be, bordering on the lily pool, is "White oak, *Quercus alba*," a common native article, of which in the diagram there do appear to be two.

And what about the stair carpet she tacked up the front stairs, "for Mother," because Father would not let Mother have one? "Drugget," said Miss Brayton, with a droll little sniff to show she was speaking figuratively, drugget being a lowly cotton material, brown or dun colored, that one read about in old novels where the characters are struggling to make ends meet. With the memory of tears in her old gray-blue eyes, she drew a word picture of herself on her knees on the bare treads, with hammer and carpet tacks hastening to finish the loving task before Father came home. It was her notion that I, though in less cruel circumstances, might use a strip of tan canvas (from Wilmarth's in Newport) for our front stairs in the old Coggeshall house on Union Street. I obeyed, and there is still a runner of tan duck (no, not the same one) on the front and back stairs of my house in Maine—people often ask me how I came to think of the idea.

Concede her her mother's stair carpet and the Little Dorrit figure kneeling with tacks in its mouth while Father thunders, concede her the Turkish oaks of Victorian taste, but what of her claim to have run welfare for the city of Fall River during the Depression? The city was bankrupt; unemployment figures stood at 50,000—half the population; Roosevelt had not yet moved in with the Civilian Conservation Corps and Public Works Administration or perhaps he had not yet taken office. In the background was a history of strikes and labor violence. Into the crisis stepped Alice Brayton, enlisted by a desperate mayor to run a relief program. It was not clear how the city happened to turn to her. She had had no previous experience; her education had stopped with Fall River High School, where they gave Greek and Latin but scarcely economics or urban administration. Yet for her, embarking on the story, apparently it went without saying that her city should have called her in its hour of need. And matter-of-factly (as she told it) she put up the money, out of her own pocket, to tide over the initial crisis. How much that amounted to she did not say—only that every cent was repaid.

I forget all the unique features of the relief plan she ran. The main outlines were that it was cheap and gave value. She cited her first decision: every man on relief should receive a pair of shoes. To ensure good quality (cheaper in the long run), she checked on where the men in her family got their shoes and ordered the same, with the choice of low shoes like her brother's or high like her father's. Next she bought shirts: every unemployed man had the choice of work shirt or dress shirt of Father's or Brother's brand. That was her picture of democracy in action—every man jack wearing Father's shoes.

For groceries she issued food stamps redeemable at the family grocer's. In fact, she claimed to have invented the food-stamp idea. The mayor of a big English city—Manchester or Leeds—came to Fall River, she well remembered, to study how her methods worked. As with any public-spirited action, criticism was inevitable. But upholding her hand throughout was the Catholic bishop of Fall River—Bishop Cassidy, I think it was—who became a friend and steady admirer, figuring in more than one of her narratives.

Naturally, she was anti-bureaucratic. From a small office in City Hall she administered the program single-handed, receiving all complaints personally. And complaints were what Alice Brayton knew how to handle. She liked to tell the story of the man who objected because his groceries weren't being delivered. Your average welfare administrator would have used the rough side of his tongue on him, giving fresh grounds for complaint. Not Alice Brayton; she agreed to delivery and *outsmarted* him. She hired a boy to follow the complainer from the office and observe his goings and comings. That done, the same little boy was detailed to wait in a doorway opposite the man's house till he had gone out for the day, then quickly deliver the bags of food to his doorstep, making sure to leave them in the sun. Soon the man was back in Miss Brayton's office asking to have the special service discontinued. . . .

The anecdote, of course, is a story against the poor, of the classical coal-in-the-bathtub type but with retribution added. Miss Brayton was a prankish moralist. Most of the fables she related of human wickedness showed people getting what they asked for, in perfect justice. The Christmas party she gave every year was a neat illustration of a morality play. Neighbors and relatives, old and young, arriving by tradition in mid-morning, found the tall spruce tree by the back door hung with brightly wrapped presents and beside it in the snow little Miss Brayton, wearing a hat and muffler and stamping her feet to keep warm. There were no names on the presents, and when you began to unwrap the one she had pulled down for you, you knew—or if it was your first time somebody explained—that what you got now didn't matter, you would be able to exchange it inside. That was the point of this Christmas.

Inside, in the dining-room, the long table had been converted into an exchange, and the guests, having taken off their outdoor things and been given a glass of hot mulled wine and a biscuit, circled slowly around the table, on which were laid out bolts of tweed and silk, cars and tracks for electric trains, paint boxes, gloves, golf balls, scarves, sweaters, stockings, bottles of sherry and claret, flower vases, books, games, perhaps a chess set of little ivory men, delicate batiste place mats, a French cheese, a piece of old lace . . . Some years there was a lazy Susan in the middle to hold more presents, and once a whole electric train was whirring around on a sort of trestle. You turned in your door-present and chose from the table the thing you wanted most. Some chose fast and some kept circling, undecided, fingering, looking at a label.

The exchange was a character test. Whatever you took, or failed to take, you gave yourself away. Children, inclined to grab without second thoughts, came off better than their elders, inhibited by an awareness of our hostess's watching eyes. But there was one year when a ferrety youth earned, I thought, Miss Brayton's eternal contempt (not to mention that of his brothers and sister) by picking *something for his mother, to help her in her cooking,* rather than the top or kite his natural heart should have craved.

The table was full of traps for hypocrites. One year she set out her bait almost too crudely. A single small flower—

let's say an unseasonal hyacinth—stood in a small container between a large box of Louis Sherry chocolates and a Nuits St. Georges. "Food for the soul," Miss Brayton, behind us like a tempter, could not forbear hinting. Whereupon the silly man next to me in line leapt forward with abandon to claim the *spiritual* remembrance.

As usual, that year I picked the most expensive thing on the table. Those traps of hers held no terror for me. Being a hypocrite about my wants was never one of my faults. Hence I greatly enjoyed those Christmas mornings, though for some of her guests (and I fear she intended it) they must have been quite an ordeal. To covetous children who, intoxicated by the display, chafed at being limited to *one* present, to adults who felt they had taken a present that was much too big or else not big enough, the exchange "taught a lesson," and "learning your lesson" was maybe not in the Christmas spirit. Was it our Redeemer or our Judge whose birth we were celebrating?

Possibly Christmas brought out an ambivalent imp in Miss Brayton. The giving of gifts was a provocation to naughtiness. With many generous people, the pleasures of bestowing have their counterpart in the joy of withholding, or at any rate in a barely controllable reluctance to part with something one has. The coexistence of the two in Miss Brayton was never more marked than in her Christmas-morning reception of the monks from the Priory across Cory's Lane. Every year an invitation went out, though relations were never what they had been with Bishop Cassidy of Fall River and were strained almost to the breaking-point sometimes by a boundary dispute. But Christmas was Christmas, and the monks always came—last, after the guests had gone and after the servants had received their gifts.

The once-groaning exchange table must have been down to the hard-core remains when the Prior, by appointment, knocked. There were never witnesses to what happened next,

334

but doubtless it varied from year to year. Sometimes it seems to have been a decidedly convivial party. Then there was the dreadful time referred to only in reminiscence: "Yes [musing], that was the year I gave the Father Prior bubble bath." Often, I suspect, the exchange-table procedure was followed normally, albeit with diminished stocks. But I remember hearing of a time that was still close to the telling when she was boasting of it, like a bantam cock. That was the wicked Christmas when the monks were shown to a sumptuously laden table: wines and cordials, fruit pastes, cheeses, liqueur chocolates, Turkish delight, nuts—everything calculated to speak to the Friar Tuck in a "black" Benedictine. Then, having allowed the poor men a full minute of contemplation, she barked, "Well, you're monks, aren't you? You've renounced all that," and marched them out of the room. And there was another year, I think, when in the same taunting spirit she gave them all *books*. Religious books, irreligious books, books on the Index, the story did not specify. But they might have been books written by herself and published at her own expense.

Rather surprisingly, Miss Brayton was an author, an historian, and not a bad one. Her books—*George Berkeley in Apulia, George Berkeley in Newport, Scrabbletown*—were handsomely produced, well written, and carefully proofread. She is thought to have got her start as a garden-club chronicler. She had been attracted to Berkeley for the obvious reason that the idealist philosopher had spent three years in "Whitehall," a house in Middletown, near Newport and the rocks called Purgatory and Paradise. But I am not sure to what extent she had looked into his philosophical writings. After Bishop Berkeley came *Scrabbletown*, a biting analysis of records found in a trunk in a Massachusetts town between Fall River and New Bedford; this is the most personal and the best, in my view, of her books. There were the makings of an intellectual

335

in Miss Brayton, I always thought. That she did not use her mind more fully, direct it to more interesting ends, was her own doing and represented a choice in life.

It must have had to do with "Father." During my years in Portsmouth, it was my firm conviction that she had made a devil's pact with him. It partly concerned the house. She wanted the house and garden, and in order to get them she had to wed herself to him, stay with him, turning into a spinster, while her sisters left home (one went to Bryn Mawr) and made their own lives. She loved her mother and she may have put it to herself that she stayed to protect her, interpose her small figure between her and the tyrant, fight her battles for her, including the Battle of the Stair Carpet.

But her mother died, and Alice stayed on with him, doubtless thinking that, having made the loving sacrifice, now at least she should get the good out of it—the house and old Joe's topiary. There must have been a large share of the money too, to judge by her *train de vie*—winters at the Colony Club, a well-paid pair of nice servants, Joe and Bertha (Bertha must have been French Canadian but Miss Brayton called her French, pretending that that was why she cooked so well), gardener and gardener's helpers, the cost of publishing her books, donations to the Preservation Society, membership in Bailey's Beach, furs, and couturier clothes from Bergdorf. She had the usual charities and subscriptions of a society woman. Yet the strange thing was that when you saw her, winters, in New York in her long mink coat and smart small gray hat on her way to a wedding or a matinée, she looked like an old rural body—liver-spotted hands under the white gloves, weathered cheeks, strawy white disobedient hair rearing up beneath the hat brim. Toil had left its signature on her.

She emphatically did not belong, and much of that emphasis was her own. She capitalized on her homely traits, on the Scrabbletown in her. The Lizzie Borden connection, for instance, which may once have been an embarrassment ("Not a cousin," her nephew firmly told me). Now she plumed herself on it; someone had sent her a record that she delighted in putting on the phonograph: "Oh, you *can't* chop your *mama up* in *Massachusetts, Not* even if it's done as a *surprise.* . . ." She was proud of her Yankee cunning. In dealing with the New York maids at the Colony Club, she boasted, she always got her room made up before anyone else's; that was simply because she always left her door ajar and an open box of chocolates on her dresser ("Never fails to lure 'em"). Her laconic wit put you in mind of a sharp rustic having the last word.

My favorite illustration of that is a true story that took place in Portsmouth one Sunday morning when I brought an old White Russian, Serge Cheremetev, to see her and her garden. Both of these old people were what they claimed to be—he was a former governor of Galicia under the Tsar, his uncle invented Boeuf Strogonoff—yet there was something spurious somewhere about both of them, and each felt it in the other. Ignoring her topiary, Cheremetev, dressed in an ancient suit of coffee-colored silk and carrying a stick, began to talk of the roses on his former estate in Grasse; she countered with a terse dismissal of roses, having only a few "pernettys" to show. Her rows of espaliered fruit trees, so exciting at the time to Americans, said little to him. Still less did her gourds. If he tapped her Sensitive Plant lightly with his cane, he did not stay to witness the quivering response. I was dying with shame for both of them: *she* was boasting more than usual, and in Cheremetev's hoarse rasping voice, a repeated "honored lady" crackled like gunfire.

Since things were not going well in the garden, I suggested that she show him the house. He glanced at the library, somewhat overstocked with detective stories, that lined the walls of the billiard room; he was a rare-book dealer in Washington and she was a member of the Hroswitha Society, but no common chord was struck. In the front parlor, he peered at a Piranesi on the wall. Just below it on a table stood a small bronze statue that echoed a detail in the engraving; the arrangement was one of Miss Brayton's witty visual puns, and underneath the statue or beside it was a rare edition of Piranesi plates—I forget which—that had belonged to the Tsar. Cheremetev, by invitation, examined the flyleaf, which stated in the imperial handwriting that the book had been the property of Nicholas II of Russia. "Ah, dear lady," he croaked, "I see you have the book of my godfather, the Tsar." Miss Brayton started, as if for once taken aback; her blue eyes took in her dark-eyed visitor with his Tartar cheekbones. Then she let out a sort of cackle: "You've got the blood. I've got the book." Mr. Cheremetev bowed. She had won. Yet if I had had only her word for the story, I would not have believed it.

She had come a long way up from the cotton mills to be able to meet the Tsar's godson in single combat in her front parlor, and he of course had come a long way down. On her side, it was the privet animals—the legacy of her pact with the devil—that had put her in a position to score. First of all, they had put her on the social map, marked Cory's Lane as an outlying bastion of Newport, which was still *the* society to get into while the summer lasted. But first Father had to die for her to emerge as a debutante on the Newport scene. That happened in 1939. She was sixty-one years old.

Despite the late start, when I met her ten years later, she had made it. Her social strategy, as carefully worked out as a Napoleonic battle plan, was based on reaching the child that she counted on finding in every Newport dowager and tycoon.

After Father was gone, she started giving her lawn parties, featuring a big rented merry-go-round near the gate on the Priory side and a clambake on the beach below the railroad tracks, with well-stocked bars dotted about in between. These parties were an instant success; old-time leaders like the

Misses Wetmore were teetering down the slope in their heels
and long dresses to view the oddity of the clambake.

It was the child in Miss Brayton who knew that to suc-
ceed you must make a party an adventure or a treat. Even an
ordinary afternoon visit to her garden, ending with a tray of
strong martinis, obeyed a canonical rule of children's parties:
each guest must get a present to take home. In the summer
it was flowers from the garden, which she picked as you walked
along and unexpectedly handed you on the front porch as you
left, or fruit (her white clingstone peaches, a variety no longer
to be found in catalogues, a basket of figs, or her slipskin
grapes, Delaware or Catawba). Then—aside from the clipped
animal and geometric figures, appealing to the scissors artist
in all of us—she had funny plants like that Sensitive Plant,
which quails when you strike it, carnivores like the flycatcher
and pitcher plants, freaks like the parrot tulip (new then), and
the tropical-looking bamboo.

With these arts and wiles, she swiftly conquered the territory she had designs on, designs perhaps dating back to her
maiden visit to Bellevue Avenue with the Fall River or Tiv-
erton Garden Club, where the society bug may have first bitten her—why not in Mrs. Arthur Curtiss James's blue garden, whose grass was once said to be dyed? It was at about
the same time that she had got her start as a writer, too, in
her local *Garden Club Bulletin*. Father's death, when it finally came, had had a double effect, opening the gate of ivory
as well as the gate of horn. It had not only set her free to
pursue her social ambition. It was what had allowed her to
become an author. The first of her Berkeley books, *George
Berkeley in Apulia*, came out in 1946; Thomas Brayton had
been dead seven years, some of which she must have used for
travel and self-education. After that came *George Berkeley in
Newport* (1954) and after that *Scrabbletown*, which peculiarly
has no date but which I know came out toward the end of

my years on Union Street—1949–54. Following that, her publications were of less interest, probably because she was no longer interested herself. The two paths that had been opened up to her by her father's death, though she may not have thought so, were divergent. She could not take both even if suddenly having so much more money seemed to promise it. She chose society—the Chilton Club, the Colony, opera seats, Joe's chauffeur's uniforms.

She could not have maintained "Green Animals" and herself in the Bellevue Avenue orbit and continued to be a scholarly historian with a lively pen for the simple reason that she had run out of local material—after Berkeley, what? There were only Governor Arnold's burying-ground and the so-called Viking tower. If she was determined to stay put at the place where she had arrived, she could not move on mentally. That she should become a *social* historian in the line of Henry James and Edith Wharton was out of the question. To do that would have required a real break, and probably she was not up to it because she had stayed with Father too long, bargaining for freedom. Who sups with the devil must bring a long spoon.

Though she claimed off and on to be a Quaker I think she had no particular religion. She was a natural rebel (that was the great thing about her), naturally independent in her views, and what she worshipped was a kind of intelligence that, given her self-imposed limitations, had to be visual and aesthetic. Once I heard her enunciate almost fiercely the principle she lived for, standing by her mantelpiece, chin out, like one willing to be counted. *"Taste!"* she cried, virtually shouting. "T-A-S-T-E." She spelled it out as if we might fail to understand her and then struck her small chest. "I have it. T-A-S-T-E." She stared at us all belligerently. "Yes, Miss Brayton. Of course you have." We laughed. "Obviously you have." The proof was all around us, in the flames leaping in the fireplace, in the shaker of unbeatable martinis, in the sandwiches of thin-cut soft white bread, thick white meat of chicken, and "Bertha's mayonnaise." But it was tasteless of her to say so. Once the word was pronounced, you had lost the thing it was meant to designate: an eye, an ear. It was embarrassing and sad, as if poor little Psyche had spilled the hot wax of her taper on a sleeping Cupid. Wishing she wouldn't, we hastily left.

She was ninety-four when she died in 1972, leaving "Green Animals" to The Preservation Society of Newport County. I was no longer living in the U.S. and had not seen her or had news of her for more than ten years. Her relatives, probably forgetting about me or thinking I would not be interested, did not send me an announcement of decease or an obituary notice from the paper. But I see from *The Great Public Gardens of the Eastern United States* that she left no endowment and the garden depends for its maintenance on gate receipts and profits from the gift shop. Does this mean she was living on capital at the end, like the grasshopper in the fable? Or expressing in that spare legacy her Yankee faith in the self-help principle? "Green Animals," like a relief client, should learn to be self-supporting. Somehow the end and final secret of her story must lie laconically in the willing of her property. If she intended "to live on," she may have hoped to be planted, warts and all, like a tiny rugged Turkish acorn up by the lily pool and turn by force of character into an indomitable tree.

December 1983